Spitting in the Wind

Billy Furious

Mag Publishing

First Published in Great Britain in 2011 by
Mag Publishing
Baltic Business Centre
Saltmeadows Road
Gateshead
NE8 3DA

For further information or ordering,
email mark.jensen@themag.co.uk

ISBN: 0-9544089-4-2
A catalogue record of this title is available from The British Library

Typesetting Phil Burns

Printed in Great Britain by Xpresslitho Limited

Contents

Introduction

We often hear that "there are two sides to every argument." Billy Furious was born in my silly head to try and find the argument's third side. Or failing that, starting an entirely different argument with zero sides or maybe five.

Nobody likes being told what they think. People also don't like being misrepresented, lied to and made victims of malicious fabricated gossip. Yet for some reason all of that comes with the territory when you are a Newcastle United fan. Perhaps the handful of dingle-berries prepared to goon up to television cameras are to blame.

I live in Newcastle, I go to the match. I don't drink brown ale down the Bigg Market on a Friday neet-oot. I'm not a racist, homophobe, sexist or, worse, have Mark Knopfler's *Local Hero* as the ring tone on my phone. I wouldn't rather my football team lost 4-3 than won 1-0, I don't think Kevin Keegan is particularly God-like, I don't think Alan Shearer is the Lord Jesus Christ himself, I know the purchase of Tino Asprilla didn't cost us the league title in 1996 or think that the 5-0 win over Manchester United the following season was of any lasting importance. I don't think the decline of Newcastle United started with the sacking of Bobby Robson.

I feel no sense of entitlement towards the winning of trophies, I have never gone bare-chested at an away match in January, worn a jester hat or painted a slogan on a bed-sheet.

And neither has any of my friends (except Nick who wore a matching chequered harlequin hat and trousers for the return of Kevin Keegan – but he doesn't count because he's daft).

I do not claim to speak for all Newcastle fans and will look to take issue with anyone who does. I liked Kenny Dalglish, I thought Bobby Robson should have been removed as manager sooner but with considerably more dignity, I have publicly stuck up for Joey Barton and I have often been proved wrong. None of which matters. What matters is fighting lazy stereotypes, avoiding clichés, wilful disobedience and being funny. What defines funny is what makes me laugh, what makes me laugh goes into the Billy Furious column in *The Mag* and the books I write. And as I find somebody shouting "Bollocks" hilarious I am easily pleased.

I started shouting "Bollocks" for independent Newcastle United supporters' magazine *The Mag* in1991 and accidentally wrote something good in 1992. By 1994 I was getting the hang of it. The following is a revisiting of some of the more entertaining stuff I have written since. Many of the jokes that my editor removed and deemed "in poor taste" for *The Mag* have been lovingly restored. Any other changes made have only been to improve the flow and never to make myself seem clever, (even with the benefit of hindsight that would be too big a task) so what you have in the fat bit of book to your right is essentially a remixed and re-mastered best of Billy Furious. *(Anything written in italics was added later)*. The Distorted View chapters are my own take on each individual season and should not be relied on as entirely relevant or factual.

This book is a year late and I did promise to call it 'Pissing in the Wind' but the more I thought about it the more the image of indecent exposure troubled me. 'Spitting' is much more punk rock and as such is a nod to my other tribe.

More recent stuff is included because I covered 1992 to 2002 in *A Mag For All Seasons* and 2003 to 2006 pretty comprehensively in *And They Wonder Why We Drink*. But please remember this is not a reference book and many facts have been ignored, overlooked or twisted for our collective amusement.

Thanks as always first and foremost to Lynn for everything.

Then to Mark Jensen for unwavering support, my match crew for unwavering abuse and to Bully, ADD, Big Al, Davie Todd, Peter Knights and Cathi Unsworth for the required kicks up the arse.

The soundtrack to this book is Frank Turner's *Photosynthesise,* Killing Joke's *Exorcism* and virtually every song by Rise Against, but especially *Behind Closed Doors* and *Satellite.*

Chapter 1

1991/92 postscript - A Distorted View

I liked Ossie Ardiles and certainly didn't want Kevin Keegan to be Newcastle United's manager. Ossie fashioned a team bursting with local youth (Watson, Elliott, Clark, Appleby to name but four) (Roche to name but a fifth) blessed with pace and with a determination to pass a football quickly on the grass.
Micky Quinn and Gavin Peacock would get the goals and Franz Carr would be too quick for everybody in Division Two. And Franz Carr scored on the first game of the season at Upton Park, temporary home of Charlton Athletic. I travelled down with Bront on a bus that never looked like it was going to make it down there, let alone back. There was a kid on the same bus who smiled happily whilst emitting farts from (and I quote Bront here) "the mingiest arse in the fucking world". It was my birthday – we lost 2-1 – our exciting "Team of the 90s" (as it said on the hooded sweatshirts you could buy from the supporters' shop) was somewhat undone by Ossie's apparent belief that we didn't need central defenders.
In October a load of us went down to Scotswood to Kev's house because he had got one of them new-fangled satellite dishes. We saw the definitive Ardiles game in the Zenith Systems Data Cup as Newcastle, 5-3 down in extra time, came back to lead 6-5 only to give away a penalty, then lose on penalties in a match that was so insane Wifey still insists it made her ill for weeks.
Bront, Kev, Wifey and I were at Roker Park to see the first of Liam O'Brien's two classics against sunderland in a 1-1 draw. We were in the Gallowgate End on Boxing Day to see us batter promotion-chasing Middlesbrough for the entire match, where not only did we fail to score, we let Paul Wilkinson run unmolested from the halfway line to score the only goal for them then Wifey and I got home to find our Benwell flat had been robbed. I'd seen the weasel-boy who lived over the road from us in the legendary Gallowgate bogs the previous

home match and he had casually asked if we went to all the home games.

Robert Lee single-handedly destroyed us in a 3-4 home loss to Charlton in January; a 5-2 defeat at Oxford was Ossie's last game in charge before Chairman John Hall sacked him and appointed Keegan. Keegan's first game was a 3-0 win over Bristol City and Newcastle moved away from the bottom of the League with some creditable results. A midweek 2-0 win away against John Beck's (Stoke City prototype) Cambridge United we heard in the car outside Glasgow Barrowlands where we walked out of The Red Hot Chilli Peppers show because they had already been blasted off stage by support act, The Rollins Band.

A run of five losses included a 6-2 at Wolves: the lead singer of Newcastle band The Sunflowers, Mr Paul Schofield , interrupted their set at The Broken Doll to ask if anybody knew the final score from Molineux and responded with an "oh fucking hell" when I told him.

The wins against Portsmouth and Leicester that saved us from the Third Division long ago passed into legend.

Player of the Season: Gavin Peacock.

Goal of the Season: Gavin Peacock at Leicester.

Leeds United won the First Division, Ipswich the second, Liverpool beat sunderland in the FA Cup final.

Chapter 2

September 1992

An Apology

It has come to my attention that remarks made by myself in the last issue of *The Mag* concerning Tyne Tees Television and their coverage of Newcastle United may have caused some misunderstanding. Is has been stated that my comments suggested that said coverage was not all it could be. Upon reviewing, both material from this season and events since, I can only say that these remarks were erroneous and unnecessary.

What should have been said from the start is that Tyne Tees' coverage is utter and unmitigated fucking crap, bollocks, eye-wateringly unprofessional shit and the sooner the BBC gets to cover us the better. The Sunday afternoon, after our 5-0 demolition of Bristol City the previous day, I tuned into *The Back Page* five minutes before it was due to start (according to the time shown at the end of the previous week's programme and both the Sunday newspapers I bought) only to see Roger Tames talking about League tables and Hartlepool. I had, through no fault of my own, missed Newcastle's bloody goals and consequently the only part of ITV's schedule for the whole day that didn't warrant puking on.

I phoned to complain, was told that there has been some reorganisation, that the Sunday Mirror had the new time in and the new time had been announced on air. "When bloody when?" I demanded. "Yesterday," came the somewhat conceited reply.

"I was at the sodding match yesterday. And after the match I was in the pub getting ridiculously drunk. We had just won 5-0. I am entitled, nay obliged, to celebrate." "You fucking sack of monkey shit," I didn't add, but thought really, really hard.

"We also said earlier today."

"Oh, I'm supposed to sit through five hours of Morning Worship, amateur drainpipe making and other assorted piffle just in case some muppet has decided to change all the programmes around, am I?"

"The goals might be on again at the end," said the man. So I slammed the phone down and ran back to the telly in time to hear Roger say, "…we like to share the honours around – here are York City's goals again." York City? We had more people locked out than they had at that game.

Never mind, calm down, the goals will be on the local news tomorrow, none of the million chances but at least the goals, I told myself. Ha ha, what a poor misguided fool. After a positively riveting story about 18th century basket weaving (or whatever) that went on for a good ten minutes, we finally got to the sport which from a Newcastle United point of view showed the signing of Robert Lee, then two of the goals. Then they were back to the goals from York. Bastards! They are blatantly punishing us for being too good and scoring too many goals.

The next Sunday, so as not to miss the action from Peterborough I put the telly on an hour early and sat through a programme about stupid dogs, then a programme about greenhouses that had a special feature on slug killing. Oh, I was in raptures.

When, Mr. Tyne Tees scheduler, 30,000 people turn up to see someone kill a slug I will apologise. Not before.

For once this isn't entirely the fault of the people who make *The Back Page* (although whoever thought a pink blazer would improve the show needs a word with themselves, unless it was to deliberately distract from the woodenness of the presenter). It must be difficult for them with Newcastle having between twenty and thirty shots on goal per game when they are only used to four or five. Although if I was Tommy Wright I would be round there with a baseball bat for them not showing the brilliant save he made to prevent an almost certain goal in the first half. Also to cover up the fact that ITV can't show goals from the Premiership we have to endure the "David Mills On The Boro" spot where David Mills *(wearing enormous spectacles if memory serves)* spends what feels like half an hour describing the action that we all saw on *Match of the Day* the night before. I wonder if Boro fans video Millsie's match reports to keep to look back on. Oh Lord, they probably do.

Speaking of Boro, a less level headed acquaintance of mine suggested Newcastle fans should retaliate for Boro fans smashing up the Three Bulls Heads before the first leg of the League Cup match by going down for the return leg and breaking things. I told him it was a stupid idea. I mean how much damage would you have to do to Middlesbrough before anybody noticed? It's already a dump with chemical slurry flowing through the streets and mutants with two heads eating each other outside their filthy homes. The most offensive thing we could do is go down there and tidy up a bit. A bit of landscape gardening, indoor plumbing, maybe put some actual windows in the holes in their houses? They would be outraged.

Much football coverage is still guilty of showing interviews with people instead of action from the match but with Sky + you can whizz through the waffle and the invention of the internet means you never have to miss a Newcastle goal again. Perversely I am now having terrible trouble stopping slugs eating my lilies.

Chapter 3

1992/93 postscript – A Distorted View

I flatly refuse to talk about the 92/93 season. I wrote the definitive review of that campaign, capturing the dizzying excitement of our promotion dash which included all the social and historical context I could throw at it and released it in a book, *A Mag For All Seasons*. Unfortunately because of the twin stumbling blocks of my own failure to publicise myself (to the extent that many of my oldest friends and people in my own family didn't know I'd written it) and what I consider to be a malicious campaign of lending, whereby every copy seems to have be read by ten different people, I was not catapulted into a world of fame and adulation. I did not become darling of the chat shows, have to avoid the unwelcome attentions of the paparazzi, cross wits with Stephen Fry on *QI* or have to turn down appearances on All Star Celebrity Pig Fondling On Ice.
Good.
Fame looks rubbish and nuisensical (which is a word so brilliant that Google refuses to recognise it). It seems to involve a lot of having to be nice to idiots, avoiding making an arse of yourself in public (a shame, because that's an art at which I am spectacularly adept), having to pay Max Clifford to stop people making up stories about you and having unflattering pictures of yourself in a bikini shown to everybody in the world. I haven't got a bikini and you should be bloody grateful to the point of buying my book and refusing to lend it to anyone.

Player of the Season: Lee Clark.

Goal of the Season: O'Brien at sunderland (obviously).

Chapter 4

January 1994

On Thin Ice

The Winter Olympics were on TV, live from Lillehammer, Norway – a little closer to home Newcastle United were allowing no away fans due to the renovation of the Gallowgate End.

It's been quite hard to give football my undivided attention recently. Why? Well, I'm sure it's been the same for us all – how could anybody even think of irrelevancies like the fourth round of the FA Cup with so much of this delightful ice dancing going on. Hasn't the nation been gripped, it's amazing anyone has slept a wink. The return of Torvill & Dean *(they relaxed the rules on professional competitors to allow their re-entry after ten years, like you could give a damn)* – don't they make you proud to be British?
Yeah right!
My patriotic fervour is stirred more by someone farting the national anthem. Mincing about on ice-skates would never have won us the Battle of Britain and chucking half an hour of it between the footage of FA Cup replays on *Sportsnight* is simply too much. Des Lynam knows it as well, the swine. That naughty flicker in his eye, you could almost see him stifling a chuckle at the thought of so many of us having to sit through such twaddle before they showed Everton getting humiliated by Bolton.
Ice dancing is not a sport. Nothing where marks are awarded for artistic interpretation is a sport. It's a circus act and should be kept in its place; between fire-eating elephants and clowns with enormous trousers falling over and bumping into one another. Wearside ice-dancer Joanne Conway understood this and used to fall over onto her generously proportioned rump in a hilariously undignified fashion for our communal amusement at every available opportunity.

Joanne of course now lives with sunderland's Gary Owers and given her sense of balance and the way he plays football (clumsily charging back and forth with no regard for his, or anyone else's, personal safety) their house must be in quite a sorry state; Gary shouting and barging through doors, knocking over tasteless fitted units while Joanne keeps tripping herself up over the sofa and falling through smoked glass coffee tables, while a never ending supply of plant pots land on their stupid heads. They do that every day as well. Probably.

(Note – wanting to shag Katrina Witt does not constitute an interest in ice-dancing.)

So having dragged myself away from endless re-runs of this televisual feast as well as the rugby (stupid, stupid, stupid fucking game only played by people too fat or inept to play football) what was I left with? Newcastle at home to Southampton?

Firstly not allowing any away support stinks, it's morally wrong. They could have put fifty of them in that little corner section at the bottom right of the East Stand that for no obvious reason has its own little wall around it and I wouldn't feel as guilty. How anyone from Newcastle's board can expect to look anybody from Arsenal in the eye this season when they gave us 5,000 tickets for the game at Highbury is beyond me.

The atmosphere was non-existent against Southampton. The players didn't help by wandering around looking like they had only just met in the first half but opposition support having the gall to enjoy themselves within St James' Park usually kick-starts the crowd to some extent.

It was eerie and weird *(Southampton won 2-1)* a feeling that was only enhanced by the presence of Southampton's Ian Dowie. I mean, who was the cruel joker who told Dowie he could be a footballer. He is at best a living reason as to why men must not be allowed to breed with chickens. Look at him; clucking away at the ref – half man, half hen.

It was a very frustrating afternoon but that happens from time to time and hopefully it won't happen again in our next game against Luton. Unfortunately the Southampton game confirmed what many of us have suspected for some time: that Kevin Keegan has a fixed idea of what the team should be and will pick it regardless of form or fitness (heresy alert heresy alert!!) I'm not going to blame goalkeeper Mike Hooper for us losing, that would be pathetic and not reflective of the facts but he's not better than Pavel Srnicek and we can all see he's not. Also does anyone in the world, apart from Keegan, think that Mark Robinson is a better right back than Steve Watson? Please say if you do because, try as I might, I can't find anyone who does. I taped *Match of the Day* and watched it twice – did you see Scott Sellars? He didn't look well enough to be out of bed, let alone trying to play football. He did very well considering but for Christ's sake we've got a squad. Surely we could have bunged Malcolm Allen or Nicky Papavasiliou in and wrapped Sellars up in a blanket with a hot Beechams and half a bottle of whisky. The same goes for the normally superb Bracewell who exacted no influence whatsoever. Brace was another late fitness test job who was rushed in when Robbie Elliott was coping adequately in his absence.

No one would be stupid enough to question Keegan's ability to manage considering what we've seen in the past two years – it just seems that "not being scared to change a winning team" only applies to some members of the squad which isn't doing anybody any favours.

Chapter 5

April 1994

Liverpool 0 v Newcastle United 2

Nobody in my family liked football – my Dad, although a child of Newcastle, only had a passing interest, my mam died when I was two so I never got to quiz her on her knowledge of the offside trap. My Grandparents, who looked after me until I was seven, despite running The North Terrace bar before the Second World War, only saw the football results because they came on straight after they had finished shouting at the wrestling on *World of Sport*. At school I didn't like football because I was shit at it. Wearing less clothes to stand in the cold and rain seemed a peculiar thing to be forced to do. From the point of view of a malnourished child, playing football in the North East of England, was either boring, frightening or painful, depending on where you stood. I came to view my Darlington Primary School football field like a British P.O.W. would view the Burma Railway.

While my dad struggled to come to terms with the death of his beautiful wife (I inherited his looks) I was bounced around various aunts, uncles and grandparents at weekends and football didn't exist in any of their houses. None except my Dad's sister, Ally and her husband, John.

John was fascinating. He was a Scouser, which meant he spoke like the Beatles, and watched *Match of the Day*. He let me stay up late with him and this new, exciting and exotic experience in a darkened front-room in Newton Aycliffe had me hooked.

I saw John at a funeral a couple of years back and told him my obsession with football was all his fault and that he owed me tens of thousands of pounds, a new liver and a head full of hair.

I liked Peter Osgood because there was a slow motion clip on TV of him beating four or five players whilst *Something In The Way He Moves* was played. This brought on neither latent homosexuality nor support for Chelsea so my

allegiance bobbed about like drowning dog in a restless sea. I wasn't born in Darlington, none of my friends supported Darlington and I had no interest it tying my allegiance to what appeared to be a joke team – so don't even go there. At this crucial point my dad remarried, I was 8 and my new (3 ? years older) step-brother, Lee, supported Newcastle United who had Malcolm MacDonald. I had still never been to a match but Super Mac was now my hero, partly because this meant that Lee would throw me down the stairs slightly less often and partly because Mac looked like a hero: powerful build, heroic stance and he could grow facial hair in places I'd never understood possible before or since.
I was 9 by the time the '74 Cup Final was live on our new colour telly and we got to see a full 90 minutes of Newcastle United playing. The first in my life. A full 90 minutes of Newcastle United - being battered to hell by Liverpool.
An early pointer – Liverpool = good. Newcastle = disappointment.

By which point (and to my tearful disapproval), my family had moved to Norfolk, where Lee and I were the only Newcastle fans in our schools. Newcastle lost and people took the piss, Newcastle won and nobody cared. My first ever live game was at Carrow Road, where I saw Liverpool (with our Alan Kennedy fresh into their team) thrash Norwich 4-1. Dalglish, Heighway, Case and Terry Mac were all playing but Emlyn Hughes was missing and some nobody called Alan Hansen was in his place.

In retrospect I relished being different to my friends, one of the upsides about being an outsider is that peer pressure is way down on your list of priorities. I hung out with smokers and glue sniffers as I got older but never joined in so my love and loyalty for Newcastle United never waned, even in the face of us getting relegated. My Granny sent me match reports from *The Northern Echo* - but quite simply Newcastle were never on the telly. We were rarely on *Match of the Day* and ITV's Sunday highlights were regionalised which meant I knew plenty about Norwich, Ipswich and Cambridge. But little about Newcastle United. Liverpool were on all the time – winning thrilling games in Europe.
My dad did his fatherly duty and took me to St James' on a family trip north. Despite the game being the infamous 1-4 against sunderland I was bedazzled and instantly considered myself a blooded and hardcore fan. He hated it and let me go by myself the next year. We beat Fulham 2-0, Rafferty and a Peter Withe

diving header that can't be as good as I remember it.

Through the late '70s and the '80s we all learnt to hate Liverpool and by the time I realised my lifelong dream and came to live in Newcastle, The Reds were at their peak in terms of winning stuff and getting on everybody else's nerves. They were on the TV far too often, they were often boring, they were dirty, cynical and worst of all the media assumed everybody loved them.

But deep down I think many of us saw them as a role model – they were where we wanted to be. We could have lived with Newcastle being occasionally tedious if we won trophies and we wanted to be so respected that we too were given crucial penalties at important times regardless of whether or not any actual offence had been committed. We wanted to have a team of awesome self-belief and a knowledge going into every game that we were probably going to win.

Most of all, Newcastle fans know a good player when they see one (unless he's playing in black & white, but that's another matter) and sometimes you simply had to ignore your petty prejudices and jealousy and admit Liverpool were brilliant.

What they also had were excellent fans. However much we've insulted them over the years, when we won 2-1 at Anfield in October of '88 their supporters clapped our team off the pitch despite the fact that we were damn lucky not to have been slaughtered by a clearly superior team.

If we ever got to be that good, I hoped I would be that big and that sporting. We did and I'm not.

Some of you may remember the first drawings on the local news of the plans for the revamped St James' Park. Stands reaching up to the skies and Newcastle going head to head with Liverpool on the pitch, at a time when we were languishing at the wrong end of the old Second Division. The idea that we could ever seriously compete with Liverpool only existed in a drawing.

Keegan and McDermott brought a lot of good Liverpool habits to Newcastle along with Venison and Beardsley. And our respect for them was tangible. Freshly promoted in '93, upstarts that we were, we wanted to pick a fight with the Champions, Manchester United, but going up against Liverpool had a *Star Wars* style master versus pupil factor – where we wanted to prove ourselves worthy adversaries.

There was a four year gap between Feb 3rd 1989 when we drew 2-2 with the Scousers at our place (rip-snorting game - Mirandinha and Pingel scored for us, with a bar hit in the last minute) and them returning to visit us in November '93 when we ripped them to bits in the first half. An Andy Cole hat-trick in swirling snow followed by a tense second half when we fearfully expected them to come crashing back at us. They tried but this wasn't a classic Liverpool team.

Going to Anfield on April 16th 1994 felt like a pilgrimage. It was the fifth anniversary of Hillsborough. Fans I knew from Newcastle had travelled down to Merseyside with flowers and scarves the week after the disaster and some formed strong and lasting friendships with the locals.
Before the game the NUFC team bus pulled up outside the ground and Terry Mac laid a wreath and a couple of fans did the same on the pitch before the kick off. As if this didn't make the game emotionally charged enough the match was the second last to be played before an all-standing Kop.

We are noisy and bolshy behind the goal as our team grabs the game by the scruff of the neck. "C'MON NEWCASTLE!" But we've all seen our team have its moments against The Reds before and everybody knows they can win without playing well – yes we look sharp and we've had our chances but do we really think we can win? Do you think about such things, away from home and up against the odds or do you just sing your head off, clap your hands raw and concentrate with every fibre of your being?
Cole picks up a short pass from Sellars, swivels and puts in Robert Lee who is flashing through the Liverpool rearguard on a diagonal run – a surge crackles through the away hoard, eyes widen and breath is held as Lee takes the ball in his stride, clips it over the keeper, David James, and the world goes instantly insane. Our celebrations are hysterical and thrillingly, the expected Liverpool counter-punch doesn't happen because we won't let them have the ball. Cole hits another shot – but straight at David James. Cole races through again, skips over James but the angle is now too tight and he shoots agonisingly close. But wide. We are totally in control. Then, from nowhere, a defensive slip and McManaman is clean through. "Oh yeah, here we fuckin' go." No we fuckin' don't cos Pav batters the shot away and we cheer with relief.

The second half is racing over in a flurry of colour and tight passing but when Lee gets up head and shoulders above everybody else to meet a perfect Sellars cross, only to see James claw the chance away, we begin to fear the worst. Liverpool are muscling their way back into the game.

Liverpool have a free-kick wide of our area, the ball is lofted in, a scramble ensues, a red shirt goes down – The Kop roars, red arms are waved – we've definitely seen this before… no we bloody well haven't, "play on" waves the ref to our surprise and relief. Pav clutches the ball to his chest and we think, "Hold it. Give us a breather."

This team doesn't do "breathers" – Pav throws to Sellars, "Salty" expertly slides the ball into the path of the wide running Fox who bursts over the halfway line at full-tilt. As Liverpool players struggle to make up ground, Fox passes to Cole who explodes clear and rifles the ball into the bottom corner of the net. Utter fuckin' bedlam.

I am still worried. The team are not and see the game out comfortably. Keegan takes off Beardsley and Venison to generous applause from the home fans but their finest moment is yet to come.

Newcastle fans start to sing, "You'll Never Walk Alone". The Scousers to our sides think we are taking the piss and boo us. Mags can be seen shaking their heads and pointing to the opposite end. The Kop comes to life. Full voice, giant flags waving, an awesome sight for the second last time ever. The Newcastle fans stop singing and clap the Kop – the Liverpool fans to the sides catch on and clap us – The Kop sings "Newcastle, Newcastle", we sing "Liverpool, Liverpool". People wave and cry as both teams leave the field to rapturous applause. If I hadn't been there (and been mostly sober) I would think I was making this shit up. I'm not.

Outside fans are shaking hands – a friend of mine, Podger, goes onto The Kop for a look and it is still packed. An enormous Scouse kid with tears streaming down his face embraces him like a lost brother.

Nearly back at the car, away from the crowds, with arms full of the fanzines we'd been selling – three dodgy looking fuckers stroll up to us and we think, "oh bollocks." Then one of them sez in an accent like my Uncles John's, "Ere lads – you lot were fukkin' magic today. T'anks a lot."

Aye, you n'all.

The Newcastle starting 11 that day was: Srnicek, Venison, Beresford, Bracewell, Peacock, Neilson, Lee, Beardsley, Cole, Fox, Sellars.

The crowd was 44,601.

I saw my Liverpool supporting friend Martin at the wedding of the Big J.Bizzle a couple of years back for the first time since Berlin (an adventure included in And They Wonder Why We Drink). And while he said he hoped Newcastle won a trophy because it would make so many of his mates happy I said that he was just about the only thing about Liverpool that I now didn't find utterly reprehensible.

Previously unpublished

Chapter 6

1993/94 postscript - A Distorted View

It seemed like a bloody long summer waiting for our season tickets to turn up. There was a mad scramble for them, with the new Leazes End being built, but there should have been no need to panic because existing ticket holders were given priority. Somehow in the panic Wifey and I ended up amongst total strangers for the first game of the season. Middle tier looking up the left wing when Newcastle attacked the Gallowgate.

We had always stood on the terraces, distrusting seats because you couldn't move away from knob-heads or towards friends. But we were instantly astonished at being able to see all four corner flags without having to bounce about looking over people's shoulders, the sun was bright and we sat blinking at the beauty of our surroundings. Unfortunately so did our team and we lost 1-0 to Spurs.

Then we lost at Coventry and you couldn't help but wonder where the bloody points were going to come from. Kevin Keegan had sold both David Kelly and Gavin Peacock and replaced them with Peter Beardsley, bought from Everton. But Beardsley got injured by Neil Ruddock's elbow in a pre-season friendly and was expected to be out for months. To make matters worse our next game was at Old Trafford, but we played brilliantly and got a creditable draw thanks to an Andy Cole goal.

Malcolm Allen scored the only goal in a 1-0 win over Everton then we had a couple of draws before an astonishing Monday night when Newcastle played Sheffield Wednesday who, because they are from Yorkshire, were sure they had brought the correct kit despite the fact that they hadn't. So Newcastle played in blue and Wednesday played in white and yellow. It was pissing down and I was selling *The Mag* outside the East Stand so I was drenched by the time I took my seat and horribly dispirited as Sheffield Wednesday, inspired by Chris Waddle, were clearly better than Newcastle. It's hard to imagine it now but Sheffield Wednesday used to be good. Waddle looked like he was revelling in the abuse he was getting from the crowd and seemed to be actively taking the piss out of the home players. But Newcastle turned it round and won the match 4-2 with two Andy Cole goals, one from Malcolm Allen and goal from Alex Mathie that looked brilliant at the time as the 25 yard shot looped into the Leazes End net but turned out to be off his shin.

As the game got away from Wednesday, Waddle went down under a challenge and as he went to get up a laughing Lee Clark pushed his face into the grass. And Waddle had the nerve to complain. In the next game Malcolm Allen scored a brilliant penalty at Swindon. Unless a player really wallops it or does one of those daring little chips (that gets them slaughtered if they miss) penalties are rarely brilliant. The Allen penalty was special because we were standing low on the terrace behind the Swindon goal and I could see it was going to go outside the post before it curled in viciously. The game was a 2-2 draw and remarkable for little else other than that it marked the return of Peter Beardsley.

Peter Beardsley: intelligent, brilliant, impudent, charming, passionate, modest, inspirational and once again ours.

Beardsley instantly clicked with Andy Cole and within eight games Newcastle has gone from 13th to 4th. By the end of the season we had nailed down third place and European qualification, Cole had scored 41 goals. Andy Cole AndyCole Andy Andy Cole had repeatedly stated he wasn't bothered about getting the ball and scoring 40 goals in a season or breaking any kind of record.

But the look on his face after he smashed in the 40th in a 5-1 massacre of Aston Villa told the truth.

Newcastle United was only part of the story of a resurgent Newcastle – in '93/94 the city seemed to be buzzing. Since Sonic Youth and Mudhoney had played the Riverside a couple of years before and Nirvana had played their first European show at the same venue no band national or international missed us out when they toured. We had a venue for any size of crowd and that crowd would generally be more enthusiastic than anywhere else in England. Not only that but Newcastle was producing its own bands who were amazing. Not just "local and not bad actually" – genuinely fucking good. China Drum, Crane, Hug, Drill, The

Sunflowers would be as exciting a night out as anything happening at St James' Park and if two or three bands got together for a single show the turn outs would be astonishing.

I was selling *The Mag* to help pay for away tickets. Repeated burglaries had convinced us to abandon Benwell for Jesmond where we lived to the very limit of our means with the world's most handsome and wilful cat. But the world was full of fun and potential and the strangers in the Leazes End had begun to grow into a family. Like a family insofar as we argued all the time, took the piss out of each other and bitched about whoever wasn't there.

Player of the Season: Andy Cole.

Goal of the Season: Peter Beardsley at Spurs.

Man Utd won the League, Blackburn were second, Chelsea were 14th, sunderland were hiding from us in a different division. According to Wikipedia, Joe Kinnear won manager of the month three times in the '93/94 season and Kevin Keegan won it once – that can't be right, can it?

Chapter 7

September 1994

Carry On Swearing

The first seven games of the season went: (a)Leicester 3-1, (h)Coventry 4-0, (h)Southampton 5-1, (a)West Ham 3-1, (h)Chelsea 4-2, (a)Antwerp 5-0, (a),Arsenal 3-2. However, a friend of The Mag was arrested in Leicester for urinating in an alleyway hours after the game had finished.

You would think seven games of Newcastle United stampeding over all-comers would leave little room for complaint at the present moment in time. And in many ways you would be right; averaging four goals a game with experts from far and wide purring over us and even the most hardened Mags filling up at the sight of Barry Venison in an England shirt – heady days indeed.

Unfortunately injustice is still abroad in the land and it's up to us at *The Mag* to have a good moan about it. Firstly: did you listen to the Radio 5 programme from St James' Park the other week? On the panel were our chairman John Hall, Don Goodman, John Hendrie, Alan Mullery and former referee George Courtney. George Courtney, who gives a gnat's knacker what he thinks? "Swearing is a cancer in the game that must be stamped out," he said.

What?

Out of all the things wrong with the modern game, swearing is considered the most serious problem? I don't think so. What about the continued existence of Dennis Wise? What about cretin opposition fans thinking that waving their arms like a conductor when the Newcastle support is drowning out their own feeble efforts is clever or witty? What about the fact that Graham Kelly gets paid or Peter Schmeichel wears lime green shorts?

Swearing is big and clever. People who don't like swearing read the *Daily Express,* don't like noisy music and think that sex is for having babies. Swearing gives language rhythm and statements fucking impact you daft twat. We should be suspicious of people who don't swear.

Obviously, we don't want to hear small children swearing but then the idea of encouraging small children to talk at all has always been beyond me. George Courtney refereed like a maladjusted halfwit with only the most tenuous grip on reality and letting him share his ludicrous opinions with the general public was merely inviting more of the same.

"Swearing is a cancer in the game and must be stamped out" – I'm glad I didn't take up my invitation to attend as the temptation to shout "Bollocks!" would have been overwhelming. And it got worse as John Hall went on to boast how Newcastle fans had had their season tickets taken away for "urinating in public". I would probably have been asked to leave after shouting "Big fat hairy monkey bollocks!" at our chairman on live radio.

Incidentally, don't you think that being banned from football for weeing is a bit much? Nobody sets out with the express intention of doing such a thing ("Hey everybody, let's all go out and piss in the street!" That would mark the start of the anarcho-revolution don't you think?) When you've got to go you've got to go and if Leicester is lacking in public conveniences there's not a lot to be spoiled, it's not like Leicester is the Queen's best hat. I'm sure all but the most bored or spiteful policeman see public urination as nothing more than a minor offence – so what's next? If you get caught speeding, not having a TV licence or being drunk in charge of a pushbike whilst wearing a replica football shirt you can be banned from football grounds? With the imminent implementation of the evil Criminal Justice Bill the police will soon be able to nick you for going to a party – so don't wear your colours when going to the toilet, or ever, then if you get caught short you can claim you were on your way to the rugby where such behaviour is actively encouraged.

Incidentally a friend of mine literally crapped himself at White Hart Lane when Vinnie Samways hit the post (dodgy curry or something) last season. Naturally we all thought this was extremely funny because he wasn't sitting or travelling with us but if John Hall found out Shitey's next appearance at St James' Park would presumably be to have his head cut off at half-time.

Not everything is football's fault; our 4-2 win against Chelsea, with Dennis "the Maggot" Wise being sent off as a delicious bonus, was due to be on *Match of the Day* but what to do whilst waiting for it apart from eat curry and drink beer? The thrilling Nigel Benn fight was live on ITV, although the pitched battle as rival boxing fans from Birmingham and Manchester beat each other over the head with plastic chairs took most of the attention. All wholesome family entertainment until Reg Gutteridge then Frank Warren (whose only positive feature appears to be him not being Barry Hearn) referred to the troublemakers as "football fans who have been drinking all day." I'm sorry but they were boxing fans at a boxing event and they were there to support boxers – it was a boxing problem, you sort it out. Of course when there used to be fan violence in football grounds people used to blame the antics of footballers for sparking that violence, yet at the boxing the sporting participants were blatantly thumping each other and no one even thought to point a finger at them.

Finally: respect to Arsenal and England goalkeeper David Seaman following Newcastle's game at Arsenal for taking the barracking of our fans in such good humour; putting his palms out and shrugging his shoulders when they sang "Where's your wife?" at him; turning to us and tapping his heart when the Gunners pulled the score back to 3-2 and giving us all a clap at the end. What a nice man but I bet he swears and has widdled al fresco.

The lad caught short in Leicester had to write a letter of apology and got a three game ban – which he ignored.

Chapter 8

May 1995

Billy Furious R.I.P.

Crystal Palace fan Paul Nixon was killed in fan violence before an FA Cup semi-final against Manchester United. Palace asked for the replay to be postponed, the FA refused so Palace asked their fans to boycott the game. Palace lost the game 2-0 in front of the lowest FA Cup semi-final crowd recorded in 50 years. The game included an incident where Roy Keane was sent off for stamping on Gareth Southgate.

I, William Bastard Furious, being of sound mind hereby state that it be my profound wish that if I be killed at a football match next season – that my football club, Newcastle United FC, are under no circumstances allowed to ask its supporters to boycott the next game as a protest.

Got that?
Good.
The FA decision to play the FA Cup semi-final replay regardless of the fact that a Palace fan was murdered outside the first game was horribly wrong. Saying the police advised them to do so was a cop-out as well as being tactless, disrespectful, heartless and shameful. A man died for Christ-sake, show some bloody dignity.
However, Palace were in my opinion also wrong to ask their fans not to go as a protest –hence the above statement. If it was me that was killed I would not see whimpering out of the FA Cup as a mark of respect. I would want 20,000 Newcastle fans to turn up for the replay, drunk as bastards singing their heads off, carrying my decaying corpse along with them. Then for the final, dress me up in my best boots, jeans and China Drum T-shirt, wrap my stinking remains in a black and white shroud, strap me to the front of an Inter-city 125 and descend

on Wembley. After Barry Venison has lifted the trophy you can do what you want with me – nothing matters after that – throw me in the river for all I care. I would do the same thing for you if you want.

Anyway, seeing as I'm not dead just yet could I take this opportunity to apply for the job of answering the sporting letters in the *Sunday Sun*. For example;

Dear Sunday Sun,
                    When oh when is Kevin Keegan going to admit that buying Paul Kitson and Darren Peacock was a mistake. I don't actually attend the match myself but…
Me: in that case no one needs to hear your opinion – goodbye.

or

Dear Sunday Sun,
                    why oh why do the media keep ignoring Middles…..
Me: Next!

Dear Sunday Sun,
                    I'm 86 years old….
Me: Well done.

Dear Sunday Sun,
                    Modern footballers are overpaid. If they had to play for no money you would soon see a stop to spitting, swearing, cocaine addiction, cruelty to animals and global warming. And another thing….
Me: Shut the fuck up! Next!

etc etc. You could get the job done in five minutes. You could then join in with the rest of the staff in making up bizarre letters to confuse and frighten professional Geordie and double glazing peddler Alan Robson who answers the non-sporting post.

Dear Alan,
      My mum keeps climbing up lampposts with a pair of my fathers greying Y-fronts on her head and singing "Wonderful Wonderful Copenhagen" to passers by. Quite frankly it's become embarrassing because she keeps getting the words wrong. I'm thinking of having her killed – do you have the phone number for Hannibal Lecter?
Yours sincerely,
      The Archbishop of York

I blame the Post Office myself. Stamps are too cheap – if stamps were a tenner each even unmitigated ding-bats would think twice before pestering local newspapers with their half-arsed musings and might actually sit down and think for a moment. There are lots of people in the North East of England with interesting views on all things football; articulate, passionate people with wit and imagination so why (oh why) are more than half the letters in the *Sunday Sun* submitted by mental people? Is it some sort of community scheme or is it an elaborate ruse? We should be told. It's not a regional thing – have you listened to *606* on BBC Radio 5 recently. David fucking Mellor anybody? Every week there are queues of people ringing up and demanding sin bins, fourth officials, or points docked off clubs for sendings off. Every other week somebody is on saying players get paid too much money and transfer fees are too high. And Mellor actively encourages them.
They should have a recorded message on the line before any caller even gets to speak to a researcher saying, "Welcome to *606*, please be aware that sin bins would actually encourage more violence from players (I mean, have you seen the ice hockey film *Slapshot*)? Three officials arse the game up enough we don't need another one and points docked for sendings off would double the punishment for the victims of their idiocy. Players do earn too much money in this country but when they didn't people used to complain about a player drain to Italy, Germany or Rangers and if you think transfer fees are too high now, wait until the summer when £7 million for Andy Cole will probably start to look like a bargain. Now anyone with anything interesting to say, please wait a moment." David Mellor: "Next we have Billy from Newcastle on the line who apparently wants his decaying corpse to be strapped to the front of a train."

As one gets older one learns to take advantage of things rather than moan about them. So I went through a short period of writing letters to the Sunday Sun using the names and addresses of friends. Anything that supports the region as a whole and looks south for unfairness works– FA Cup semi-finals being at Wembley used to be a nailed-on twenty quid. Which I thought was funny until they asked me to write some stuff for them and didn't use it or pay me. Which damaged my sense of self-worth and irony to the point that I couldn't buy the paper anymore without crying.

Chapter 9

1994/95 postscript - A Distorted View

The spectacular start to the season kept going. Experts said Keegan would have to adapt our expansive game when playing in Europe then we beat Royal Antwerp 10-2 on aggregate.

Newcastle didn't lose a game until very late October when we went down 2-0 at Manchester United. The Andy Cole song and "We are top of the League, I said we are top of the League" boast felt like ours to keep, sung fast and confidently by bouncing Mags, they provided a soundtrack that matched the team. Bristling with spiky charm and a law unto ourselves, we rocked. We rocked Manchester United out of the League Cup and beat Athletic Bilbao in the UEFA Cup at St James'.

But there was something that Johnny Rotten/Lydon said about The Clash – that they always came on too fast and burnt themselves out. Newcastle took a breather and went Straight to Hell. 3-0 up against Bilbao a Mexican wave went round St James' and everybody switched off. Two late goals for our Basque guests meant a 1-0 win for them at their place would put us out and that is exactly what happened. We only won three of our next 17 games which saw us out of the League Cup and Europe and drop to fourth in the League which cost us our second best song. In the meantime Kevin Keegan sold the source of our best, most energetic song to Manchester United. The sale of Andy Cole to the team we most wanted to beat seemed insane. Keegan asked us to trust him. Like we had any choice.

One of the three wins in that period was an FA Cup replay against Blackburn who drew in the North East and probably expected to beat an injury-hit and

Cole-less Newcastle in the North West. Lee Clark and a screamer from Swiss full back Marc Hottiger sent Newcastle into Round Four in a 2-1 win.

A Paul Kitson hat-trick put out Swansea in the next round, and a goal from John Beresford plus two from Keith Gillespie (who came to Newcastle + £6 million from Man U as part of the Cole deal) saw off Manchester City in February.

The season is remembered by many as falling apart after Andy Cole left but Keith Gillespie hit the ground running and Cole initially struggled at Manchester United. At the time if you asked Newcastle fans if they would swap Gillespie back for Cole you couldn't find one who would sanction the deal – except maybe the lad who had an Andy Cole tattoo on his leg. Newcastle won seven out of their next 11 League games and pushed back up to third but in the meantime lost at Everton in the FA Cup. Wifey and I had tickets and a lift sorted but some unnecessary tidying up meant the tickets got accidentally thrown away. Everton won 1-0 and went on to beat Man Utd in the final. Man Utd lost out in the League to Blackburn Rovers largely because Eric Cantona was suspended after attacking a fan at Crystal Palace. Which for the record I thought was fucking hilarious.

Newcastle finished the season without an out and out striker after Paul Kitson was injured and fell away to finish sixth, just missing out on European qualification.

Player of the Season: Darren Peacock (because the local press and idiots never gave him any credit).

Goal of the Season: Andy Cole at home to Chelsea (because they said he had no left foot and he used it to nearly uproot the Leazes End goal).

Nottingham Forest finished third, Arsenal 12th, Villa 18th in the last year The Premiership had 22 teams.

China Drum released the *Great Fire* and *Barrier* singles.

Chapter 10

December 1995

Would The Real Glory Hunters Please Stand Up

So I was standing outside Hillsborough flogging The Mag back in the August of '95; as ever, Sheffield Wednesday had been generous with their ticket allocation and swarms of folk in black and white were descending on the away end. On the Tuesday we had seen a 3-1 win at Bolton with two goals from Les Ferdinand and one from Robert Lee in a scintillating performance. Prior to the game I had dropped in at The Riverside to pick up my 3-day tickets for the Reading Festival courtesy of my friends in China Drum who were due to be the first band on the main stage on the Friday. Bill and Dave from the band shouted, "We are top of the league, I said we are top of the league!" and threw inflatable Newcastle Brown Ale bottles into the crowd. A crowd that had more than a few of our then new grand-dad style shirts that had the distinctive stiff beer mat Brown Ale logo on the front. Apparently you could parcel-tape narcotics to the inside of them to deceive a security body-search. We cut out of Reading on the Saturday to be back in Newcastle for a lift down to Sheffield on the Sunday. The game was on Sky TV, we could have stayed a-hob-nobbing with our backstage passes and wandered into Reading itself to see the game but David Ginola was on fire and you felt you would be physically ill not to be there in person. Demand was outstripping supply for every game, by December Newcastle had only lost twice, so many people's main fear was not getting a ticket. I remembered standing in the sunshine outside Hillsborough, knackered, hung-over and buzzing and overhearing a couple of veterans...

"Where were all these fuckers at Old Trafford the week after we got beat at Hereford in the FA Cup, that's what I want to know?"

I honestly heard somebody say that outside a match this season. It would have been funny except it was said with such obvious bitterness. It could easily be ignored if it wasn't the kind of thing we are starting to hear all the time and what's the point of saying: "Listen, I would have loved to have joined you mate but it was 197 (fucking) 1 and I was really busy shitting in my nappy and vomiting up baby food at the time (I was only seven, after all). And those lads and lasses over there would have gone too if only their parents had met each other ten years earlier – divvy."

The truth is every Newcastle fan over 16, without exception, has got a game they can point to and say, "Ha, I was at that game – it was miles away, midweek, pissing down, we had two hundred fans there, tops, and our entire team was bollocks." We've all been going for years; only some people have gone at different times, now is the only time we have all wanted to go at once. I have heard tell of people who only started going recently but they are children and if you stop kids going the rest of us will all eventually die of old age and there will be nobody left to support the team. I don't like this nasty feeling of distrust that has crept into some people's minds, it used to be that if you were in a strange town the first Newcastle fan you saw may as well have been your best mate in the world. Now you need a C.V. of your supporting career as well as your birth certificate to prove that you are allowed to support your bloody team. It's bullshit and it's really starting to get on my tits. If you are a Newcastle fan I don't give a hamster's bollock who you are or when your first match was – shut the fuck up and get the beers in....

I used the rest of the page to moan about official travel club members getting priority for tickets and said that the P.A. announcer playing some god-awful club band singing a song about being Champions was asking for trouble.

Incidentally we won that match 2-0 (Tudor, Barrowclough) at Old Trafford in 1971 and at the time of writing (and long into the future in all likelihood) it was the last time we won there. Also interesting is that if there ever has been such a thing as a "glory hunter" within our ranks, they have been fucking rubbish at it.

The day of the game at Bolton the boys from China Drum gave me a bright yellow t-shirt from their US tour. They had played the legendary CGGB's in New York and some dates with Green Day (check out the Green Day bass player's shirt on the "When I Come Around" video). I wouldn't normally wear yellow but so as not to lose such a thoughtful gift I put it on and can be seen on the match highlights celebrating our third goal at Bolton a full second after everybody else in the away end. I don't know what that tells us about anything.

Chapter 11

1995/96 postscript – A Distorted View

Have we got to do this?

It is a horrible truth that the best Newcastle team of the last 50 years is the one some of us fans are least keen to talk about. To many, the 1995/96 season is what defines Newcastle United as famous failures, so some of our best ever players are remembered for what they didn't do. A generation of non-Newcastle fans can trot out "12 points clear", "Keegan losing it at Leeds", "4-3 loss at Liverpool" and all the good stuff about that season is crushed by fact that Manchester United won the League instead of us.

I went back over what I wrote for the season at the time and it is all too horrible in retrospect. Reading about hope that we all know died; useless defiance in the face of media criticism; a short bit about how Peter Beardsley should be fined a week's wages for his insistence on taking quick and short corners (we scored four goals from corners to Man Utd's 12); complaints about tiny incidents that tipped the scales against us (e.g. "Man Utd haven't had a serious decision go against them for weeks and all of a sudden we are getting five players booked in games for nothing challenges").

I was reminded of an Arsenal fan who came up to me after we had lost at Highbury to apologise to me for his team losing to Man Utd and beating us. He said he had never wanted Spurs to win a game before in his life but would be doing so when they played Man Utd the following day – I had forgotten how much goodwill we carried from other teams that season in the wake of all the abuse they have poured on us since. Going to Man City and Leeds and having the locals urge us on, being in stark contrast to Liverpool breaking their fucking necks to beat us in the 4-3. As Man Utd close in on Liverpool's record number of titles, that game sticks out a mile. Liverpool also beat Blackburn on the last day of the season in 1995 which would have given Manchester United another title if not for West Ham beating the Salford mob the same day. At the end of the

2010/11 season Liverpool scored an equaliser in the 12th minute of injury time to put a nasty dent in Arsenal's hope of catching Manchester United and yet Liverpool fans claim to hate Manchester United when few teams have done them as many favours.

The '95/96 season, because it remains so vivid and painful, is chock full of bitterness and what ifs: 1-0 down at home to Man Utd, Keegan had Lee Clark and Keith Gillespie still on the bench as unused substitutes as the final whistle went. The Manchester United supporting Nottingham Forest goalkeeper letting in five at Old Trafford who then single-handedly kept us to a draw at the City Ground. The fact that we had to play three games in the last week of the season. Away at West Ham being postponed due to the weather, with us in good form, when the game a stone's throw away at Dagenham went ahead, and then losing the rearranged game after some shocking refereeing. Graham Fenton scoring twice for Blackburn then never doing anything else, ever. That dopey fucker with his shirt on backwards with "Champions" written on it crying on the telly. All these things leap to mind ahead of how brilliant and bewitching our team was and how proud we were of our manager, players, city and selves and it is very, very hard to imagine us ever being that thrilled and hopeful again. The best argument was made by Paul Nunn of the Journal, as I reflected in *The Mag* at the time: "easily the most sensible and talented writer in the local media, Paul pointed out that Newcastle got more points against the rest of the teams in the Premiership than Man Utd did. Man U won the league on the points they got against us." This undermines any squabbles about tactics, the purchase of Tino Asprilla, our supposedly dodgy defence, Fenton, Collymore, referees and fixture congestion. We lost the League title because we lost at home to Manchester United and we fucking battered them that night. We battered them harder than when we beat them 5-0 a season later – but they still beat us and that season being defined by how we "lost it" does not do Manchester United justice for how they won it.

Paul Nunn unfortunately died prematurely and the North East lost one of its most perceptive voices.

Player of the Season: Les Ferdinand.

Goal of the Season: Ferdinand at Bolton, when the season was young and we could watch games with pure joy, without constantly consulting the league table that lived in our heads and wouldn't let us relax from January.

Chapter 12

November 1996

Liar Liar

Trying to convince the world that David Ginola didn't dive feels like taking on the fucking world, especially when listening to some people that's all he ever did. Apart from being lazy, shit and weak in the head. And that was just some Newcastle fans, everywhere we went in England he got booed, presumably because people had confused him with Eric Cantona. He had suffered a dip in form at the start of 1996/97 but he came back in style, torturing fullbacks and smashing in a couple of cracking goals. It was unfortunately all too easy for opposition managers who had seen their defenders humiliated to accuse him of cheating.

Doubters. Detractors. Poison pen weasels. Experts and critics. Get on you knees! Beg for forgiveness and prostrate yourselves before the majesty of David Ginola. God bless every one of you who never lost the faith and God bless Kevin Keegan above all others because our Frenchman's recent performances have vindicated our manager's loyalty and knowledge of the game beyond all doubt. Now the hard part starts: we saw it last season and it has started again already. Git-pigs who aren't fit to unblock Ginola's toilet, let alone share a football pitch with him, are assaulting him and then claming he dived. Witness the ginger gobshite at Leicester elbowing him in the face and Ginola getting booked for 'play-acting'. *(That would be Neil Lennon who has kept a low profile ever since.) Match of the Day* and Sky TV had the pictures to prove our man's innocence but neither saw fit to do so. The bastards!

Witness Middlesbrough manager Bryan Robson smiling wryly and saying, "Ginola looks for penalties and free kicks all the time." Point of order Mr Robson – an already booked Emerson boots Ginola up into the air during a run at goal, but which player's sportsmanship is called into question? Of our penalty, which Ginola won, Robson says, "Neil Cox said he didn't touch him," says Robbo – in that case as well as being a pretty god-awful footballer he's a fucking liar too, Bryan.

After studying our last three televised games painstakingly (if you call sitting in front of the TV with a four pack, a bag of Kettles and the remote control every day for a fortnight painstaking) I'll admit Ginola flicks his feet up from time to time, but only to avoid some nasty and late tackles and he never does that silly waving an imaginary card thing that Ravanelli does down at Boro. Our Frenchman also took a tremendous amount of punishment against Man U and to his credit kept getting up and having another go. It's obviously harder to do this away from home, especially in a hostile environment, and the next few weeks may see games like we saw at Arsenal last year. I don't often agree with *The Chronicle's* Alan Oliver but Daveed seemed to take a long time getting over the way he was bullied and cheated out of the game at Highbury last season. Ginola's new mental toughness might have to get even stronger. Middlesbrough away in the League Cup will be the first real test; it's bad enough at the best of times but now the cloth-eared smogsters think we have been racist towards Emerson (instead of shortist towards Juninho) they'll be riding their high horses around their silly plastic stadium before the game even starts.

In all fairness, I do applaud the Boro fans' reaction to perceived racist abuse but clean your lugs out people, you're not in sunderland now.

Speaking of liars...... after the Man Utd game (that we won 5-0) we had Alex Ferguson saying of our first goal, "all my players say the ball didn't cross the line." Did you hear that, boys and girls? "All my players...". It must have been pretty hot on the coach back to Salford with an entire team's pants on fire.

No-one is going to call Jack Charlton a liar – he is often applauded for his honesty and it is difficult to imagine him wilfully deceiving anybody. Punching people up the throat and shooting at things with a big fucking gun, yes, but not telling porkie pies.

No – Jack has simply got a bad memory – arguably the worst memory in football in fact. So who had the bloody bright idea of getting a man who could never remember the names of his players from one day to the next to write an autobiography? *The Journal* recently ran some excerpts from Big Jack's publication and I must say it is without doubt some of the best comedy I've seen for ages. Remember being 4-2 up at QPR and Peter Beardsley not wasting time at a corner and the game finishing 4-4? No, me neither. Remember the time Jack came onto the pitch to tell off Beardsley after we played Watford? Can you remember why? Yes, I can – but Jack can't. Doesn't stop him telling us about it at great length, though. But the best stuff is his reason for leaving us; apparently he got a load of abuse at a pre-season friendly – true enough, but do you know why? Apparently it was because Eric Gates chose to sign for sunderland instead of us. Honestly, I'm not making this up, that's what he says. Nothing to do with selling Chris Waddle then, eh Jack? Nothing to do with buying George Reilly, Gary Megson, and Pat Heard at all? Nothing to do with turning an exciting, attacking young team full of potential into an ugly fucking shambles? No, no, of course not.

All these years we've remembered Jack for the wrong reasons it seems, but then what do we know, according to wor Jack the people who wanted him out were "hooligans" and wor Jack isn't going to be dictated to by "yobs" – nice that he remembers us so fondly, isn't it?

Chapter 13

1996/97 postscript – A Distorted View

You know when bands that have been going 20 years put out a "Best of" album and they ignore the concept album about moon blood and dragon dreams they did when they were all fucked up and on hard drugs and weren't even talking to each other? Or better yet, consider the *Cut The Crap* album by The Clash, where only *This Is England* is redeemable. Well, between '96 and late '97 I appear to have been having my dodgy fourth album syndrome. And I wasn't even on drugs (well not hard ones anyway, I've rarely had the disposable income.) There were, however, lots of distractions. On revisiting the Furious page in *The Mag* for that season I now think: "what the fuck are you on about?" at my younger, less distinguished and finely tuned self. My younger self replies, "I'm doing two jobs, one of which involves DJing at The Riverside until 3 o'clock in the morning – you only see 3 o'clock in the morning when you shuffle to the toilet after being in bed for five hours, you old wanker."

My older self shakes his head and wonders how I lived so long.

Not concentrating at this time was all the rage: it was the year Newcastle United took their eye off the ball. John & Douglas Hall and Freddie Shepherd were giving themselves seven figure payouts and talk was of new grounds and share issues. If it wasn't for the small matter of buying Alan Shearer for £15 million we all might have thought we had turned into fucking accountants rather than football supporters.

In the cold light of day Newcastle United didn't need Alan Shearer, scoring goals had rarely been a problem but there was no cold light of day, only hot and sweaty delirium. Keegan bought Shearer and the city of Newcastle went insane. Newcastle United, on the other hand, went to the Far East where hot and sweaty delirium is more than a metaphor. Then they came home, played a nearly full-strength team at Lincoln to thank them for selling us Darren Huckerby two days before the Charity Shield against Manchester United. A game we played with a reckless number of strikers.

People wondered why we lost 4-0.

As we left Wembley the heavens opened so my own less-than-happy band cheered themselves up by starting a rumour that, on lifting the trophy, Eric Cantona had been struck by lightning and horribly killed. Which seemed to lift people's spirits considerably.

Newcastle lost two of their first three games including a home loss to Sheffield Wednesday when I (and everybody else for that matter) should have gone to the Reading Festival to see China Drum and The Prodigy instead.

Things picked up – Newcastle won their next seven league games, starting with a 2-1 win at sunderland, (where we weren't supposed to have any fans in attendance), fired Halmstads out of the UEFA Cup and consolidated our place at the top of the league by beating Man Utd 5-0.

Because we are Newcastle United we spoiled this by losing at Leicester the following week.

By the end of November we were out of the League Cup but still in Europe and still top of the League thanks to a 1-0 win at Arsenal.

By Christmas we were sixth and all was clearly not well; in January Kevin Keegan walked out. Kenny Dalglish came in as manager but before everybody could adjust we were out of the FA Cup and 1-0 down at home against Everton, for whom Gary Speed had scored. With 15 minutes left we came back to win 4-1. In the next game at home to Leicester we were 3-1 down with 15 minutes left but thanks to a Shearer hat-trick we won 4-3.

Monaco dumped us out of the UEFA Cup but a nine game unbeaten run in the League, culminating in a 5-0 last day win over Nottingham Forest, fired us to second in the League. It was the first year second place qualified for the Champions League which seemed to piss a lot of people off but as both Middlesbrough and sunderland were both relegated on the same gloriously sunny day you would have struggled to find a Newcastle fan who gave a shit.

Player of the Season: Alan Shearer.

Goal of the Season: "Phillipe Albeaaaaaaaaarrrrrrrrrrt!" (as Sky commentator Martin Tyler so memorably shouted.)

Chapter 14

September 1997

Don Howe's Dog Skin Trilby

Football statistics eh, what do you reckon? 67% of them are made up or bollocks according to the imaginary scientist who lives in my wardrobe.

Obviously the important ones matter, like how many games your team has won and how good your goal difference is, but beyond that? I mean, you can use them to factually point out that Newcastle United's notoriously dodgy defence has conceded less league goals than Manchester ("rock solid at the back – best goalkeeper in the world" etc) United in total over the last two seasons but most people outside the black and white masses will ignore you. *(True that – '95/96 + '96/97 = Man U conceded 79 to our 77.)*

According to Sky stats, Sheffield Wednesday had 50% of the possession in a recent game which isn't that big a deal until you find out another slightly more important stat from the same match.

They lost 7-2.

So where does that leave us? With the bloody OPTA Index, that's where. Last season Don Howe (doddering old duffer in a dog skin trilby) and a team of experts (grubby little men with thick glasses, bad skin, sweaty palms and no friends), set about the mind -numbing task of breaking down every Premiership game into its tiniest pieces to compile this OPTA Index thing to show who the best players are. Points are awarded for completed passes, goals and stuff while points are deducted for bad things like bookings, own goals and giving the ball away. Andy Gray used to feature the resulting tables on a Monday night on Sky but he's dumped them now presumably because they were rubbish, unrepresentative and irrelevant. For example, Liverpool passing the ball around in circles when they were 1-0 down with only ten minutes left was seen as a good thing because they didn't give the ball away. They may have lost the match but their midfield could take much consolation from knowing that they had three of the top ten places in the OPTA Midfielders list. Also, all the top marked defenders who didn't take penalties were full backs.

Points were not awarded for running off the ball and they were not taken away for having bad hair (Mikkel Beck) or looking like a murderer (Kvarme) so the whole thing was nonsense. Enter an unnamed regional newspaper with "the expert analysis that only the managers used to see." So what's my problem with it?

Well, seeing as you asked – I hate it because it takes away my supporter's right to exaggerate. What's the point of me standing in the pub after the recent Aston Villa game *(a 1-0 home win with a John Beresford goal)* getting excitable about how "Warren Barton won 50 tackles and cleared the ball 200 hundred times in the last ten minutes of the match!" (which to my recollection he did) if some swotty-arse with a computer is going to tell everybody different. It's just not right.

Keeping with statistics and things that just aren't right, 100% of the people I asked thought there was no need to call off the Liverpool v Newcastle match which was due to be played live on Sky for the nation because of the unfortunate demise of the former Princess of Wales in that tunnel in Paris. In fact I haven't spoken to one single person who thought postponing the game was the right thing to do. Yet there wasn't a dissenting voice across the entire media as far as I could tell.

Now even the most virulent anti-royal has got to admit that Diana did good work on stuff like AIDS, landmines and reportedly calling the last Tory government hopeless BUT the most bonkers pro-royal has to see that the whole thing has little to do with Liverpool or Newcastle football clubs or their followers. This isn't a criticism of anything except the crazy media-led society we live in; because I don't know about you but I was still expected to go to work the next day.

The game, we were told, was called off as a mark of respect. Despite Diana having no obvious interest in football. She had a soft spot for rugby, that she apparently put to good use – *(Yee-ha I've waited years to put that line back in)* – so were the rugby games that took place while Newcastle weren't playing at Liverpool disrespectful?

And what were we all supposed to do instead – sit around all day watching sycophantic hypocrites and parasites from the media wailing and gnashing their teeth because they'd finally seen off their chief supplier of golden goose eggs? Maybe, but the Metro Centre was apparently packed, presumably where the people working had to struggle on through their tears. I'm not even suggesting that people aren't or shouldn't be allowed to be upset but that's the way life goes. I personally found going to see Newcastle play at Manchester City and drinking beer with a load of mates the day after Kurt Cobain died a very comforting experience.

Finally, a bit of gossip – a reliable source informs me that during Newcastle's appearance at Goodison pre-season, a very bad person from within our ranks tried to punch former footballer, and Saint out of *The Saint & Greavsie*, Ian St John. This seems like an over-reaction to, and very late criticism of, an admittedly terrible TV show but might go some way to explain why in his role of co-commentator he sounded so desperate for Croatia Zagreb to beat us in the recent Champions League qualifier. Never mind that a load of Nazis in the crowd were racially abusing Tino Asprilla, never mind that the home team were diving all over the place or that Warren Barton was playing with blood pissing out of his head – we were the villains. We were lucky and the ref was cheating, an opinion that seemed to be echoed through the large section of the press that resents Newcastle United being in the Champions League despite having only finished second in our League. *(That's: "only second in our League.")*

Personally, all the crap we heard around that game made our victory all the sweeter – remember how nobody gave us a chance after the first game and all that stuff coming out of Zagreb about them winning 6-0? Then afterwards it's all, "we're only a little country and this isn't fair." Well for the record they were a damn good team and we beat them and it's about time somebody gave us some bloody credit for being in the Champions League instead of all this sniping. Bastards!

Of course these days finishing fourth is considered better than winning the FA Cup and Newcastle United have done well if they finish at all.

Chapter 15

September 1997

Barcelona at St James'

Like us, Barcelona only finished second in their domestic league but we didn't hear anyone bitching about how unworthy they are – on the contrary.

Everybody seemed to be falling over themselves to point out what small fry we are; how their team is valued at 400 hundred million quid or something and how they are the best supported team in the world.

Perhaps it's just me but I also got the impression that they didn't see us as much of a threat at all. Certainly Barca coach Van Gaal's remarks about what "English teams are like," gave me the impression that he didn't know or care a great deal about Newcastle United. This attitude (and some beer) changed my feeling from; "Who cares if we lose, we're playing Barcelona" to "We can beat these bastards, C'MON!" – and judging by the atmosphere at the ground I wasn't alone in that. The best supported team in the world brought about 200 fans, none of whom got a look in once the most fantastic atmosphere most of us have ever been part of took hold. For days after, people must have had sore throats as the black and white masses fuelled an inspired performance from our team. We were fantastic and got louder as the team was clearly responding. By about the 17th/18th minute we actually seemed to making the air shake such was the noise, which culminated in Tino Asprilla winning and scoring a penalty. Jon Dahl Tomasson, who had looked a bit nervy and had missed a couple of chances, knocked an exquisite ball into the area, the keeper came out and Asprilla tumbled over him. A nonchalant thwack from the spot, into the Gallowgate net, 1-0.

All over the pitch there were outstanding performances: Steve Watson was in exceptional form at centre-half and Phillipe Albert was immaculate but most eye-catching was a rejuvenated Keith Gillespie who defended heroically when required but more importantly attacked with speed and determination. Keithy ran his marker to death and crossed with startling accuracy. Tino timing his runs beautifully and leaping higher than looks physically possible scored twice to put us 3-0 up with the second half barely started. By which point most of us in the crowd had been rudely introduced to people in seats some distance from our own as we bundled chaotically all over each other in screaming, wild-eyed disbelief. Incredibly the Gillespie/Asprilla combination nearly made it four before our guests woke up to the fact that merely being Barcelona wasn't going to cut it here and they started to find their feet. Luis Enrique forced the ball home with his chest from close range to introduce some anxiety, Rivaldo hit the bar from a free kick and the crowd were at the point of barely contained hysteria when Figo shot through a forest of legs to make it 3-2 with time still on the clock. Fortunately our team showed more composure than us fans and held on to assure us of a result that sent shock waves out of Tyneside which will have been felt right across the world. Nice one.

Crowd 35,274

Chapter 16

December 1997

Christmas Was Ruined By the Christians

Thousands and thousands of years ago, pagan people all over Northern Europe would endure a bleak, tedious, long and dark winter with no tellies, video games or curry. It was obviously a bit depressing and parts of the world that were hot in December hadn't been invented yet so they had a big fuck-off party with loads of booze, food, shagging and football ("Football, are you sure?" – Ed) ("Yes!" – BF). Then Jesus was born. Jesus was basically a hippy communist revolutionary who said, "Hey, why don't we all be nice to each other?" – so they nailed the poor bugger to a couple of pieces of wood for being a trouble maker. In the meantime the people in Northern Europe continued to look forward to drinking, eating, shagging and playing football to cheer themselves up while they patiently waited for BBC 2 to be invented so they could watch *Some Like It Hot* every year.

"The Establishment" later decided that if little bits of what Jesus said could be re-packaged and made law people would behave themselves, stop mucking about and go to work, stop complaining about being invaded, ripped off and buggered by an increasingly powerful church – so they started celebrating Jesus' birth by giving each other Gold pants, Frankincense bath salts and Myrrh pie every October.

Not surprisingly, this didn't catch on so the Christians (many of whom Jesus would have hated by the way) switched Jesus' birthday to the same time as the pagans' mid-winter celebrations, claimed them as their own and built churches on pagan holy places and invited people to turn up pissed to sing *O Little Town of Bethlehem* at midnight mass. They tried to discourage the shagging and the football but people had been doing it for years and they liked it and wouldn't stop.

So if some lily-livered god-botherer tries to tell you to "remember what Christmas is supposed to be about," tell them to fuck right off because it wasn't their festival in the first place and remind them that the only bit of the nativity that is represented in December is gift giving and that it's rampant commercialism that has ruined Christmas anyway. So HA!

In an ideal world, Bar Oz on Percy Street would be open for 24 hours on Christmas Day but they would change its name to Bar Humbug, there would be no decorations except black ones, no Queen's speech, no new jumpers, no fat old perverts in red pyjamas and anyone putting *Last Christmas* by Wham on the jukebox would be squirted in the eyes with Jif lemon. Then on Boxing Day we could all go to the football to see Newcastle lose. A traditional Christmas, that's what the city needs.

Speaking of bastards: most football supporters have a league table of hate in their head. There is no such thing as a neutral. Most of us aren't really interested in a game on TV where we don't care who wins. So every fan has a League table of hate burrowed away in their head that they can refer to when teams other than their own take to the field. Some placings in this distinctly personal and individual League are obvious but when bored you can go through the entire fixture list and decide who you want to win. Or more likely who you want to lose because football supporters bear grudges longer than the Neapolitan Camorra which means Newcastle fans still think Brighton, Luton, Exeter, Chester and Hereford are all bastards. Still.

I mention this because Bolton were probably low on all out hate lists; four ex-Newcastle players, partisan supporters and a healthy dislike for Man Utd and Blackburn. My, how that has changed in recent weeks.

Newcastle have three away games in six days (Barcelona, Crystal Palace and Bolton) so we ask if it's possible for the last game to be put back 24 hours. The Premier League agrees, Sky Television agree but Bolton manager Colin Todd at Bolton feels, "it wouldn't be appropriate." Newcastle lose 1-0. Kenny Dalglish is asked about it and ever so politely suggests Bolton were seeking to take advantage of the situation. Todd accuses him of "sour grapes."

No Colin, The Sour Grapes were the annoying little girls who would run into the Banana Splits house and dance the jitterbug while Fleagle, Bingo, Drooper and

Snorky fell over each other's tails – Kenny was actually being over-polite when he should have called you a pack of cheating twats.

Turns out not to have been appropriate for Bolton to stay in the division in 1997/98: they were relegated and Colin Todd was all nice and sacked.

Chapter 17

May 1998

My Game Is Hanging Upside Down

I've sat in the Leazes End, middle tier, since that dewy-eyed summer afternoon when it first reopened. I like it and I have become fond of the people around me. The crazy drunk argumentative loons who sit behind me and have been known to beat me on the head to the tune of The Blaydon Races; Ken on my left who spends the second half listening to the radio and takes it upon himself to keep us all abreast of other pertinent scores. It's also comforting to know that no matter how late Wifey and I arrive, the chunky well-built bloke along from us will need to have us upstanding because he is later. I appreciate the way the people in front of me are so patient when I jump on their heads when we score and the fact that the people to my right don't complain about me having to go to the toilet at 3.43 pm every single game.

I would sooner give up a liver than my seat but recently our friend got a chance of a ticket and we didn't want her to have to sit alone. Also our seats are quite close to the away support and I felt I needed a break from treading that fine line between passionate backing of my team and the increasingly accusing eye of Br'er Plod and the Swear Patrol. Our happy band do look after each other to the extent of calming each other down – and you learn not to look at, or gesticulate at, the sweaty faced monkey who is insulting you and your team from within the enemy's ranks. There is the rare opportunity to have a bit crack-on with the away supporters, (Tranmere were cool and Liverpool and West Ham are always all right for a laugh or two), but mostly it's just having to come up with a witty retort to "Where were you when you were shit?" The best, in my opinion, being; "Looking for my hubcaps – hey you, yes you, you took them, stop thief!" (Liverpool); "Filling your poxy ground" (Everton); "Where were YOU when we were shit?" (Bolton) and increasingly, until very recently, "we were here a fortnight ago" (everybody else). Although you have to go a long way to beat the happy drunk who responded to the Stevenage following singing, "Where were you at Broadhall Way?" by rising unsteadily to his full height and shouting, "Shagging your fucking mother, now fuck off!" to much hilarity. *(yeah OK, it was me – is there a statute of limitations on swearing at the football; if not I would like several other offences to be taken into consideration.)*

So I entered into the lucky dip of getting one of those lone tickets that turn up from time to time and found myself in the lower tier of the Gallowgate for the recent game against Leeds – and entered the Twilight Zone. At home, yet totally unfamiliar. Among "my people" yet not knowing a soul. Not only that but I'm close enough to the pitch to see how scabby and awful it is and everything is backwards!

I cheer on my own when Newcastle elect to kick towards the Leazes End in the second half because that's what I have done for years and am genuinely shocked to discover that the atmosphere is the same. You see, from the Leazes we rarely hear the Gallowgate sing – to the extent of cheering sarcastically when we do. Now I can't hear the Leazes and people around me are complaining because my end "is full of black and white zombies who don't pull their weight."

People jump up and scream abuse at the hackers, butchers and cheats who are presently pulling on the Leeds shirt and again I am shocked. Not because of the bad language itself but because they use it without an instinctive nervous glance towards the nearest copper – lucky buggers. Also the team appeared to be playing better from this view but I later discovered that this was simply because we actually did play better which is interesting because the last time our friend got the chance to go was against Dynamo Kiev and we played well and won 2-0. Perhaps I should do this more often – but I want my seat back, damn it.

Chapter 18

May 1998

The Death of the Cup Final Song

In May 1998 The Mag was full of stuff about Newcastle United reaching an FA Cup Final for the first time in 24 years and further reaction to Freddie Shepherd and Douggy Hall's careless comments made to an undercover reporter from the News of the World supposedly whilst in a house of ill-repute. My only direct reference to this is the Gobshite in a Brothel gag. Freddie Fletcher was brought to the club by John Hall and many Newcastle fans recall him being some kind of Chief Executive/ Childcatcher hybrid. He had the unenviable task of maximizing the club's revenue and defending Hall Junior and Shepherd. He was later held responsible for moving many fans out of their seats whilst expanding the club's corporate facilities. I waved politely to him one morning just outside Ponteland – he seemed unnerved by this but waved back. He left the club in 2000.

The strangest thing happened the other morning – my alarm went off like the hateful bastard that it is and another day bullied its way into my previously happy little beer-soaked head. No more roasty-toasty duvet and lots more rainy-wet morning and idiots fucking with my life. No change there then. Neither was there much unusual about an ungainly stumble to the coffee jar and a hopeful switch on of Radio 5 to see if Kenny Dalglish had made a late bid for a seriously under-priced Georgi Kinkladze.

As it happened they were talking about Newcastle United and yes, they were slagging us off. It seems that two Newcastle fans have penned a jaunty little ditty that they planned to release upon the pop charts in order to celebrate our team's forthcoming trip to the FA Cup Final. No doubt with dreams of appearing on *Top Of The Pops* with the players, they approached the club for support and were surprised that instead of the slightest hint of encouragement they were told in no uncertain terms (and I paraphrase for my own amusement here), "You release that shit and we'll sue your fucking bollocks off!"

Now the strange bit: while the interviewer clucked along about how the hierarchy at Newcastle United were terrible spoilsports who should be more conscious of their public relations ("especially after all that has gone on up there recently") I'm standing in my matching Rupert Bear pyjamas and slippers uttering the most unlikely sentence: "Thank you Freddie Fletcher. Thank you from the bottom of my heart, thank you." You see the song (a tatty piece of nauseating, weak-arsed drivel backed by a pathetic euro-disco beat) had the words Toon Army repeated over and over in it and the club owns the copyright on "Toon Army", specifically so that grotty little back street peddlers can't legally stick it on their shoddy wares and pieces of shit and try and sell it to people. And a bloody good job too.

Hopefully this massive overreaction to a novelty song will discourage Busker from his latest comeback. Busker (whose song *Home Newcastle* is the first track on *Now That's What I Call Sentimental Geordie Claptrap)*, you will remember, cost us the League title the other year by releasing a song called *"Champions"* in bloody February and I feared he would be planning a follow-up.

It turns out the club, far from providing quality control, was actually just squishing any competition for the official song. The club obviously wanted a song for the FA Cup because... well...er...everybody has one and presumably having been turned down by Napalm Death and the Chemical Brothers they approached Sting. Sting took time off his busy schedule of writing songs about rainforests and Quentin Crisp to churn out a song called *Walking on the Goon (er)* or *Gobshite in a Brothel* or some such but wasn't prepared to dirty his hands by actually singing on it so they found some tramp to warble along with 250 of his mates. It's rubbish by the way. No, I haven't actually heard it but of course it's rubbish, only a fool would expect anything else.

But why do we need a song at all? Singles don't make any money anymore, they are just adverts for albums, and the last thing we need is an album of Cup Final songs, unless it is to trap them all in the same barn before setting it on fire like in *Braveheart.*

Football and pop music can work together *(World in Motion, Three Lions, England's Irie,* Sky's end of programme clips) but all too often the people who make the decisions are hopelessly out of their depth and before you know it we have the equivalent of your dad being in charge of the youth club disco at which he is prepared to dance. Witness the semi-final at Old Trafford and the announcement that two songs had been chosen by each club to be played before the game. How we cringed as the Newcastle choices were *Simply The Best*, sung by that shabby old fortune teller from *Mad Max 3* having some sort of fit, and *Local* (bloody bastard) *Hero*. We were only saved from shrivelling like 30,000 salted snails by the fact that Sheffield United chose *Sailing* by Rod Stewart and *Annie's Song* by John Denver to celebrate their big day. At least we had the decency to look sheepish, the Blades fans started singing along. Have you people no shame?

Finally, credit to sunderland chairman Bob Murray for handing over his club's quota of 80 tickets to Newcastle season ticket holders. The local press have called it a drop in the ocean but if you think about it that's two coach loads of Newcastle fans who won't miss a game they shouldn't have been in any danger of missing. If more clubs followed this example there would more genuine fans at future finals and less free-loading scum-sucking fucking bastards.

Cheers.

This article was originally entitled "Oi Busker Don't You Fuckin' Dare" - but the artist formally known as Busker has since died and so out of compassion for his friends and family I changed the title and removed some of my criticism of him and his music. Despite my personal opinion being that the artist was a fucking nuisance and his music irredeemably awful. At a Spanish airport departure lounge in 2010 waiting for a flight back to Tyneside was a group of seriously hungover Geordie lads, one of whom kept singing "I'm Coming Home Newcastle" until one of his mates said (and I cuff away a tear of pride as I remember this), "Howay man, fuck off!"

The wonder of Google tells us that the Sting written song was called Black and White Army (Bringing the Pride Back Home). I read the lyrics while trying to muster the courage to click the Play button. Pausing briefly to remember that bringing any pride home was the last thing our team managed in a charmless 2-0 surrender to Arsenal I held my breath and went for it. What I got was a catchy Punjabi sound which may or may not have been the same song but as I unfortunately don't speak Punjabi, Urdu or Bangla I couldn't tell you. I chose to look on the whole event as a narrow escape and fled the site like it was makemnazipaedoporn.com – which you must never put into your search engine, however tempted.

Chapter 19

1997/98 postscript – A Distorted View

I liked Kenny Dalglish, still do for that matter, fucking live with it. As a player he was so brilliant that you had to be constantly careful not to forget that Liverpool were functional, deliberately tedious and horrible spoilsports. All organised and winning things. Bastards.

Kenny had to follow the Sainted Keegan as Newcastle manager and never complained about what he was left with. Despite what he was left with being an ageing and thin squad, no reserves or youth set-up to speak of, and a board of directors that was intent on cutting costs. Supposedly, David Ginola spent most of this time under Dalglish having a colossal strop on because Keegan had talked him out of joining Barcelona before buggering off himself the second somebody hid the cheque book. So Ginola had to go and we had to gamble on young and cheap which is always going to throw up some lads who just don't cut it. Which is a shame because Des Hamilton and Brian Pinas looked good at a pre-season game at Bradford. A game memorable for Stuart Pearce and David Batty both closing down a Bradford player who kicked the ball into the crowd rather than face up to such a dangerous prospect as well as the Newcastle fans camping it something wicked. I doubt any player ever got a higher songs to pitch-time ratio than young master Pinas.

All of Dalglish's mistakes make sense if you believe that he thought he could get Robbie Fowler out of Liverpool in the January of '98: letting Les Ferdinand leave, not getting a proper replacement when Alan Shearer got seriously injured in a pre-season game that put him out for five months. Bringing in a creaking Ian Rush as a stopgap. When Fowler got injured playing for Liverpool, Dalglish immediately spent the money he had made from flogging Ginola and Sir Les to

Spurs. OK, that money was spent on Andreas Andersson but I can't be doing with "Dalglish sold good players and bought shit" when he had to deal with Shearer being injured, The Honourable Lord Peter Beardsley being past his best and Ginola being so damned French. I'm delighted Stuart Pearce was a Newcastle player (he ran to our corner of SJP and shouted "Fucking C'mon!" at us on his home debut – which was brilliant); you could see Pistone was quality and Jon Dahl Tomasson went on to prove those wrong who condemned him as rubbish by winning stacks of silver shit at AC Milan. Gary Speed anybody, Nicos Dabizas at all? Shay Given... hmmm. People still scoff and name check an aged Ian Rush as a Dalglish buy, forgetting that Rush's goal at Everton helped get us to the FA Cup Final. And without John Barnes' goals we might have got relegated.

Circumstance and a refusal to toady up to the more significant shithouses in the local and national media did for Dalglish. Look at the team that played in the magnificent 3-2 win over Barcelona, it is well under-strength. We also beat Dynamo Kiev and were immaculate in qualifying for the group stage of the Champions League against Croatia Zagreb. The same season we got to the quarter final of the League Cup (lost in extra time to Liverpool) as well as the FA Cup Final. Dalglish had to deal with a hostile press thanks to Stevenage being jumped up little shit-pots and Hall and Shepherd talking bollocks to a dastardly sneak from *The News of the World*. Kenny was funny if you bothered listening and was charming when Wifey met him for an interview for *The Mag*. He must have remembered her as well because he waved when he saw her at Barcelona airport. I loved him for that and for the fact that, thanks to him, we were in fucking Barcelona. Our draw at Manchester United (the much maligned Andersson scoring in a 1-1 draw) helped the Salford mob lose a 13 point lead in the title race to Arsenal, something we were told would never happen to them.

Dalglish was hobbled when Newcastle manager by terrible luck and a catastrophic injury record. Arsenal had better players than us in the Cup Final obviously, they had just won the League while we were 13th, and Kenny tried to keep the game tight and nick it. People forget that at 1-0 to The Gunners, Newcastle had a couple of really good chances. I'm not saying we played well, we clearly didn't, but like a lot of that season Dalglish did damn well with what he had. And we qualified for Europe because we got to the Cup Final while Arsenal did the double during Arsene Wenger's first full season in charge.

That said, Dalglish did buy bloody Ketsbaia.

Player of the Season: Rob Lee and David fucking Batty.

Goal of the Season: Ketsbaia against Zagreb. It meant we qualified for the Champions League Group stage and while I was running up the street screaming I swear I could hear people doing the same all across Newcastle. At least that's what I told the nice policeman.

Chapter 20

January 1999

Irn Bru & Egg Sandwiches

It's the first of January 1999 as I write this. Hung-over and actually in Newcastle for the first time in three years, thanks to our civic leaders and cops who, by letting the pubs stay open, finally woke up to the fact that people might actually want to go out and celebrate New Year in this city.

Irn Bru, egg sandwiches and (eventually) more beer will cure much, but not the gnawing sense of disappointment that I feel.

You see, in the 1970s the popular TV show *Space 1999* promised me that I could be living on the moon, whizzing about in a rocket ship, wearing (and flirting with space-girls in) a shiny nylon jump suit and never having to worry about going to the toilet again by this exact date.

Instead I find myself here... (dramatic pause to survey the world)... enduring ghastly little pop stars like 911 and Billie, still having to put up with referees who think Liverpool's God-given right to win at Anfield is a law more powerful than the actual rules of the game AND having, on a daily sodding basis, to put up with a sporting press that could only be more malicious if it wasn't so incompetent and lazy.

If EVER any doubters needed a snapshot view of how the press operates in this country you only have to look at the whole "Ruud Gullit spends more time in Amsterdam than in Newcastle" bollocks. One ill-informed muppet wrote it a few weeks ago and now it's gospel truth and that's it. All the other ill-informed muppets can repeat it without fear of contradiction. Nothing like actual facts are allowed to get in the way and no witnesses for the defence need be called. So Ruud Gullit spends more time in Amsterdam than in Newcastle, it's a disgrace. Apparently.

Strange, because Warren Barton said in a recent TV interview that he himself turns up for training early but that Gullit is always there before him and that

Ruudi stays on after the first team players have gone to train the kids. Over Christmas I spoke to a splendid gentleman who lives in Chester-le-Street near to where the team trains and he told me that Gullit is there every day. It's not like he is hard to miss and it would be so easy to find out the real truth. But where would be the scandal in that?

Within a matter of days, Ruud Gullit has learnt that at Newcastle a dignified silence is not allowed – like Kenny Dalglish he tried it but ended up in a spectacular press conference looking at the pack of bastards representing the national press with fury and fire in his eyes saying, "You bitch-assed fuckers, write one more lie about me or bother my family again and I will sue you within an inch of your worthless fucking lives!" (Not his actual words but I personally like to think that's what he meant). Not since Keegan went righteously bonkers at Leeds have I felt such pride in a manager reacting to unfairness. The press claim not to like this sort of thing and get very sniffy about it but it has got to be better for them than the recent televised Alex Ferguson interview which involved him droning on after the Chelsea/Man Utd match where nothing he said was interesting enough to draw the viewers attention away from, what certainly looked like, a great big bogey stuck to the end of his shiny red hooter.

Speaking of people's appearances on TV, Mark Lawrenson's moustache has now become so preposterously enormous that he has gone from looking like a Village People
reject to looking like a man who is carping at us whilst peering over a privet hedge.

Welcome to Newcastle Ruudi – people don't like us. Witness perennial Mag hater Tony Gubba's mumbled "Charvet scores" as the ball ripped into the Middlesbrough net at over 80 miles an hour compared to his "YES!" when Cooper accidentally deflected the ball over Steve Harper.

Witness the *Daily Mirror* reporting the crowd were actually booing Gullit rather than the daft ref and the bloody horrible Leeds team at the end of their ridiculous 0-3 win at St James' Park recently.

Witness the regional reporter for *The Guardian* writing like he would rather have rusty nails banged into his eyes than have to suffer another 90 minutes watching Newcastle play (if you don't like it – fuck off and get a proper job).

Paranoid?

You had better believe it and with good fucking reason.

History has not been at all kind to Ruud Gullit as far as his time at Newcastle is concerned. It obviously all ended very badly as everybody within either football or Newcastle knows. When he turns up on Sky Sports sitting next to Graham Souness and offering expert analysis I am surely not the only Newcastle fan scoffing audibly at the screen; "Look at this pair of discredited fuck-wits pretending to know what the fuck they are talking about." But there was a time where we liked him, when he was doing well and where we thought he had our best interests at heart. One should never forget that, unlike Souness, when he saw his job was going tits up he left without financial remuneration. Interesting too that 10 years later Joe Kinnear, whilst Newcastle manager, was also driven to shouting at the press over their malicious lies. Amazingly Billie went from being a detestable pop star to being a bloody good actress - which surely nobody saw coming.

Chapter 21

February 1999

True Romance

It always seems pointless to me when the media announce the bookmakers' odds for who is going to win the FA Cup before at least the quarter finals. There are so many variables, the most obvious being that the two top favourites could be drawn to play each other. This occurs because the media don't think like football fans. They don't understand what the FA Cup is, which is why they try and sell us the same lies every year and expect us all to buy into them blindly. Well no more. Let's nail a couple of smelly great lies now and forever, shall we?

Firstly: "Giant-killing is part of the romance of the FA Cup" – cobblers! Giant-killing is only either hilarious or a bloody nightmare. Example; West Ham got dumped out by Swansea in the Third Round. Imagine asking a West Ham supporter how romantic they felt after that? Romance is candlelit bubble baths or a weekend in Paris (preferably involving someone as well as yourself). Romance is not suddenly finding yourself in Wales, on a freezing Wednesday night, sobering up quickly to the thought that you have a long journey home, work tomorrow, piss-taking to endure forever and the fact that some hairy-arsed Welsh bloke in a ten foot swan suit is dancing up and down on your last hope of doing anything at all this season.

Naturally everyone except West Ham fans thinks it's amusing but no one thinks it is "romantic". Romance is surely more to do with giving flowers for no reason or driving to Los Angeles in an open top car with Patricia Arquette than it has to do with watching fat smelly pub players trying to make a name for themselves by kicking real footballers up in the air.

I tell you what I'm sick of seeing every bloody year as well; every time a pokey little market town or commuter belt shit-hole full of wannerbe cockneys gets to the Third Round of the FA Cup, we have exactly the same pre-match feature. Picture the scene (you've seen it a thousand times), some doddering old biddy (who by rights should be locked in someone's attic) wearing a home knitted scarf, covered in badges, with little plastic flags sticking out of her hat is doing a clumsy can-can for the cameras while skinny youths pull faces and shout a lot. Behind them is the local butcher shop where the owner, using food dye, tripe and other offal is displaying a grotesque representation of the club badge, while the town mayor is lying unconvincingly about what an up and coming place they all live in, despite the local nightlife being entirely dependent on hard drugs and trying not to get stabbed.

Come match day, the crowd sing songs they have only ever heard on the telly, hopefully they lose. Tony Gubba says how brave and spirited they have all been (despite the fact that their only chance was a deflected back pass), the old woman vanishes until the next Tory party conference where she can be seen doing the same dance but now waving little union jacks, the youths will go back to sniffing glue and getting each other pregnant whilst pretending to support Spurs or Man Utd and the butcher will go back to putting people's pets' eyelids and testicles into his sausages.

Is that your idea of romance? Because if it is you ain't going to be getting much when those youthful good looks fade, I can tell you.

Secondly: "Everybody in this country loves the underdog" – lies lies lies. What we love in this country is taking the piss out of people. If a member of the Royal Family or the detestable pop star Billie were to slip on a great big dog turd and crack their head open on the pavement we would all think it top entertainment. We would laugh and rewind the video again and again. This doesn't mean we love great big dog turds, does it? When Rushden and Diamonds went 1-0 up against Leeds no football supporter thought, "Hoorah for the plucky underdog!" We all thought of a Leeds fan we know who we could point at and giggle at when next we saw them. You can tell no one really likes the underdog because as soon as the little team goes a second goal down you instantly want the big team to score 12 or preferably 50.

Granted, giant-killing is a gift that keeps giving. It has been over 40 years since Yeovil selected a team of shit-kicking pig-fuckers and beat sunderland. No one has any lasting affection for the shit-kicking pig-fuckers but the whole country shouts "Wa-hey!" whenever they show the grainy old footage of the goal that did the damage. Similarly no one in sunderland knows where Hereford even is, but even the most slack-jawed inbreed in a red and white shirt (fill in own joke here) raises a smile when Ronnie bastard Radford's goal is shown a hundred times each season.

Similarly, I had little more than the most passing of interests in Bishop Auckland beating Colchester in the FA Cup. I was aware that they were vaguely local but I don't know any of their players or anyone who goes, so who gives a fuck? BUT then I remembered that I know some poor sap who supports Colchester and suddenly, it's the best result of the year. What larks.

And that's the point – underdogs aren't for loving, even at Christmas, they are for people (who aren't us) to fall over and hurt themselves on. Because let the little bastards start to believe that everyone loves them and you end up with a Stevenage situation and that simply will not do.

Chapter 22

1998/99 postscript – A Distorted View

The best thing about the '98/99 season was our away kit; electric blue with a yellow trim. I was instantly besotted with it to the extent that my friend Kev Broon threatened to murder me when I suggested it should be our first kit instead of silly old black and white stripes.

Kenny Dalglish continued ruining the Keegan legacy by bringing in sub-standard rubbish like Dietmar Hamman and Nobby Solano (that's sarcasm by the way) but I do step sharply away from Stephane Guivarc'h. Guivarc'h must have been some good – he was top scorer in France the season before Dalglish bought him and was first choice striker for the French as they began what turned out to be a successful charge at the World Cup. His injury and consequential absence from the later rounds was probably an advantage to the French, having subsequently witnessed him play for Newcastle United. Although "play" seems something of an exaggeration because apart from popping in a consolation goal in a home mauling by Liverpool he didn't do anything, in fact you couldn't see why or how he had ever been any good. He wasn't quick, clever, skilful or brave, he wasn't good in the air, didn't bring other players into the game and marking him looked a piece of piss. We stood in lashing rain at White Hart Lane in the October watching him and Alan Shearer up front for us and they clearly didn't get on, so much that they wouldn't even look at each other, never mind consider passing a football in each other's direction. Guivarc'h was part of a squad that won the World Cup but he refused to move faster than an idle trot; Shearer would have set himself on fire and run through walls for club and country (probably – we should ask him): proof, if ever it were needed, that life and football ain't fair. Speaking of unfair, I was so disgusted with the sacking of Dalglish two games into the new season that I stopped writing for *The Mag* in protest. Fight the Power! In the next game we got battered 1-4 at home against Liverpool and I thought it served us right. Not a popular opinion especially as it was drunkenly expressed by my clapping and shouting, "what's the matter, I thought we all wanted to see more goals?" as Liverpool banged in the fourth.

But what can the disgruntled fan do? Shut up and get behind the new manager, usually, which was easy because Ruud Gullit was smart and glamorous and handsome and confident. Newcastle would become more European on and off the pitch with such a man at the helm. We would become more tolerant and open-minded and we would drink espressos in the street and the bars would stay open all night.

Wouldn't we?

Not really, Gullit couldn't do anything about the awful weather and Partizan Belgrade knocked us straight out of the Cup Winners Cup, which to be fair we had little business being in anyway. It started well: during September Newcastle won four games and scored 13 goals in the process. It felt like Dalglish had been telling us not to attack and Ruudi simply flicked the switch to 'on' and said, "let's enjoy ourselves shall we? Go on lads, get about them!" Newcastle were suddenly third in the League table.

By the end of October we were out of Europe and 11th. Near the end of November we were out of the League Cup and 14th. We were particularly bad at Everton so how or why Duncan Ferguson left them to join us provoked some scepticism. He cost £8 million (+ Newcastle not trying at Goodison Park, cynics suggested), but he scored twice on his debut against Wimbledon and we spent the rest of the season thinking, "when we get Shearer and Ferguson fit at the same time we will be unplayable" – but it rarely happened. After his debut, Ferguson played eight other games and didn't score again.

Indifferent form and injuries meant Newcastle dithered about in the League (although the 4-3 win at Derby was a laugh) but the FA Cup run was something else, culminating in Gullit out-manoeuvring George Graham's Spurs in the semi-final at Old Trafford. A game where we Newcastle fans again made the main stand bounce, in a way that visibly startled the local stewards, after Alan Shearer howitzered in the second goal.

After the game Gullit and Shearer were photographed smiling at each other and shaking hands. The band Gene has a song *As Good as it Gets* which always reminds me of this never to be repeated occasion.

Contrary to popular opinion, we played quite well in the final that Manchester United won as part of their historic treble.

Player of the Season: Dietmar Hamman.

Goal of the Season: Louis Saha at Blackburn in the FA Cup.

Chapter 23

November 1999

Mascots

In the winter of 1999 editorial meetings for The Mag would take place in The Strawberry public house over plates of cheesy chips. England manager Kevin Keegan was presiding over the vital European Championship play-off match versus arch enemy Scotland but I was keen on starting what has turned out to be a ten year war against Newcastle United's players coming on to the pitch to Mark Knopfler's Local Hero – dreary fucking dirge that it is.

When discussions began at *The Mag* about what we could do about stopping our team coming out to the revolting *Local Hero* the editor's eyes glazed over. He frowned and became momentarily confused by the idea of anything happening before five, or even ten, past three on a Saturday or Sunday afternoon at all. You see, it is considered frightfully bad form for any of us to be seen entering the ground before kick-off. What better time than five minutes before the match actually begins to buy some more beer? After all there isn't a queue at the bar for the first time in two hours. Many of you clearly feel the same. Long gone are the days when you would have to get into the ground an hour before kick-off with nothing else to do to pass the time except make loads of fucking noise. Nowadays most of us wander into the ground, sit down and think, "Well go on Newcastle, start scoring," before starting to complain about how the atmosphere isn't what it used to be.

Having made such a fuss about what music the team comes out to I thought it only polite to start turning up a little earlier. Rob the club DJ has done a terrific job with the music but he could use some help I'm sure and that help will not be coming from our two new club mascots. Two people in flea-bitten old black and white costumes that have flat duck-like beaks sticking out of their heads and spindly legs in what (God help us) look like white tights sticking down from the body. I am reliably informed that they represent "two for joy" magpies. Unfortunately foreign visitors will leave thinking, "nice people, nice stadium (when it's finished), some good players but why is the club mascot two dead ducks impaled on a cocktail stick. Twice?"

I could not put it better than the chap (Paul) who sits behind me, who had clearly drunk his last pint too quickly, and was in the ground earlier than he had been for some time. On clapping eyes on the ducks he visibly wobbled, peered through the beer haze, pointed a shaky finger and shouted, "AND WHAT THE FUCK IS THAT SUPPOSED TO BE??!!"

Like anything at SJP that doesn't make somebody a lot richer, the mascot idea is half-arsed. They tried it before, when we first got promoted into the Premier League. Again there were two magpies but the old ones looked like birds and not like a pissed pig on stilts at a fancy dress party. One was male and one was female – you could tell one was female because it differed from the male in that it carried a handbag. This was the early days of Sky Television's coverage and afeared that everybody would suddenly stop going to football if it was on the telly they provided dancing girls to stem our straying loyalty. I was very drunk at the time so forgive me if I've remembered this incorrectly but the male magpie approached a dancing girl and made the universally recognized open-handed palms-out gesture that denotes intended breast grapplage. At which point the female magpie flew into a terrible rage and, wielding her handbag over her head, pursued the errant male around the pitch while the crowd laughed and roared its approval. Following this distressing insight into Mr. & Mrs. Magpie's domestic life they never appeared again – I think there were letters of complaint in *The Evening Chronicle*.

The new ones are rubbish and worse than that they are lazy. Simply walking around waving and patting the child-mascot on the head isn't a day's work now is it? They should take penalties or race over hurdles against opposition mascots or better still they should, after the kick-off, be employed as stewards in the away support section of the stadium. Seeing people dressed as contestants from *It's A Knockout* manhandling foul-mouthed troublemakers (i.e. away fans who stand up) out of the ground is something we would surely all like to see.

But what's the point of offering up such sensible ideas – the people who run football don't understand fans and they prove it on an almost daily basis. They think they can chuck people out of their seats and give their Cup Final ticket to a knob in a suit and we won't fucking notice.

Kevin Keegan should know better than "hope the English fans would respect the Scots' national anthem" – sorry Kev old stick but bollocks! BOOOOOOOOOOO! And indeed the England fans responded with one of the most fantastic examples of booing Wembley has ever witnessed and those fans watching at home, laughed and laughed and laughed.

And then England were rubbish and we stopped laughing and started asking what is it that Jamie Redknapp is actually supposed to be doing?

My other favourite comment recently (apart from someone suggesting that Silvio Maric might be struggling because he is not used to the cold weather – like Croatia is a suburb of fuckin' Kingston, Jamaica) is one that is being used so often that it is danger of being taken seriously. You've all heard it, here we go: - "Football supporters pay to see 11 against 11 – all these sendings off ruin the game as a spectacle."

I'm sorry, when did being a football supporter start equating with some quaint old idea about fairness? When was the last time a player got sent off against Newcastle and you thought, "Oh no, that's the game ruined. What a pity the ref didn't show some common sense."

Nope, you were standing on your seat cheering and waving as the poor lemon stomped off towards the touchline. Not only that but you expect any opposing fan to do the same when one of our players gets a red card. We are not fair people. We are mean spirited and spiteful, vengeful to a point when even the mafia would say "let it go".

Admit it, what is your dream goal against sunderland for any team playing them; a bicycle kick at the end of a free flowing attacking move? Nonsense sir! Here it is. It's nil nil, the 4th official has held up the board indicating three minutes remaining, yet despite this five minutes have elapsed with no new injuries, the game goes on. A free kick is given after a sunderland player is incorrectly flagged offside. A quickly taken free kick is dispatched towards a forward who is clearly offside and who has just pushed the last defender over. He shoots, the shot hits the bar and bounces a good foot in front of the line but the goal is given anyway. The opposition celebrates, the sunderland bench is apoplectic with rage, fans have to be restrained by stewards and two players are sent off for arguing before the ref blows for full time. Perfect – now remind me about that 11 against 11 thing again please.

Chapter 24

April 2000

Wembley – Knock It Down

Newcastle lost the FA Cup semi-final to Chelsea 2-1 – this was written the day after when we were still feeling hard done by. 10 years later that feeling has only partially faded.

Well I don't know about you but I shall be wanting Chelsea to win the old piss-pot that is the FA Cup now, despite the presence of Frank Lebeouf who in my not very humble opinion is a cheating TART! of a footballer.
I think that of all the indignities the FA Cup has suffered this season (Third Round in December, games spread all over the place, semi-finals at Wembley etc etc) I think having a team as lousy as the present Aston Villa mob winning it would be just too much. Pundits pointed, quite rightly, at their semi-final with Bolton and said it was poor (piss-poor to be more precise). Where the press got it wrong was when they said Villa could play better than that. No they can't. That's how Villa play: bore the opposition to death, waste time, defend deep and hope to sneak a goal. I don't care that they've got some lovely Geordie lads *(Steve Watson and Alan Thompson)* their manager *(John Gregory)* is an odious sneaking lizard of a man AND it's pretty fuckin' rich of them to complain about their ticket allocation for the final when they haven't been able to fill Villa Park all season on account of the team being so deliberately tedious.
But how much do we really care – it's the day after the semi-final as I waffle, our hearts are heavy and football has bitten off another piece of our soul and spat it down the toilet. I forced myself to watch the video and came to the conclusion that it hurt more than the two Final losses we have endured because we played so well. I squirmed at the missed chances, whinged about the rolling ball before their first goal and the foul on Kieron Dyer in the build-up to their second, squealed at Lebeouf's constant gamesmanship and remembered that during our

game at sunderland ref De-mott Gallagher gave us fuck all then as well. You have to wonder how Chelsea played flat out on the previous Wednesday but were at full strength while we had the week off but were without Helder, Gallacher and Ferguson. Desailly was fantastic for Chelsea and Poyet took his goals well but (along with conceding last minute goals at Anfield) I am utterly sick of coming away from Wembley with a brave face masking unbearable gnawing frustration. Whatever it is that we're being punished for isn't that enough now. Never mind the unfairness of Newcastle fans being forced into a 500 hundred mile round trip while Chelsea's supporters had to do little more than roll out of bastard bed.

A couple of things it was impossible for those of us lucky enough to be at the game to have noticed that the video threw up: firstly co-commentator Andy Gray saying, "For God's sake referee" as Lebeouf flattened Dyer seconds after a blatant edge of the area handball that also went unpunished, and secondly Alan Shearer shouting at an off-screen Chelsea player (hopefully Lebeouf) "Fuck off! Twat!" which made me smile.

I'm with Shearer on Wembley as well – knock it down, blow up the rubble and fire the bits into the sun. I'm sick of the sight of the bastard.

Looking on the bright side – we scored at Wembley, I kind of thought we would never do that - Robert Lee's tremendous header is playing over and over on my brain-telly. This season has not been a disaster because a football season is not only about League position – like the fools down the road seem to think. sunderland's claim to be "Top Dogs" reckons without Newcastle winning more games and scoring more goals than them, including a thrilling European campaign culminating in seeing our boys run out at the Olympic Stadium in Rome, we beat up on Man Utd *(3-0)* and we all got the opportunity to enjoy a day drinking in the sunshine going to Wembley.

St James' Park is going to look fantastic, Bobby Robson has got us playing again and some of our players are, quite frankly, fucking brilliant.

As if that wasn't enough to be hopeful about we have returned to wearing black socks instead of the terrible white ones Gullit insisted on.

So like I said, I hope Chelsea win the Cup – but I won't be bloody well watching the bastard.

Chapter 25

May 2000

The 1980s Were Bollocks

'Twas the night before the season started and I bumped into my mate John. Always a cheerful soul John, one of those fellows it gladdens your soul to come across. "Alright?" he beamed. But John's smile had a slightly manic twist and the gleam in his eye worried me. "Alright," says I, fixing him with a stare. "What?" says he, somewhat defensively. Then it struck me what was wrong, "Oh my God," I breathed.
"What?" He is noticeably more defensive and thus confirming my suspicions.
"You think we are going to win the League."
He briefly considered denying it before nodding ferociously and grinning even wider. "Aye!"
Now John is a good friend and I love him very much, so naturally I was keen to exploit this temporary delirium towards my own financial gain. Obviously my conscience forbids me betting against Newcastle so I ask him who he thinks will be relegated. I forget who he said but crucially he didn't say Watford. I assume he has overlooked them and press the point. "No. I think they will stay up." We make The Bet.

The Bet: every point Watford are above third bottom I will give John a shiny new pound for. But every point Watford are behind fourth bottom he will give me a pound. We shake hands.
This is a splendid bet for two reasons. Reason 1; Watford are awful. They got in the Premiership by accident, they will finish so bottom that footballing administrators, annoyed with themselves for allowing Watford up in the first

place, will try to hide their shame by relegating Watford straight into the Third Division where they belong. Watford won't complain because having been beaten like a red-headed stepchild every time they take the field are hiding under a table and refusing to play anymore. They are subsequently docked enough points for myself and Wifey to enjoy a fortnight in Disneyland at John's expense. Hoorah!

Reason 2: I get to explain my seemingly irrational hatred of Watford. They are a team from the 1980s and their reappearance in the top flight has coincided with Culture Club and ABC reforming and people having '80s parties and those people saying what a great time we all had.

UTTER UTTER UTTER DONKEY'S ARSE AND FUCKING LIES THE '80s WERE SHITE!!!!!!!

People seem to have forgotten that pubs in Newcastle only sold Exhibition and rancid fucking lager (Except for The Broken Doll that sold Slalom D which was brilliant but was likely to render the drinker somewhat dead) and that all pubs shut in the afternoon and again at half past ten at night. Half past fucking ten.

All chart music (except Siouxsie and the Banshees) was bloody horrible. All girls (except girls who liked Siouxsie and the Banshees) looked terrible because they thought the only fashionable way to go out was with grotesque dollops of scarlet blusher and ugly smears of blue eye-shadow plastered under a Princess Diana haircut. Watch the audience in those repeats of *Top of the Pops* if you don't believe me, damn it.

Kids, don't be taken in by the lies. Apologists racing towards middle age will give you a knowing look and talk of endless drinking and shagging. Well obviously – what else was there to do? All TV except *Hill Street Blues* and *Dangermouse* was fucking garbage and there was no such thing as Playstations. Being a football supporter meant you got treated like a leper with a chainsaw by the police and general public and we had to spend games peering through fences at shit footballers with skinny arms and big hair. We were told that watching a Liverpool team, wearing obscenely tight shorts, pass the ball back to the goalkeeper for 90 minutes was good football and told that Watford were the way all football clubs should be run in the future; lots of lovely families in garish colours smiling and bringing picnics to the match. Never mind the fact that their ground was rotten and in the middle of nowhere, or that the team made lumping the ball towards George Reilly a tactical option that even Newcastle United (with some all too rare good footballers in the team) eventually fell for.

The 1980s is defined by The Miners Strike, Yuppies, Aids, Kajagoogoo, *3-2-bastard 1* and bloody Watford.

Watford disappearing into the darkness coincided with The Poll Tax Riots, back-passes to goalkeepers and tight shorts being outlawed, fences coming down, Nirvana, all-day opening and better clothes. Things started to happen that eventually brought down the Tory government and gave us *Tekken 3* and *Fightclub*.

If Watford had survived just one season in the Premiership we would all have Flock of Seagulls haircuts, Ra-ra skirts, be voting Tory and have nothing to do until the pubs re-opened at 5-o'clock. Honest.

Watford finished bottom of the League, a full 12 points from safety. John paid up but we didn't go to Disneyland and an '80s revival withered on the vine. 10 years later I just saw The Drums on television and see someone is trying it again. They must be stopped if not killed and burned. And we must remain ever vigilant.

Chapter 26

1999/2000 postscript – A Distorted View

Liverpool continued their long and notable tradition of scooping up another team's best player surprisingly swiftly and cheaply by taking Dietmar Hamman to Anfield before the new season even started. No one is saying Hamman was tapped up, the very idea. You must be thinking of Christian Ziege, who Liverpool picked up from Middlesbrough a year later for £5.5 million when other teams had bid £8 million. Liverpool were later found guilty of an illegal approach for the player – this despite that their manager Gerrard Houllier described Middlesbrough's complaint at the time as "laughable" *(The Telegraph).* So it is very important for you to understand that I am not saying Liverpool have a long history of tapping players up. I'm not saying anything of the sort, despite them being found guilty of doing so after protesting their innocence.

Ruud Gullit bought Kieron Dyer, as well as Alain Goma and Marcelino and Franck Dumas. However the season got off to a wretched start when referee Uriah Rennie sent off Alan Shearer for backing into a player in a game Aston Villa won 1-0. The decision, incredibly, was upheld on appeal despite there being no evidence to justify the punishment and thus began a long and hateful war between Mr Rennie and Newcastle United's supporters. He armed with cards, a whistle and an apparent unflinching conceit that all rules were open to his own bizarre interpretation and us with a righteous and noisy outrage, which was to prove no defence against such a monster.

Newcastle took one point from their opening five games despite having been at least a goal up in four of them. This ended for Gullit in the notorious game where he dropped Shearer and Ferguson, amid freakish weather conditions and circumstances, against sunderland. The city was a maelstrom of hate and misinformation, everything was annoying, frustrating and you didn't know whose side you were supposed to be on; the blood-thirsty media apparently bent on Gullit's downfall and Newcastle's relegation, or the bonkers bloke with the dreadlocks whose team of internationals was a hideous bloody shambles. Gullit walked, Newcastle got slaughtered 5-1 at Man Utd and Bobby Robson came in as manager.

Wifey and I buggered off to Prague but did get in a conversation with a Dutch lad between flights at Schiphol Airport in Amsterdam. "With Gullit it is always a woman," he said and I assumed he must have been high. Gullit was always complaining about the press taking pictures of him in restaurants when no pictures of him eating were ever published. Why so sensitive? Again, my intention of making it to the bottom of the page with being sued means I couldn't possibly speculate.

Robson's first home game in charge was an 8-0 win against Sheffield Wednesday. It is testament to how shell-shocked we had become that even at 5-0 up the crowd was nervous. Bobby Robson slowly pulled the team round; he got a run of games out of Duncan Ferguson, revitalised Alan Shearer, recalled Rob Lee who Gullit had shamefully ostracised and brought in Kevin Gallacher. A 0-0 draw at Arsenal was tactically the best defensive display many of us could remember from a Newcastle team (Dumas' finest hour and a half), while a 3-0 win over Manchester United showed how good we could be. Bobby dragged us up to 11th place when his job was to stop us getting relegated. In Europe we rattled past CSKA Sofia and FC Zurich before we got to wander around Rome in shirtsleeves in November, only getting knocked out by a dubious penalty.

But the FA Cup should have been ours; we smashed Spurs 6-1 in a replay, knocked over Sheffield Utd 4-1, won at Blackburn and beat a spirited Tranmere before our best Wembley display in a generation ended in a cruel 2-1 loss to bloody Chelsea.

Crucially, Bobby Robson had galvanised us and given us back our heart, pride and belief.

Player of the Season: 87% of *The Mag* readership said "Alan Shearer" – I'm not going to argue with that many people.

Goal of the Season: Kieron Dyer at Everton; exploded clear from the halfway line and chipped the keeper, an act of great beauty in a terrible, terrible game.

Chapter 27

June 2000

Silvio Maric

In the summer of 2000 Newcastle's first Croatian footballer failed to turn up for a club tour of Trinidad and Tobago and publicly stated that the club should give him a free transfer.

I have a couple of strict rules regarding Newcastle United players that I like to stick to. I broke one of those rules recently and now I have to break the other. Rule 1: Never talk to them. Unless I'm interviewing them for *The Mag* or in the highly unlikely circumstance that they talk to me first (e.g. "What are you doing in my house?") I can't imagine how a clumsy conversation with an awe-struck idiot is going to enhance either of our lives. For example, Robert Lee is one of my favourite ever players and I've vocally encouraged him at home, away and in Europe for years now. I shared his joy and his pain but he doesn't know who the fuck I am, which seems to suit us both fine. I mean, what the bloody hell would we talk about in the improbable scenario where we found ourselves trapped in the same lift? He recently went to see Simply (bloody) Red, for Christ sake. With his good friend Alan Shearer. With whom he plays fucking golf.

I have as much interest in Simply (bloody) Red and fucking golf as he has in *Medievil 2* on the Playstation and the new Eminem and Slipknot albums. Plus he must get hundreds of fools yapping at him every day. I figure one less is doing the man a favour.

Rule 2: Never slag them off in this column. In a match report you can't say every player was brilliant when you have just lost 0-2 at home to Leicester City but to the best of my knowledge I have never scapegoated a player who was still in the employ of NUFC on this page. They are on the same side as me so I don't see why it would help. I am constantly appalled that people will waste the price of a stamp writing to the local papers slagging off their own players. What pleasure is there to be had in being proved right, and is turning up the heat on a player going to make them play better? If you want to write to the paper, how about someone pointing out that we actually won more games and scored a ton more goals than sunderland last season because nobody in the local press bleating on about them being "top dogs" seems to have noticed.

Granted the temptation to criticise a player has often been overwhelming. I firmly believed that John Barnes deliberately slowing the game down when he got here was a cancer that spread through the club that we still have yet to fully recover from. The urge to get after Ketsbaia …ahhhh. And most of all, the fact that there are now some players within our club who think their job description precisely matches that of The Queen Mother; namely smiling weakly and waving in the general direction of some peasants once every couple of weeks before vigorously plunging their snouts back into the trough marked 'Other People's Money.'

I broke Rule 1 a couple of months ago when I spoke to Silvio Maric. I shook him warmly by the hand, professed my belief in his footballing abilities and wished him well. You see, when we played Croatia Zagreb it was my firm belief that during both games he was the best player on the pitch. The idle-assed media whittered on about Prosinecki because they had heard of him despite the fact that he lumbered around like a werewolf/pie-monster hybrid. I insisted we should purchase this splendid young fellow post-haste to all who would listen or to many who would not. I followed his career and confidently wrote "Maric" in the space marked "Which players would you like us to buy?" in *The Mag's* end of season poll. When Ruud Gullit surprisingly bought him I was ecstatic as this proved not only our manager's vision and genius but my own. Within an hour of finding which number he had been allocated (the very prestigious 10) I had it and his name on the back of my beautiful blue away shirt. I wrote to my friend in Australia about it.

Well Mr. Maric has made me look like a right twat hasn't he readers? Those of you unfortunate enough to have shared a beer with me over the past year have been endlessly argued with over the man's merits. "It takes time for foreign players to settle in – especially midfielders"; "How many people didn't rate Gary Speed or Nolberto Solano at first and look at them now"; "I know he missed an open goal but he made the chance himself, confidence, that's what he needs, love and confidence."

When Silvio rifled in that goal away to Zurich the relief on his face was like a ton weight had been taken off his back, now we'd see the real Maric. He scored again in the return leg. I watched the away game drinking nothing but Red Bull because I was due to play 5-a-side at 9.30 that night. I must have done four laps of the Strawberry and, in an unprecedented and unrepeated display at the Lightfoot Centre, scored six times in my Maric shirt. My team mates were astonished (as was I) but me and Silvio (and a probably dangerous amount of sugary taurine based drinks) were putting the world to rights. Now surely Silvio would thrive and knowing that people had enough confidence in him to stop him in the street to offer him love and encouragement – well he would surely smile and redouble his efforts. Not come off the bench in the very next game and wander around like an aged and inebriated moose.

Now he doesn't bother even turning up for work and wants a free transfer? Well that's it, I'm washing my hands of the fool and here goes Rule 2: you sir, are an idle fucking parasite and I despise you for it. How dare you? How dare you sit about stuffing your pockets with my fucking money WHINING about wanting a free transfer – don't you think we've wasted enough money on your miserable, lazy fucking backside? We want some back and whatever we can't recoup from whatever mugs you end up at, you should pay us out of your own bloody pocket. We should sue and pursue you for it like we were the bastard Russian Mafia. You fucker! You get a free trip to Trinidad and Tobago where your "work" consists of trotting around in the sunshine and smiling at local dignitaries and YOU can't be bothered. YOU would rather sit at home feeling sorry for yourself – bellyaching about wanting a free transfer. You rotten ungrateful fucking swine! After all I've done for you. How dare you?

(Bobby Robson managed to get over £2 million from Porto for a player who never scored a League goal for Newcastle. He scored twice for Porto before returning to Zagreb, then he had two years at Panathinaikos, going back again to Croatia before retiring. My Maric shirt was destroyed by a German washing machine in 2004.)

Chapter 28

October 2000

Memories

Under manager Kevin Keegan, England lost to Germany in the last game played at Wembley under the famous old twin towers.

Women know where "things" are. It's true, they just do. I have it on very good authority that all TV and film continuity people are female. Continuity people, as you may well know, are the people who make sure all the props and actors are in exactly the same place on scene changes and in re-shoots and stuff. Their job is to know precisely where "things" are all the time – and they are all women. I rest my case. Girlies may get all cross and shout "Why don't you look?" when a chap says, "Have you seen my keys/drink/shoe/house/head?" and they will also tut loudly in exasperation when you decide not to ask and instead wander aimlessly from room to room feeling helpless. But it's an inbred and special skill, a gift if you will, and they should celebrate it and understand that not all of us were born so fortunate.

Men's corresponding skill is to keep "things" for years and years. We attach feelings to "things" and keep them forever. Women obviously keep "things" as well but not as many "things" of absolutely no practical use or worth, what-so-bloody-ever.

If you are male and reading this, chances are you will almost certainly have an enormous hoard of records you don't listen to, videos you don't watch, clothes you don't wear and books you wouldn't ever read even if you were nailed into your house for a decade BUT the thought of giving them away or throwing them out fills you with a horror on a par with giving away or throwing out a kidney or a testicle.

How many of you have got that really bad episode of the *Black & White* video magazine that features a dismal run of losses and draws for our team as well as

Mrs. Pavel Srnicek's recipe for traditional Czechoslovakian biscuits (that looked bloody awful)? They sold thousands of them, they have got to be somewhere – in your loft, that's where they are. What kind of debilitating disease do you expect to contract that will mean you have the time and the inclination to watch it again? Can you imagine anyone you know wanting to see it? Have you thrown it out? Have you bollocks.

I can't remember the last time I played a vinyl record so, as the house was bursting at the seams with "things", I promised to get rid of some.

Oh the trauma.

Your head says, "you've got the CD of that, it's scratched, tatty and worth nothing".

Your heart simpers, "but I've had it for 20 years and the picture on the cover is bigger than the one on the CD." It's pathetic.

I got brutal, went through the lot. Got drunk and went through them again. Got sober, panicked and lovingly put many of them away again but still took an alarming part of my personal heritage to Steel Wheels. I felt fantastic. My whole life felt fresher and less cluttered.

This is what we must do with Wembley; set aside misplaced sentiment and bin the bastard. For weeks going up the last game there, against Germany, the media was wailing and gnashing its teeth about the destruction of the Twin Towers. Phone-ins demanded we ring in and share our favourite Wembley memories. The goals, the occasions, the heroes, the villains, Geoff Hurst, Ricky Villa, Alan Sunderland….

Will you please fuck off!!!!

Wembley is a ghastly, ugly, outdated monstrosity and the sooner they tear the bastard down the better. Most of the seats were crap and afforded an appalling view of the pitch which was failing on the only job a stadium needs to do. It smells like a tramp's trousers and has long been little more than a haven for extortionists and thieves. My memories of Wembley?

My memories of bastard Wembley consist entirely of laughing at the prices of stuff on Wembley Way to cover trembling drunken nerves, not being able to see the lines on the pitch from my seat, scuffing my new Cats by trying to stand on said seat and bitter disappointment followed by long and agonisingly painful journeys home.

The country is being soppy and mawkishly sentimental and should give itself a shake. Losing to Germany amidst pouring rain with hopes crushed amid nationwide frustration was an entirely fitting finale for the old shitpile.

They should have stuffed the fucker full of dynamite and blown it to rubble the same day. With the FA still in it.

Everyone would have felt better.

HELP

I have a good friend Tim, a Spurs fan, who seems fixated by all sport which he absorbs for days at a time due to him also being a lifelong insomniac. As a child he would listen to test match cricket from the other side of the world on a transistor radio beneath the sheets. He was rewarded for this peculiar behaviour by hearing, from the infamous commentary of the game between the West Indies and England, "The bowler is Holding the batsman's Willie" so can confirm the story is not an urban myth. This was well documented. What I have seen or heard nothing of is his most recent report and I want it confirming. Apart from claiming that every goal Newcastle have scored against Spurs was illegal or unfair, I am not aware of him ever having lied to me but he reckons in the small hours of the morning during The Women's Clean & Jerk Weightlifting that David Coleman uttered the phrase, "I saw her snatch this morning and it was tremendous."

Thank you for your time.

Ten years later and the above mentioned video along with dozens of others were still piled up in my loft. Recently on Twitter I offered to deliver them personally to anybody who wanted them. Are they now A) in a skip; B) still piled up in my loft; or C) sold to a lad from Killingworth?

Chapter 29

February 2001

Larry - The Gay Chicken

I usually allow myself two hours to write all this shite. That includes the time I need to: a) wander to the fridge for liquid inspiration; b) rush into the garden to frighten pigeons or burst stray children's footballs with a big garden fork; c) scurry back in for a good giggle; d) write abusive letters to the many celebrities I'm stalking; e) go back through the stuff I have written to take out the excessive fucking bastarding bad bastard language.

Well, in celebration of Newcastle United's performance at Charlton, I considered simply sitting in front of the screen for two hours doing little more than attending work. Feet up, swigging cold beer and munching chocolate Hob-Nobs. Perhaps occasionally I could randomly clatter away at the computer keys before remembering that I'm off on holiday next week and, not wanting to injure myself with any over strenuous typing, I could have a little rest. Then after the required two hours I could e-mail an incomprehensible load of old bollocks to *The Mag* HQ, wait patiently for my big fat pay cheque to clear, then fuck off to Spain for two weeks to play sodding golf.

This seems pretty much an accurate reflection of what our players did at the weekend and what's good enough for the goose, etc…

Except I'm not a goose (or a gay chicken – more of that later) so this splendid plan is somewhat undone by a few minor details; I send in incomprehensible bollocks every month, I don't get big fat pay cheques and I would sooner sit on a rusty fucking spike watching *Stars In Their Eyes* for ten hours than play bastard golf (And I hate *Stars In Their Eyes* – Bleach in Their Eyes or Spikes In Their Eyes, that's what they need).

Like the rest of you I am completely frustrated and infuriated by our team's ability to be instantly and utterly rubbish for no apparent reason. We have got good players and we have played really well this season against some good teams but this latest and most public of humiliations, without any viable excuse, really makes you wonder why we fucking bother. *The Mag* generally has a very positive outlook even when results have been poor, most of the regular writers have been watching Newcastle United long enough to have seen some really shit teams under-performing and can recognise that we have better players than in the days when we were waiting for Wayne Fereday to cross a ball, Kevin Dillon to score or Bill Rafferty to do anything of any use whatsoever. But there really was nothing positive to take out of that game.

It was probably best for all concerned that the entire squad buggered off to Spain – I for one didn't want anything to do with any of the bastards and actually refused to buy a newspaper for over a week because the very thought of them turned my stomach.

Normally not soaking up the news would be bad for this column but I have been gathering material from different sources and my gloom has been exorcised considerably. For a start, I have taken to watching **Banzai** on the television wherein bizarre stunts are performed while an oriental gentleman shouts a lot and you the viewer have to guess the outcome. Recently we had 'Old Lady Wheelchair Chicken Challenge' wherein a couple of old dears in electric wheelchairs were encouraged to race towards each other across a car park like James Dean in *Rebel Without a Cause* and we were expected to guess which one of them had the strongest nerve and which one of them would steer herself out of the other's way. There was also a game where we viewers had to guess how many helium balloons it would take to float 'Larry The Gay Chicken' straight up into the sky and they finished on a lingering shot of Larry floating away. At no point did they explain why Larry (generally a man's name, all chickens are female) was homosexual. They also had Harold from Neighbours knocking on people's doors and running away and hiding behind a hedge. 'The Vertically Challenged Vertical Challenge' featuring two men under three feet tall climbing up the body of a basketball player to see which of them could be first to stick a little flag into his big hat nearly caused me to rupture a lung – I can't recommend it highly enough.

My spirits were also raised this week by the fact that I have been working with a Darlington fan. For those of you who have no interest in lower league football you need to know that Darlington are without doubt the funniest team in the country. My colleague laughs hysterically and constantly but with tear filled eyes at the on going sit-com that is his chosen team. All of the following information he swears is true: last season Darlington Chairman, George Reynolds, took over the club, paid off all their debts and built them a £1 million stand. They only failed to get promoted because they lost the play-off final. This year work started on a brand new ground. "Very nice but not very funny," I hear you say. Well OK, until you find out that "Mad King George" (his words, not mine) is a former safe cracker who reportedly once got caught smuggling gelignite in an ice-cream van. Next up was the idea to improve Darlington's Feethams pitch's poor drainage which involved the club paying Manchester United tens of thousands of pounds for a consignment of the European super worms that apparently keep the Old Trafford turf in tip-top shape. Revolutionary thinking, except the Darlington drainage problem was so severe that the pitch flooded and all the European worms (many of whom had learnt English on the way) were tragically drowned.

Following the play-off defeat, George slagged all the best players off for earning too much money and systematically sold them. Despite this, he happily announced that the club could expect to take 5,000 fans each from Newcastle, sunderland and Middlesbrough once the new stadium was completed. Prices were to be frozen for the next ten years.

Bereft of their better players Darlington have been losing games. The fans are understandably unhappy and the crowd behind one of the goals began to complain during matches. George announced that this "loutish behaviour" was causing distress to his 80 year old mother and threatened to ban anyone under 16 from standing behind the goal before adding, more confusingly, that he "didn't want anybody lying in front of his car."

Mr. Reynolds recently employed a joiner from his work-top factory in Shildon to be the club's new director of football – a factory where urban legend has it that George, spotting an employee with the sole hanging off the bottom of his shoe, summoned the fellow over and demanded to know why he was flapping about his factory in such shoddy footwear. The chap explained that he was too poor and busy to replace his shoes. George at once pulled a fat roll of notes from his suit pocket and loudly announcing that none of *his* workers were going to suffer such conditions – removed the elastic band from the roll... and gave it to the bloke to hold his shoe together.

So in summary, we may be pissed off because our team are occasionally indolent swine but at least we are not gay chickens being floated over the rooftops or worse, Darlington fans.

Chapter 30

March 2001

BADGER!

In last month's edition of *The Mag* one of our writers, Dave Edwards, met Chairman of Newcastle United, Mr. Freddie Shepherd via a competition in *The Evening Chronicle*. He and the other winners got to speak to our illustrious leader over a specially arranged dinner. I was thrilled and excited for him, "Go on Dave!" I cried, plumping up a cushion; as I settled down to read what happened, "Get about the bugger!"

Perhaps my hopes that the boy Edwards would have taken a photo of an arse and another photo of an elbow along with him and asked our Chairman in front of impartial witnesses if he could tell which was which, were a little high – but I was disappointed, Dave lad, you didn't even make him cry.

I would love to believe Mr. Shepherd won the fans over with his plain talking Everyfan attitude and confident plans for the future but the man thought the transfer system was about to be abolished and that this was "a good thing for Newcastle United" – ferfuxsake…

Well, the transfer system has been reshuffled for nearly a week now and there is no sign of Juan Sebastian Veron or Francesco Totti at Newcastle Airport which is probably for the best as the whole place is stinking something wicked as another herd of Friesians is thrown on the pyre. *(Foot and Mouth Disease darlings – it was all the rage in the spring of 2001, and it started on mackem soil.)*

But I digress – I don't mean any disrespect to Dave Edwards who is a fine writer, as well as being a splendid fellow and a tremendous shag if the office rumours are to be believed. BUT on top of clearly having his head turned by a square meal and a free pint he left us all hanging: he asked about our shoddy training facilities (good one) and was told that the three year long wait for our fantastic new state of the art complex near Wolsingham was nearly over as soon as the problem with badgers was sorted out. Then he went onto another subject. Wait up! Re-wind!

BADGERS?

What fucking badgers? What are these badgers doing to upset our urgent need for a new training facility? Protesting? Have they got little badger placards or is it more sinister?

Perhaps they're badger separatists with bandanas, sunglasses and military training from the Russians – with bullet belts over their shoulders, cigarettes in the corners of their mouths, turning the heads of all the young lady badgers with their devilish badger charms.

What do we know about badgers? I was going to ring Willie Poole, the rosy faced fellow who writes about the countryside for *The Journal*. Then last week he started writing about the need to start culling people's cats to stop the spread of Foot & Mouth disease and I realised he was an even bigger knob-head than I have always suspected and decided not to fucking bother.

Fortunately I work with a man called Rob who is an expert on badgers, along with everything else in the whole world. Badgers, it seems, are members of the bear family that also includes skunks – but they don't emit a defensive smell. They actually smell of jasmine and their natural habitat is lying dead on the side of the A1 and A69. They walk like an over-stuffed carpet-bag on little legs and eat mostly grubs and ice-cream. Their fur is used to make shaving brushes but you have to make sure they are dead before you use one to lather your face up because they have got a nasty bite. They build nests in oak trees from which they like to leap down and startle rabbits. The problem Newcastle United have is that it is illegal to chop down the trees they live in because all oak trees belong to Her Majesty the Queen. Thank you Rob.

Of course, would that former club enforcer Freddie Fletcher was still here. Freddie would have been round the badgers' gaff quick as you like to tell them that Newcastle United plc held the copyright on black and white faces and, as they were in breach of that copyright, they would have to piss off forthwith.

We had a similar problem with bats in The Leazes End. Many was the time when our frustration at not being able to score against Crystal Palace (or whoever) under Kenny Dalglish was interrupted by the swooping of Mr. & Mrs. Batty (named after the tough tackling Yorkshireman). I, like everybody else, didn't bother mentioning the bats because if the assorted nitwits and NIMBYs who tried to stop the recent ground improvements got wind of the situation we might have been knackered. Bats are protected and you are not allowed to disturb their nests even if they happen to be in your loft or the roof of your football stadium. The roof was ripped off, we all got soaked for a season but they built the new tier – the new roof was put on and I'm delighted to report that the bats are back as well. Isn't that lovely?

Hopefully the badger situation can be dealt with as happily because our present arrangement of making the players train on cobblestones in high heeled shoes (or so you would think given the amount of them who get injured) simply can't go on.

Sometimes I'm painfully slow on the uptake. For example it is only now that I think to say, "you were going to build the training ground in fucking Wolsingham - is that the Wolsingham which is the other side of Tow Law? The Wolsingham that is up in the fucking mountains miles away from Newcastle? The one where the residents regularly get snowed in, during April? Or perhaps that's Woolsington by Newcastle Airport."

Instead they built the new training ground in Longbenton, on top of some desecrated druids' graves. Clearly.

Chapter 31

April 2001

If You Stop Going to the Match You Might DIE!!!

The end of the 2000/01 season saw Newcastle United in a quite wretched run of form that saw them win only three of 14 games. The natives were understandably restless and Douglas Hall, son of John, attempted to stem any loss of confidence by claiming that manager Bobby Robson would have £100 million to spend in the summer.

Reading the letters in the local press is like picking at a scab; you know you shouldn't do it, you feel mildly queasy while doing so and disgusted with yourself and unfulfilled afterwards. Most letters have been in a similar vein recently to how they always are; irritating and pointless sniping between Newcastle and sunderland fans, letters from people announcing that they have been going for 50 years and have still not mustered any insight, blah blah blah "Jackie Milburn spinning in his grave" blah blah blah.

There have been no letters from fans excitedly recommending players whom Bobby Robson should start spending Douglas Hall's £100 million on what –so – bloody – ever. 'Geordies good , foreigners bad' letters don't count because Clark, Bridges, Carrick, and Elliott wouldn't cost £100 and there are no other top flight class Geordies who don't play for us already, least of all a mystery centre half who might be able to head the ball away at a corner. Is this because nobody believes there will be £100 million spent on players? What a cynical lot. But then Hall senior barked on about regional stadiums and teams full of Geordies and we didn't believe him either. Newcastle fans have a innate mistrust of any claims made from on high, which may or may not stem from the club knocking the old Leazes End down then failing in their promise to build a new one for 20 years. Who knows?

What is coming across is fans' weary, cynical hatred of their team. Hatred might seem like a strong word but the atmosphere at the recent Middlesbrough game *(Newcastle lost 2-1, at home)* ranged from trench humour to malevolent disgust. The fact that we have snatched Andy O'Brien from under the very noses of Barcelona has done very little to help matters. People were leaving at half-time and vowing not to return. And swearing a lot.

We have always boasted that supporting Newcastle United isn't a hobby or a pastime but a way of life. Unfortunately it is beginning to feel less like a lifestyle choice and more like an affliction, an incurable disease. And because this arse end of an arse end of a season has been so messy our attention is bound to wander. Thanks to previously unwelcome international breaks, whole fortnights pass with no Newcastle match and it's not like the summer where all supporters are in the same boat and you can sit in the sun with cold beer. The weather is still shite and other teams are gallivanting about in Europe.

We have had to get on with our lives and some people are reportedly enjoying football-free weekends.

Well I'm here to tell you people to BEWARE – do not get lulled into this sort of behaviour – the odd weekend bumming round the shops, socialising or maybe slumped in front of a box set of *The Sopranos* is all well and good but you have to take care that this path doesn't leave you to those dreaded three letters; D, I and – yes you guessed it – Y.

There was a report on Radio Five Live last week claiming that last year over ONE HUNDRED THOUSAND people were injured, hospitalised and in some cases killed performing D.I.Y. Detailed breakdowns on how many people fell off ladders, strimmed their own toes off, whacked themselves in the eye with claw hammers or beat family members to death with shelves over arguments about self assembly home furniture were not forthcoming. The point is no matter how annoying this present collection of Newcastle United players may be – they are unlikely to kill you.

Places like Texas and Homecare are essentially peddling death and the D.I.Y. equivalent of Leah Betts' (girl who probably died from drinking too much water with her Es) Dad (bloke who turns up full of righteous indignation any time anybody mentions legalising drugs) should be on hand to protest publicly any time a new set of garden furniture or security lamp is released onto the market. It may all be promoted as being very homely, domestic and lovely, and people who know which end of a hammer to use when banging in a screw may well look at you as if you are some emasculated half man/lady boy because you don't BUT, these people are dangerous anarchists who are tearing at the very fabric of society and they must be stopped. Think about it – people study and train for years to learn a trade that will be useful to their fellow man. They turn up, do the work, they are paid and they can then afford food for their children. These clever D.I.Y. bastards who get a socket set and a fucking drill for Christmas suddenly, and without so much as a by your leave decide they can put these honest tradesman out of work by doing things themselves, it's disgusting. At least it would be except for the fact that people make such a monumental arse of doing anything for themselves that skilled professionals end up getting paid not only to fix the initial problem but also to clean up the horrible dangerous mess fumble-thumbed dafties have inflicted on their houses.

People who make their own beer are as bad – what would happen if everybody brewed their own? Pubs would shut down and thousands of people would be put out of work. Or at least they would be if all homebrew wasn't rancid fucking dog piss. I don't care if you can knock it out for 8p a pint – I wouldn't wash a diseased ox in the fucker and that dandelion and pigscock wine you made isn't fit for pouring down the bastard sink either.

Basically if people stop going to football and take up D.I.Y. the best that will happen is that they will die. The worst is society will collapse and we'll all be living in caves. So just say no!

Chapter 32

2000/01 postscript – A Distorted View

Transitional. In retrospect this season was transitional. Bobby Robson actually got money in for worthless or irritating footballers, like £2 million for Maric and nearly £4 million for Ferguson, which was a £4 million loss on what Gullit paid for him but was £4 million more than he was worth by then. An awesome footballer on his all too irregular day. Ferguson was replaced by Carl Cort. That's replaced in the, "and when do you expect him to be fit?" kind of way.

We had a splendid all black away kit as well.

Transitional.

As I say it was transitional.

In retrospect.

At the time it was just painful and irritating – like having Scouse girls arguing with Welsh girls over who is the more classy. With megaphones. While you are strapped to a enormous vibrating cheese-grater with giggling fat children pouring salt in your eyes.

After losing the first game of the season to Manchester United, who would go on to win their third consecutive title, Newcastle won three games on the trot to go briefly top.

By the middle of January, Robson's United were out of both domestic cups and thanks to only winning three of their last 14 league games we finished a disappointing 11th. An improvement? Yet 83% of *The Mag's* readers claimed to be "less happy" than they had been in the previous year. For the most part the football was tedious and frustrating but the season had a sting in the tail as Newcastle qualified for The Intertoto Cup through the Fair Play League. This drove many of our enemies to visible annoyance, especially down on Wearside where Peter Reid's sunderland had ended up 7th. sunderland had (for the second year running) the worst disciplinary record in the Premier League. Meanwhile our failure to get stuck in (like some of our more vocal and fed up fans had been demanding all season) meant that we would be in Europe the next season. All be it in a competition that started June. Newcastle United, thanks to their proud European history, wouldn't have to play until July.

Player of the Season: Shay Given.

Goal of the Season: Solano at home to Leeds. A rare Boxing Day win in a game that Newcastle came back from a goal down to win 2-1.

Manchester City were relegated along with Coventry and Bradford.

Chapter 33

September 2001

So When is it Alright to Call a Game Off?

So Wifey and I decided to go and live in New York City. Why? Well why the hell not, given that it's the coolest, most vibrant and exciting, 24 hour Rock n' Roll city on the planet, with some of the finest food, bars, people and things to do on God's good earth?

We would have stayed there for the rest of our lives but for the small matter of neither of us having a work permit, immigration papers, jobs or anywhere to live – so after a week we came home to see Newcastle play Brentford in the Worthington Cup. *(We had a long conversation in the bar over the road from CBGB's about extending our stay for another couple of days so we could see The Strokes play live and very reluctantly decided against it)*

I was sitting in JFK Airport on September 10th (having just paid $14 for a copy of *The Times* and a bottle of beer – that's about a tenner) wondering what our adventures may provide that was of interest to you, dear reader. Not much, except to call top *Mag* writer Chris Tait a glory hunting tourist for pledging his allegiance to the New York Yankees baseball team within an article he wrote some months back, when we residents tend to follow the Mets. Apparently.

Also we continued *The Mag's* casual stalking of Mr Jake Burns (adopted Geordie front man of "the legendary Stiff Little Fingers" – as they were introduced in The Underground Bar in Greenwich Village). Apart from that what relevance would us being in New York the day before September 11th 2001 have to anything or anybody?

Our flight was delayed due to a terrible storm; by the time we got back to Newcastle we were exhausted and fell straight into bed.

We awoke to the phone ringing. The voice was James, the same fine fellow that had informed us of Newcastle's magnificent 4-1 victory at Middlesbrough, while I stood grinning like a ninny on a payphone in the scorching sunlight between the awesome World Trade Centre and the Brooklyn Bridge. Nice to hear from him again so soon, he asked if we were OK, I asked why and he said we should put the television on. The news was that the planet had suddenly gone utterly insane. Sky News confirmed James' opinion that the world was now unspeakably horrible and officially "never the same again". After 30 hours of tears, fury and "yes we're fine" phone calls we were ready for the big comfort blanket that is a Newcastle United home match. Familiar rituals and people with the chance to get blissfully distracted.

There was a murmuring of discontent from the media about sporting events taking place. With the Champions League games postponed, why were there Worthington Cup games going ahead – isn't it disrespectful? Well my feeling is that the Champions League games were put off more over security and travel fears and once the authorities had weighed up the likelihood of the Brentford team bus being hijacked, it was best if we all just got on with it – also the disrespect argument ignores the immaculate silences observed by football fans before games over the following week.

"Football is comparatively frivolous", went another argument. Well compared to a bunch of crackpots hijacking a plane and deliberately trying to murder thousands of civilians and compared to what we witnessed happening in Manhattan you tell me what isn't fucking frivolous. And having seen it again and again with no hope of the horror ever subsiding I for one could use the frivolity and if the players were distracted and the game wasn't the best then I forgive them all and understand.

Of course there is a precedent of sorts. Our game with Liverpool was postponed a matter of hours before the kick off following the death of Diana. And surely if matches can be called off over former members of the Royal family dying (despite her having as little interest in football as most football supporters had in her) then they can be stopped for anything more disastrous than one of Her Majesty's corgis being off its food. This argument ignores the deliberate mind-fascism that was imposed on the country by the media at the time – but I'm sorry – who gets to decide who has to go to work and who doesn't?

I'll ask that again because it is important. Who decides who has to go to work and who doesn't? Bus drivers, road sweepers and publicans yes; footballers and sports journalists no?

So now we're at war: well the modern equivalent of war whereby we fire 20 million dollar missiles at some peasants waving sticks. Any thoughts of games being postponed or do we now need to be distracted? Oh and don't worry about chemical attacks because we're pretty sure the enemy haven't got chemical weapons because we haven't sold them any. We have sold them a lot of weapons but not chemical ones.

Whatever, one thing to come out of this is a violent shift in my sense of perspective, friends seem dearer and idiots are being ignored. So "Stand up if you hate sunderland" when we're not actually playing sunderland, that's over. No I haven't tuned into a bloody tree-hugging hippy but if you want me to bounce up and down from my seat like Busta Rhymes on a space hopper over those poxy bastards you can forget it. "Form a human pyramid, set light to your trousers and wave them above your head if you love Newcastle" – fair enough, I'll go along with the majority. But "stand up if you hate sunderland" when we're playing Liverpool – I couldn't be fucking bothered.

I interviewed Jake Burns some years later – he was a season ticket holder at SJP at the time. I asked him about 9/11 because he was obviously in the area; he said that he heard from the mother of a lad who had been at the show in New York who died in the Towers thanking him for his band's part in her son's life. Also, after the New York gig the band were due in Washington and had the choice of two flights. The one they didn't choose was the plane that crashed into the Pentagon.

Not surprisingly, The Strokes show in New York was cancelled.

Chapter 34

December 2001

Leeds United 3 v Newcastle United 4

In the week previous to this game, Newcastle won 3-1 at Arsenal to go top of the League. We didn't expect it to last, not with our next game being at Elland Road. Leeds United's Lee Bowyer had just been cleared of an assault charge.

Games like this are pure life juice. The world seems finer, beer tastes better, music sounds cooler, friends are funnier and football is the finest, most exciting thing on the planet. When Nobby Solano rolled in the winner in injury time in front of the Newcastle fans the headrush was purest mental. The crowd reacted like The Clash had just come on as we piled over each other, seats were leapt off, strangers screamed gleefully in each other's faces, glasses were knocked Eric Morecambe style wonky and we shouted from the very depths of our black and white loving souls. The memory will make me tingle like our third against Barca and Liam O'Brien at Roker and I, like all of you who were there, will go misty-eyed when recalling it.

The day didn't start too well – Newcastle was encumbered by a thick layer of snow and squirming free of the city centre took long enough to make us doubt our chances of seeing the kick-off never mind getting a pint. But south of Scotch Corner the snow was but a pleasant seasonal dusting so the car was parked in Leeds in time for the beer to be plentiful. Hoo-rah.

"Hey ay Lee Bowyer. I wanna knowoa-wa oh oh how you're not in jail"(clap-clap clap-clap) sang a group of lads at the bottom right hand corner of our generous allocation. More people laughed and then joined in until the whole end was rocking to a piss-take beat.

Kieron Dyer in central midfield – what a job that lad did. Man of the Match nailed on from the beginning. Leeds, you can't afford what that boy is worth so don't insult our intelligence by asking. Kieron had a hand in everything and set up the opener by scorching past Harte and crossing for Craig Bellamy to rush onto and blast past Nigel Martyn in the Leeds goal.

Leeds scored a second later. Why Nicos Dabizas didn't clear out the rat-faced Bowyer we will never know but our Greek's over-cautious challenge allowed the man with the appearance of a car thief to turn and equalise before screaming "Cunts! Cunts! Cunts!" at those of us behind the goal. What a nice chap – can't imagine why anyone would want to slap his stupid head with a wheelbarrow.

Harry Kewell was making a nuisance of himself but the worst damage was being done on Dabizas by Viduka. Even if we ignore him breaking Nicos's nose with his elbow as being an accident, the late, studs up, challenge above the knee that put our man out of the game was little short of disgusting. Leeds are an evil team, full of evil men and overseen by an evil manager.

Second half and despite having an arse the size of Ayers Rock, Viduka did a dainty little pirouette past the otherwise impeccable O'Brien to slot in the second Leeds goal and Harte belted in a cruel third before we knew it. Leeds' fans now had a hateful glee about them but instead of getting shy and vulnerable our team and fans got up, dusted themselves down and produced one of the best travelling performances in living memory.

Solano and Dyer were terrorising the home defence and the former fed the latter who blasted a shot across the goal which Martyn clawed away – but straight in front of Robbie Elliott whose diving header went back across the helpless keeper and into the net.

A surprising penalty was then awarded to Newcastle after a careless handball from Bakke. Surprising in that the ref was mad Jeff Winter (who hates us). Shearer blasted in for 3-3 and most of us would have settled for that. But a magical fourth goal arrived; Dyer's ball in for Solano cutting in from the right, leaving Harte behind before calmly finding the bottom left corner *(I can see the ball coming towards me now)* and this was nearly followed by a fifth as sub Lomana Lua Lua exploded clear in the 96th minute and shot just over while Kieron Dyer, who we were told couldn't be expected to play 90 minutes, ran the full length of the field in support.

September the 22nd and Christmas was on us early – God bless us every one.

Both Mark Viduka and Lee Bowyer would later become Newcastle United players which makes this match report more than a little depressing.

Leeds manager David O'Leary claimed Bobby Robson had "lost the plot" after Robson complained about the Viduka challenge that put Dabizas out of this game. My mate Frankie was in Newcastle the following Monday and saw Bobby Robson doing a bit of late Christmas shopping with his wife Elsie. Keen to secure an autograph he politely folded his copy of the Guardian to the match report of this game. Unfortunately the picture with the article was of Mark Viduka diving studs up towards the thigh of Dabizas a half second before the injury. "Look at that! Look at that!" shouted a re-enraged Robson brandishing the picture at Elsie.

Chapter 35

February 2002

Ratshaggers!

The 24th of February to be precise and Newcastle are about to play at sunderland's Stadium of Light for the third time. The previous two occasions ended in draws.

Newcastle United's games against sunderland don't start or finish on the day of the game. The 90 minutes of football we know how to deal with (stand together, make as much noise as possible and hold your nerve). How we deal with the build up and the consequences afterwards are an entirely individual psychological battle. You are on your own.

It starts when the fixtures come out and lives deep in your mind, rising in prominence as the date approaches, scratching at your very soul and nagging at you in the night however you try to distract yourself.

(Sunday 17th, the week before) – the media tried to convince us that the return of Kevin Keegan with his Manchester City team was the date Newcastle fans were looking forward to but the conversation within the pack of degenerates I drink with was all about the sunderland game. The majority of them want sunderland relegated out of existence because they don't like playing them. I must admit I love it: sure, the stakes are high and the cost of defeat is truly appalling but the excitement and the head rush can't be duplicated anywhere else. Yes, I will raise a glass in celebration at their every misfortune and my living room ceiling still bears the dent my head put in it when Mickey Gray missed his penalty in their playoff game against Charlton but dammit I love the drama of these games.

(We beat City 1-0 in a Fifth Round F.A. Cup game with a Nolberto Solano goal.)

(Monday 18th) Starting to brace myself but distracted by fools. The media is gushing about how we were lucky to beat City. I bite spitefully at any colleague echoing this view then go home to check the tape. I wasn't that pissed, surely, we did deserve to win and Kevin's team went away heroic losers – now where have we seen that before? Watch *Shooting Stars*, drink beer and go to bed.

(Tuesday 19th) I've come up with a strategy for how to deal with the mackems at work as engaging in a battle of wits with unarmed opponents seems unfair. I simply smile nicely at them, which brings a splendid reaction "What?" snapped one of them. "Oh nothing," say I, and stroll away. Their nerve is shot – I need to hold mine.

Playstation, beer, bed. How ever did I cope on derby weeks before I had *Spyro the Dragon* and *Grand Theft Auto 3* to distract me?

(Wednesday 20th) Time to up the stakes with work's gobbiest sunderland fan. "Scared yet?" I innocently enquire.

"Of what. You lot? You must be joking."

"Just checking." He's fuming, I'm smiling. This is so much fun but the truth is my nerve ends are on fire.

Liverpool live on telly should prove a happy distraction – it doesn't. Boring bloody team and why do their fans feel the need to make banners and bring them along to the game? This is a football match not a bloody craft fair you stupid bastards. Very bored long before the end. I don't want to watch anymore football before Sunday. Get annoyed and drunk to stave off the butterflies.

(Thursday 21st) Leeds live in Europe. Again this is not our game against sunderland and I'm getting very impatient. The fact that PSV Eindhoven are actually dirtier than Leeds is hilarious but we go out before the end because Rival Schools are playing live at the University.

A fine show but the average age of the audience is about 16 which is fine for getting served at the bar and seeing the band from the back (where us old people have to stand with our partners lest the young folk in the mosh pit think you are trying to molest them) but we keep getting buffeted by gangs of 12 year olds rushing about the place. Isn't this a school night? Get to bed you scamps. Bump into Tony and Paul (Mags) at the bar, both have tickets for the match but Tony's is in the sunderland end. I wince visibly and he smiles confidently – daft get.

(Friday 22nd) Agitated beyond words by the time still left to wait and for the first time I'm contemplating the ramifications of not winning. If our quest for Champions League football falls short because of points dropped on Wearside we will never hear the last of it. The rush of panic is eased by pouring cold beer on to it. Sky Sports are starting to hype the game up with interviews and goal montages; that Phillips goal that he only scores because the ball stops in a puddle and the one he gets in the 2-2 draw where he was half a mile offside make me spit bits of my dinner onto the carpet; "Now look what you've made me do, you little rat faced bastard!"
Go out with good friends – laugh a lot – agitation subsides but I can still feel it.

(Saturday 24th) Cool as you like. Now I'm in control. I know what to do and when to do it.
True, it's before 9 a.m. and I'm drinking but like Christmas Day and being at an airport this is one of the times you can do so without being a tramp. *The Mag* crew numbers nine and we are on bus 35 out of 35 buses and we are upstairs at the back so we will be getting there last. The nerves are virtually gone – it's just excitement and we laugh a lot.
We are in the ground over an hour before kick-off. The queue for the, as yet unopened, bar is a massive scrum of thirsty Geordies. Last year I queued patiently all the way to the front before the cops came and shut the bar claiming we were vandalising it. Which was lies. I hadn't got my beer and would have personally intervened against any vandalism. This time round enough vodka to drown a baby elephant has already been consumed and I couldn't bear a repeat of the disappointment. Sure enough, the bar is shut half an hour later. Our players are warming up: Given and Harper are taking it in turns getting in each other's way as crosses are knocked in. Given is in goal and Harper doesn't run across him, the cross is mis-hit straight to Harper who turns and volleys an unstoppable shot past Given. We cheer as Harper celebrates and playfully abuse the laughing Given.
The lads are in blue – good, I don't like the white shorts thing.

Two years ago I was in the third row when the teams came out with 3,000 Geordies behind me shouting their throats raw. Grudging respect for the home support that I couldn't hear my own tribe's voice because of the noise they were making. Last year they were noticeably quieter and this year, again in row three, they are a shadow of themselves which I take as a sign of fading confidence. We are full of ourselves and we jingle our keys at them. LET'S FUCKING GO!

Bobby Robson has gone with two wingers in Robert and Solano and has Jenas in the midfield when the consensus on the bus was Acuna for his tackling. This is extraordinarily brave.

They get a quick corner and the home crowd roar but groan as we cheer a silly dribbly flag-kick that barely bobbles up to our first defender. The pitch is a mess, the ball is bouncing erratically and sunderland's players are tackling wildly. Niall Quinn is drawing fouls deceitfully from the eager Dabizas but we are coping well enough despite the lazy linesman who can't be bothered to flag them offside. His counterpart on the other side rules out a goal from Craig Bellamy at the far end, which despite my appalling view was clearly onside. Kilbane blasts a half chance well over for them before Bellamy is bizarrely booked for shouting at a sunderland player which is difficult to comprehend when it took McAteer nearly kicking Distin in half for them to earn a booking. We are cross and indignant and get angrier still when Phillips appears to handle when bursting through our defence to blast straight at Given.

Shearer apparently can't win a header without being penalised and as usual the ball uncannily spins to red and white shirts. Despite this we are playing the better football, although Given has to get down sharply to save from Kilbane.

Our chances will come – we know this and at half time 0-0 is no bad thing.

"Stand up if you hate the Mags", sing the inbred, slack-jawed, rat-shagging cave dwellers and we absolutely love it. I'm vibrating with pleasure and clenching my fists with joy as my beautiful team is clearly starting to move through the gears. Quinn was marking Nicos Dabizas at our set pieces in the first half but the big goon has been replaced with Mboma who isn't as sneaky. Dabizas clearly wants to win the game by himself, abandoning central defence to turn up on the wing or burst through his own midfield. He has a chance, stretching to meet a cross about one yard out but Sorensen in the sunderland goal throws out a desperate foot to block it. He has another chance, spinning in the box and rattling a shot against the bar but eventually he scores. Hughes feints to cross then drives on, Mboma clumsily dives in and is booked. Robert whips in the resulting free-kick, it takes a bump. Dabizas and ball are on a collision course not ten yards in front of me. Sorensen and the sunderland defence are nowhere and the world has slowed to capture the moment.

Greek head hits ball, ball hits net and world snaps back to real time as we explode. Nicos' shirt is off – we're piling over each other leaping and screaming with unconfined delirium.

There's half an hour left. What if they score? We'll get another. "CMON!" Robson's decision to play Jenas is paying off and we are fizzing the ball around. Jenas has a shot, then another and the confidence can be seen coursing through the lad and it's making us play all the better. Bellamy flashes a header that Sorensen has to be quick to save and the time is draining slowly away. With 12 minutes left, so are the locals. Our friend Mick exaggerates a look at his watch and at the departing vermin before holding his hands out in disbelief. We laugh. Out of nowhere Phillips cracks a shot hard and Given makes the save of the season.

Dabizas is still turning up on the wing – what the hell is he doing? A naked man runs around on the pitch and the ref doesn't stop play. My nerve is slowly shredding. Uncle Bobby brings on Ameobi for Robert in the last minute which nobody understands.

We are so close.

Surely this can't be taken away now?

Three minutes of stoppage time, I check my watch every 15 seconds – Shearer is wasting time near a corner flag and all our players are scrambling hungrily around the ball not giving them an inch. The three minutes have gone – why are we still playing? The ref raises his whistle to his mouth and blows.

We're there and it doesn't get any better than this.

The police keep us in – we don't care. We sing and abuse the departing locals, Bobby comes out to wave to us and we thank him from the bottom of our hearts. Amazingly, there are mackems outside still giving us the 2-1 thing. We point at them and laugh – silly stupid fuckers.

Bus number 35, naturally far and away the last of the convoy to cross the Redgie bridge, most of out compadres must be onto their second beer at least by the time we crawl into town but we are all grinning like ninnies and confident the town won't run out of beer.

The Editor is so happy and delirious that he marches into the women's toilet when we finally get to a pub but the beer is the nicest in the world and the people are all beautiful and happy. Blackburn are winning some cup or other on the telly but nobody here cares.

We move pubs and one of our number goes mad and orders a bottle of Champagne in The Forth – we drink a toast to Nicos Dabizas – this is all so brilliant. People have tears in their eyes and every detail is relived and the knowledge that those nasty poisonous tramps down the road are suffering because of us adds to the joy.

We stumble home for beer, curry and the entire match, including build up, half-time analysis and full-time interviews, and hungrily devour the lot before slumping into bed.

(Monday 25th) Hungover but still happy. It's cold, pissing down and I've got to go to the dentist but life could not be better.

Chapter 36

March 2002

Ignorant, Pissy-knickered Little Cowards

The 2001/02 season was my own personal favourite season with Bobby Robson's swift and skilful young team playing the most exciting football since the heady days of Kevin Keegan. Top of the League at Christmas and through to the Sixth Round of the FA Cup by March, Newcastle played Arsenal three times, drawing at home in the Cup before being beaten both in the replay and at home in the League to end any hope of silverware. I had my own ideas as to who was to blame.

It's the morning after our FA Cup exit and I'm trying to combat both depression and hangover with the thought that at least I'm not in Wales. Can you imagine being this pissed off AND being in Wales? But I keep being distracted by the overwhelming urge to beat Dennis Berkamp to death with Lee Dixon. I know I said recently that Arsenal were the team at the top end of the table who I hated least but that was before we had to play them (what has seemed like) every week for three months and I came to understand that despite flashes of sublime beauty they are in fact despicable.

And so another season is passing without the opportunity to wave a gaudy pot in the faces of our enemies and do you know what? We are never going to win anything. And do you know why? Because a sizeable minority of our supporters haven't got the bollocks. I'll just give you a minute to let that sink in.

As soon as we even look like doing quite well at anything the people who can't take the heat get very vocal, the pressure gets turned up to an intolerable level and the wheels come spinning off.

We are beset, dear reader, by a collection of hysterical pissy-knickered little cowards. The people in question could be six feet four, twenty stone and capable of punching holes through brick walls but mentally they are hysterical pissy-knickered little cowards and it would be better for all concerned over these next few weeks if they spent their Saturdays at the fuckin' Metro Centre because we don't need them slagging off our team, arguing amongst themselves over whose fault everything is and whistling for full time after 80 minutes.

Just about all the away following and the vast majority of the home crowd are brave of heart, strong of spirit, loyal, knowledgeable (mostly drunk) and beautiful people whom I am proud to spend any part of my weekend with. But the insidious fuckers who need a scapegoat and a hate figure are actually damaging the club's chances. Whose fucking side are you on – it's that easy – make your bastard mind up!

We have got two choices; we love Laurent Robert and accept the fact that he is not going to be brilliant every second of the game or we slag him off, make him feel unwelcome, force him out and let some other team reap the benefit of this fantastic footballer. I'm prepared to go to war over this and if that makes it me versus a certain local journalist (Alan Oliver at the *Evening Chronicle)* then so be it. Am I alone in feeling disgusted by his ongoing campaign of hate against Robert? "Robert clearly hasn't got the mentality for big matches" he wrote recently.

WHAT?

Who set up the goal against sunderland this season? Who won us the game at Arsenal? I could go on for absolutely fucking ages (and I will). He scored against Manchester United – how big a game are we talking about here?

We came out of Bolton early in the season complaining about Robert's apparent lack of effort then realised he'd scored one and set up two others in a 4-0 win. It was obvious from then that the only way to judge the lad's performance was when it was finished. Some people still, despite all the evidence, haven't caught on. I'm not trying to say he had a good game against Liverpool, he clearly didn't, but despite that who created our only chances?

Last week we had Chrissy Waddle roped into the affair claiming Robert "didn't look too interested" after watching the Ipswich match. Is he taking the fucking piss or what? Chrissy Waddle for Christ sake. We were having the same arguments about him 20 fucking years ago. Standing around in his mullet and too-tight shorts doing sod all and looking lost or bored – then suddenly winning the match for us. Of all people, dammit.

Yes Robert can be frustrating but why do you think Bobby Robson leaves him on: do you think it's out of stupidity or do you think he might actually know what he is doing?

We know foreign footballers, especially midfielders, take a season to settle into the Premier League. Look at Pires at Arsenal last year compared to this, the situation is identical. Look at Nobby Solano, he has got better every season. Why do these people slagging off Robert want to air their crass ignorance so publicly? If you want to watch 11 players who will do nothing but run around sweating for 90 minutes go and watch sunderland for a couple of games then get back to me and tell me what you would rather pay for.

It's not just Laurent, virtually every player gets it at some point – and it's time some of us grew the fuck up. Ask yourself, "Whose side am I on?"

It's that simple.

Newcastle went on to finish fourth and qualified for the Champions League.

Chapter 37

2001/02 postscript – A Distorted View

When discussing Sir Bobby Robson's time at Newcastle you have to talk about Craig Bellamy. Robson tried to buy him the year before but he went to Coventry City instead who promptly got relegated. Bellamy had a stinker in Coventry's game at St James' Park and the general feeling was that we had dodged another expensive flop. So it was confusing when Robson went back for the same player offering the same £6 million. Nearly everybody, including many Coventry fans, thought it was a daft thing to do. Robson put his faith in the irascible Bellamy and was proved right, along with my friend Kev Broon. How Bellamy eventually repaid that faith is open to individual interpretation.

Modesty does not forbid me saying I saw Laurent Robert playing for France against Brazil and thought, "we should buy him." Love at first sight darlings and I remain a bit gay for Laurent Robert to this day. As Bobby said, "You have to live and die by Laurent. There may be some aspects of his play that may irritate at times but he is a match-winner." (nufc.com)

2001/02 was my favourite Newcastle United season. It was more fun than '95/96 because there was no weight of expectation; nobody took us seriously which meant the team belonged to us and not Sky television's legion of the sofa-bound. This team was fast as fuck, vibrant and brilliantly crafted by Robson; Dyer, Robert, and Bellamy were exhilaratingly fleet of foot, but we had the guise of Nobby Solano, the imperial athleticism of Gary Speed at the peak of his powers, arguably the best goalkeeper in the league in Mr Shay Given and only Alan bloody Shearer up front and fit for the full season.

We were out of Europe before the end of August despite coming back from 1-4 down against Troyes to draw 4-4 but the early start seemed to give us an edge that would last until February. Has there been a Newcastle team in the last 20 years that was as quick, fit and indomitable as this lot? We would be a goal down against good teams and not be thinking, "I hope we score" but "we're going to win this."

We smashed Middlesbrough 4-1 at their place, we beat Manchester United 4-3 with Alan Shearer unflinching in the face of Roy Keane's impotent, red-carded rage, then we got a little carried away. We lost at Liverpool, beat Bolton before Robson played Laurent Robert as a wing back (while trying to be Obi-Wan Kenobi to Glenn Hoddle's Darth Vader in what he seemed to see as a game of Ex-England Manager *Star Wars*) in a 0-2 home loss against Spurs. But we won the next two games to go third. Then we lost to Fulham. It felt like Robson had worked out that draws were no use to us; win two, lose one earning more points than win one draw two. This process doesn't work in cups however and a 90th minute Hasslebaink goal dumped us out the League Cup quarter final in December.

But the best was yet to come with Newcastle coming from at least a goal down in three consecutive games to beat Blackburn at home then Arsenal and Leeds away to go top of the table. A pesky 0-0 draw at Leicester tipped us straight off again.

A notable insight at this point was after a 4-2 win at Peterborough in the FA Cup: Alan Shearer was asked what he thought of the more basic facilities at lower League teams and replied without the hint of a smile, "they're better than ours". Nowadays Newcastle have a state of the art training centre and the players all look knackered after 75 minutes.

Continuing the fightback theme we came from a goal behind to win 3-1 at Spurs; and from both 0-1 and 1-2 down to beat Bolton 3-2. Next we battered Southampton 3-1 and knocked Man City out the FA Cup. Dizzy on our own brilliance we beat sunderland at their hovel before Craig Bellamy got injured. Bellamy played once more in the season, as a substitute at Blackburn but he was to prove irreplaceable. The timing could not have been worse, Newcastle lost at home to eventual champions Arsenal, then lost at Liverpool and got dumped out of the FA Cup (after a replay) by Arsenal who went on to win that as well.

The horrible bastards.

Duncan Ferguson put Everton a goal up at St James' but we came back to win 6-2. Then we had a couple of draws that set the pissy-knickered little cowards off on a hysteria attack. For my patience this culminated in us being 2-0 down at Derby amidst a group of Newcastle fans in front of a TV in the Punch Bowl on The Coast Road. The relentless abuse of Robert from one party led to a stand up row. Robert smashing in a rocket of a free-kick nearly caused a fist fight and only a last minute Lua Lua winner after a Dyer equaliser calmed everybody down. People often ask me if I'm going to the pub to watch a match – this is the reason I say no.

Arsenal won the League, Liverpool were second, Man Utd third, Newcastle fourth; five points ahead of Leeds and seven clear of sixth place Chelsea.
With a fit Bellamy and a nailed on bully-boy bastard of a centre half we could have beaten anybody or as Robson said, "If we finish fourth, some of the football we've played will deserve that. But we're not good enough defensively to win titles." (nufc.com)

Player of the Season: Alan Shearer – Robert, Solano, Dyer and Bellamy made us exciting and Shay Given won *The Mag* Player of the Season, but without Shearer's 27 goals we would have been nowhere.

Goal of the Season: Solano at Leeds (which ignores a Shearer belter against Villa and at least three bitchin' Robert free kicks) because it remains so vivid.

Chapter 38

September 2002

Bringing The Game Into Disrepute

Does anybody know what the bloody hell "bringing the game into disrepute" actually means? It's a charge that seems to be being bounced around the media like an exploding space-hopper just at the minute; nobody knows where it came from, who controls it or where it's likely to go off. What the hell is it? It looks akin to "indecent exposure" (Bringing The Game Into Disrepute, not space-hoppers... I'm done with that metaphor; it wasn't working and combined with indecent exposure it was, quite frankly, beginning to make me nervous). It seems a catch-all sort of crime where the rules are grey and so well hidden that we are all likely to have been guilty of it at some time or other and could at anytime be bundled into prison as soon as someone can decide who's going to be in charge of the sentencing.

The media seems to be happy for B.T.G.I.D. to be used like tax evasion was used to get Al Capone (i.e. it doesn't matter how we get them as long as we get them) and demand the charge be brought against anyone they have got a problem with, who hasn't done anything that is actually illegal.

"What sort of example is that to be setting for our children?" seems all the evidence required for a public hanging. Roy Keane has got the noose around his neck at the minute but not for swearing at Mick McCarthy, trying to kick Alfy Haaland's legs off or even for trying to knock some sense into Jason MacAteer's silly wooden head – simply for writing a book. Damn it, we must be seen to be hard on literature and hard on the causes of literature.

From what I have read of it, Keane's ghost writer (the hilariously bad-tempered and terminally grumpy Eamon Dunphy) has put together a fascinatingly readable account of what it's like to be an intensely troubled, violently inclined, wild-eyed loon with a fat wallet and poor social skills. If Rasputin was in

Trainspotting it couldn't have been more intriguing. For the language alone (which is spectacularly extreme), some commentators want him brought down. The charge? "Bringing The Game Into Disrepute" but like I said, who can be done for it and what can happen if they are found guilty?

OK, we'll take the Jimmy Hill line of "What sort of example is that to be setting for our children?"

Arsene Wenger – charge – being a sneaky hypocrite. Blaming Gronkjaer for "over-reacting" to get Patrick Viera sent off when his own Ashley Cole has now been involved in five players being sent of for "fouls" on him in a calendar year (including our own darling Craig Bellamy who brushed him with a stray finger and watched in some disbelief as Cole went down like he had been struck with a pickaxe handle. Chance being a fine thing.)

Ken Bates – charge – piracy; by charging a mad, greedy and inexcusable £40 for away fans to get in Stamford Bridge. If that isn't Bringing The Game Into Disrepute then absolutely nothing short of leaving the England team with no place to call home and having nowhere in the country to play the FA Cup Final is…. who is responsible for that again… oh hello Ken, fancy seeing you here.

David O'Leary – charge – re-writing history, just in case outright lying is a bit harsh. Many of you have informed me one way or another that Mr O'Leary, who last year accused Sir Bobby Robson of having "lost it", is now turning up on TV claiming that Leeds United were a top four team in The Premiership last season. Fourth gets you in The Champions League David, have Leeds been in The Champions League this season David? No they haven't David, that's because you finished fifth David which the rest of us don't consider within the top four but feel free to inform us what colour the sky is in your world this week. David. You tool.

Frank McLintock – charge – defamation of character. Like many of his media chums Frank accused sunderland fans of being fickle because they turned on Peter Reid. Yes, our neighbours are fickle. They are also ill-educated, have one arm longer than the other and many of them smell like a damp goat but the evidence of this cannot be found in their attitude to Peter Reid because they have been enduring bollocks football under Reid for years and have been remarkably patient.

Most fans – charge – have you seen yourself, if a child behaved like that, you would slap it?

David Seaman – charge – going out dressed in slate grey and lemon yellow. That can't be right, can it?

Sven Goran Eriksson – charge – wanting a mid-season break. His England players were tired at the World Cup apparently. Who ran the players' bollocks off in Dubai for two weeks before the World Cup started? How many times have we got to have this stupid argument?

George W Bush – there is nothing guaranteed to Bring The Game Into Disrepute faster than a swift apocalypse and this retarded fucking psycho-hillbilly is going to get us all killed.

You are all found guilty - Judge Furious is going to the pub.

Season 2010/11 – it was £50 to get into Stamford Bridge to see Chelsea play Newcastle. It is a wonder that anybody goes to football at all.

At least twice in the last two years David O'Leary has been linked with the manager's job at Newcastle. At the time of going to print he has yet to get the job. The tool.

Other good news being that George Bush didn't get us all killed. Yet.

Chapter 39

October 2002

Sticking To Your Principles

Telesales?

Telebastards more like. I've got more time for people who beg in the fuckin' street, seriously, at least they don't ring you up the exact bastard second you sit down with your tea in front of *The Simpsons* and try and sell you shit you don't bloody need.

Hey Northern Electric, are you listening? If you ring me up one more fucking time – just once – I'm going to have my electricity cut off entirely. I'd sooner sit in the bastard dark than put up with another sugary voiced snake pestering me - LEAVE ME ALONE!

Telesales isn't a job; you're a professional nuisance, it's legal stalking and it should be outlawed on pain of death. The Government should double dole payments just so people don't have to get involved with this stupid, pointless, irritating bloody occupation. We, as a society, lock up drug dealers, who at least provide a service and yet we are not safe in our homes from cold-calling pests.

Market research people ringing? Now that's a different matter altogether. While they have got the same uncanny knack of calling during anything that involves you not having your trousers fastened, they want my opinion on stuff and baby, I've got an opinion on fucking everything. So bring it on!

A few weeks ago I got a call from a reputable marketing company asking if I could name any of the major sponsors of the World Cup. As usual I assumed they were about to shout at me if I got any wrong and nervously mumbled, "Budweiser and er… Bainbridges?" The nice man politely lost patience with my dithering and read out a load of names and asked if I thought any of them were major sponsors.

"Kodak, MasterCard, Fuji film, Pepsi, McDonalds?"

"McDonalds," I snapped. "Aye, them insidious buggers will be in there," I said.

The lad on the other end of the phone line laughed. Turns out all the other questions were about McDonalds – that's who was paying for the research. So basically (if indirectly) McDonalds were ringing me up to ask me what I thought of them.

Excellent.

"Do you think that McDonalds cares for the sport it sponsors?" asked the lad, laughing as I became increasingly animated. "No, no, no! Whadya think I just landed here off the moon? Of course it doesn't. Ian Paisley is more likely to dine with the Pope than I am likely to sit down with a bloody Happy Meal – I hate McDonalds and everything it pretends to stand for. They have infected the world like a virulent disease, insulting people's culture, taste buds and intelligence wherever they sprout up. They can be trusted for nothing except the provision of a clean lavatory – which I will poo in and leave without buying so much as a bag of chips by the way. And they try and wrap themselves tightly to the world's greatest game so we will accept them. Oh they can't be evil, scum-sucking multi-national bastards because that lovely Rio Ferdinand smiles nicely when he orders his on the television commercial. And that clown? I hate clowns, they're not funny, they are scary and malevolent. When this government eventually finds its testicles and bans fox and stag hunting they can keep the dogs, guns, horses and brutal tradition to hunt down clowns and shoot them. Do you understand?"

"So I'll just tick the 'no' box, will I?"

Even if you have the morals of a starving sewer rat you need to have lines that you won't cross. Affiliations that you won't stand for. You don't agree? Bought a car from Reg Vardy since they started having their name across the front of sunderland shirts, have you?

But it is getting increasingly difficult not to compromise yourself and that is the point I'm trying to make. With their massive sponsorships and subsequent cash injections, Vodaphone and Nike are conspiring to make Manchester United an even more dominant financial force in the game than ever before. They are already on a different planet to everybody else (Arsenal may be the better team at the moment but you can't imagine them being able to stump up the £30 million Man Utd have just paid for Rio) and we are all helping them by not throwing out our phones and trainers and refusing to buy any more until they stop it.

Pick your favourite drink in the world (mine's a Holsten Pils, a cool thirst quenching expertly brewed beverage made of only the finest hops – oo yummy – now where's my fucking cheque?) Now imagine they start sponsoring sunderland. The cross hairs are on your principles – whatcha gonna do, punk? Worse still, what if Burberry starts sponsoring Newcastle United? I live in mortal fear of such an event. We would start to have Burberry patches under the arms of our replica shirts and an entire Burberry away kit which would make us look like the biggest wankers in the universe.

If you think that sounds cool then, like telesales people and Ronald McDonald, you deserve to be chased down the street and pelted with shit.

Fight The Power!

While he has yet to be seen dining with the Pope, Mr Paisley has had dinner with Martin McGuinness, which is remarkable and really rather lovely. Now if we can just get Celtic and Rangers fans to grow the fuck up I might consider a McFlurry.

Chapter 40

November 2002

Newcastle United 1 v Juventus 0

In the weeks leading up to this game I have heard it said and, shamefully, I have seen it written in the pages *The Mag* that our games in The Champions League are "an unnecessary distraction from the real business at hand." Some fans, it seems, find the "muck and nettles" of the Premiership more to their taste than the supposedly more sophisticated fare served up in the Champions League. Granted the club itself hasn't helped with the eye-watering strain on our wallets that ensured the games against Feyenoord and Kiev were never going to sell out. Also losing the first three games without scoring a goal didn't help with the overall enthusiasm but Mother of Christ on a dancing donkey will you go back and read the first line again: Newcastle United v Juventus; 1 – bastard 0.

We played Juventus in a competitive match. A match we earned the right to play in. A match they needed to win. And we won. And we deserved to win. And we were fuckin' brilliant. And angels floated us away from the ground, with joy and pride in our hearts, to pour cold drinks over our red-raw throats. And we woke to discover it was real and we laughed off our hangovers and felt like Gods.

Seriously, you'd rather play Charlton, or Southampton or Birmingham or bloody West bloody Bromwich bloody bastard Albion? CAST THE UNBELIEVERS UNTO THE PIT! I WILL HEAR NO MORE OF THEIR MEWLING!

Even if we don't qualify for the next round, or even the UEFA Cup, we needed to win this game. The spiteful and the ignorant in the media had been saying we were out of our depth, our enemies were pointing mocking fingers and the strain was starting to show. Remember, we went into this game on the back of the 5 – 2 debacle at Blackburn. A game we played 89 minutes of with just 10 men *(Dabizas was sent off for handball the exact second I found my seat in the away end. The damn fool.)* Our confidence and resolve should have been shot to hell but dammit this team is tougher than that and our grey and blue boys came out swinging from the off.

It's got to be said that the kit change did many people's heads right in. After decades of wanting the team in black and white stripes to win the tackles, pick up the loose balls and win everything at St James' Park, to suddenly want the other team to get the ball was hard. And fans had to keep mentally checking themselves.

Griffin, who had looked shaky at Ewood Park, gave the first declaration of intent by cleaning out an opponent, then giving him a "have you got a problem with that?" look and it was from the back that this victory was built. Bramble and O'Brien were solid and controlled with the extra burst of pace required to get themselves out of trouble, while Aaron Hughes played like… well Aaron Hughes actually.

In front of them, the man of the match, ladies and gentlemen, Mr Jermaine Jenas. Is that a pistol in your pocket JJ or are you just pleased to….. no wait, it's Edgar Davids. Cool.

Steve Harper was in goal and The Leazes End gave him a stirring welcome back which he, rather sweetly, looked shocked by. Harper made one mistake, his usually faultless kicking deserted him and an open goal was presented to the cross-eyed scarecrow that is Pavel Nedved who missed and spent the rest of the game tripping over invisible but clearly very hungry crocodiles.

Newcastle had the edge but chances were few. Shearer shot and headed half chances over and Lua Lua rolled a timid shot up to Buffon when Robert was unmarked to his left. On the stroke of half-time Robert ran on to the clearest chance but couldn't allow for its awkward descent and missed the target.

Looking round the ground at half-time it was clear that Juve had brought a quite pathetic amount of fans with them – but as the Italians don't seem interested in home Champions League games at this stage I suppose we shouldn't be surprised.

The skinny lad in the salmon pink shirt was Gianluigi Buffon. He is the most expensive goalkeeper ever, costing 30 something million pounds and most of the major second half talking points involved him. He charged out brilliantly to smother a Solano shot that looked like a sure goal and made an excellent save with his forearm, diving low to his right to thwart Shearer. Later he would surpass these saves by diving high to his left hand corner to tip over a Solano shot that was dipping ferociously.

However, his contribution between saves two and three was to divert a Griffin shot into his own goal. Griff burst clear on the edge of the Juve area, resisted the temptation to dive like Nedved and thumped the ball in low. If Buffon had missed it Nobby was sliding in but he didn't and the ball squirmed swiftly through his grasp into the net. For a second Griffin looked utterly perplexed. The 48,000 people screaming eventually sunk in, as his ecstatic team mates gleefully leapt all over him.

The Champions League has been a steep learning curve for players and fans and, to be honest, the crowd was a little subdued up to this point. Our team has played well but has been cruelly treated by luck and officials and perhaps we feared getting our hopes up a fourth time. But now we started to believe.

The realisation of what our team was doing began to dawn on a crowd mentally prepared for more brave disappointment and the volume just turned up and up and up. Shearer began playing for time with ten minutes left and our nerves began to rattle. But not as hard as the bar rattled when Juve sub Zalayeta thwacked a shot off it.

Substitutions were greeted with long and rapturous ovations as we tried to clap our way to 90 minutes. A clearly injured Shearer limped painfully from the pitch after extensive treatment and bounced straight back on like a spring lamb. The determination and passion of our chosen men had us on our feet and roaring encouragement right through the two added minutes, and the final whistle brought a victorious roar which will have rattled the very bones of our detractors.

Whatever happens next, we'll look back on this night as one of the best in our club's history. Juventus manager Marcello Lippi was gallant in his praise of our team and fans which made a change from the crying of vanquished Premiership managers and damn it, we deserved it.

Interesting is the attitude to Europe amongst Newcastle fans. Many, like myself, love being in Europe and see it as a celebration of the previous year's success, relish the opportunity to travel and to see different players. Yet Newcastle got more fans in St. James' Park to see us play Scunthorpe in 2010 (despite all not being well at the club and fans having fallen out with owner Mike Ashley and the team being in the Championship) than came to see most of our games in The Champions League when all was comparatively well with our world.

Chapter 41

November 2002

Ideas Above Our Station

Apparently somebody complained about this article in a letter to The Sunderland Echo.

Something has been brought to my attention. Something which I feel I must pass on to you dear reader, despite the fact that you will find it upsetting and disgusting. It seems that "The National Glass Centre" in sunderland requires a new Chief Executive. Consequently an advert has been placed in the "quality press" inviting applicants to put themselves forward for the £55,000 a year post. If I may quote from the advert:

"NGC aims to create and sustain a world class centre, to celebrate the artistry and craftsmanship of glass through the provision of facilities for production, exhibition, education and sales.

"The Tyne & Wear conurbation is fast becoming a major centre for culture with the recently opened Baltic Centre for Contemporary Art and The Sage Centre opening in 2003. The NGC is part of that renaissance."

You're fucking joking?

No, it bloody well isn't.

The dynamic Newcastle/Gateshead "City of Culture" bid is up against some pretty hefty competition as they strive to attain what is rightfully ours for 2008 – and these manky fucking tramps are trying to hitch a ride on our magnificent bandwagon with their grotty little bottle shop. This is the sort of thing we can expect for the next seven years is it? The mayor of sunderland trying to shuffle onto the winner's podium, smiling and waving while our gallant leaders, trying to accept the award graciously, are shifting nervously. "What's that horrible smell?" they'll say. "Who is that disgusting little man and why has he brought a pig in a frock with him?"

And every time King of News Readers, Mike Neville, proudly puffs out his chest and links to another "City of Culture" piece on the local news Steve Cram is going to be there in the background, jumping up and down and waving like some snotty urchin behind Stuart Hall on *It's a Knockout*. It's like a beautiful contestant turning up for Miss World and her simple-minded, toothless, one legged, hump-backed, bald (yet moustached) next door neighbour won't let go of her gown and she keeps farting loudly and demanding more cakes. Frankly it's embarrassing.

Get away from us. You shameless conniving bastards.

When sunderland chairman Bob Murray was advertising for a new manager for his club did the advert read: "The Tyne and Wear conurbation is fast becoming a major centre for footballing excellence, with Champions League football, young quality international footballers like Craig Bellamy and Kieron Dyer and a 52,000 seater stadium sold out week after week? Sunderland AFC is part of that renaissance" – probably not but it wouldn't surprise you would it? They're all like, "We have got all the facilities to stage International Football matches. You'll have to get the train or the plane to Newcastle first, mind. Oh and you'll have to stop there as well if you want a hotel room or anything decent to eat and…" yeah, whatever.

The thing is, sunderland's shitness is actually starting to get on my nerves. For a while it was funny; Sergeant Wonko Wilkinson was proclaimed "The New King Of The Tramps" with his sidekick The Evil Howler Monkey (Steve Cotterill man, he's got a howler monkey's face and arms, he couldn't look more like a howler monkey if he hung upside down in the dugout by his fuckin' tail – and he looks well shifty) and like many Newcastle fans I brought crisps and beer to watch the funny mackems play Bolton on telly and nearly lost the will to live. They were on again, against Charlton and by the end I was crying and wailing, "that was two hours of my actual life wasted. It was awful, really really awful – I like football but what the fuck was that supposed to be, they don't even want the ball, they only want to chase round after it. Oh sweet Jesus, is this the same game that has given us Cruyff, Platini, Garrincha and Viana? Somebody shoot me please."

Fortunately, Hundred Reasons played at Newcastle Uni that night and their ferocity and brilliance made the very walls bleed and scorched the filthy mackem residue out of my wounded soul in the process.

By the time we slapped Middlesbrough stupid (again) *(2-0: Ameobi, Caldwell)* I was feeling quite calm and even Steve McClaren's pathetic crying over non-existent penalties couldn't spoil my happy mood. "We could have got a result here" – you did get a result Steve, it's called losing and you should be thankful we had five first teamers missing and three players left on our bench who are better than you have got in your entire squad. Now stop being silly and go away, I've got a job application for Chief Executive at the National Glass Centre to fill in. How many 'm's in sledgehammmer?

Unfortunately Newcastle/Gateshead did not win the City of Culture. It was stolen by some Scousers.

Chapter 42

December 2002

Be Strong Be Wrong

My editor has been telling me off for obscure cultural references for years. Be Strong Be Wrong is an album by a brilliant Canadian three piece band called Nomeansno; anyone who noticed this can have a pint, if you can find me.

Being proved wrong and admitting as much can be a wonderfully liberating thing. It is an experience that should be embraced and there is no need to cry or pull funny faces like Cherie Blair whilst doing so. The recriminations may go on but you can keep a straight back and look your detractors square in the eye, with a clean soul.

Many people purporting to be my friends will happily remind me that I once wrote of Kieron Dyer (whilst he was still at Ipswich) something along the lines of "Dyer will sign for Spurs and in two years time, like Jason Dozzell before him, people will wonder what the hell happened to him." I delight in being proved wrong on this as I do about Bobby Robson for manager, his signing of Craig Bellamy and being forced at virtual gunpoint to view the film *Strictly Ballroom*. All of which have enriched my life splendidly.

The week I write this every Newcastle fan I know (with one exception – hello Guy) had their opinion of Shola Ameobi radically shaken as he went from being "canny" to "fuckin' awesome" within the space of 90 minutes in the Nou Camp. *(We lost 3-1 but Shola scored and played a blinder and we call it the Camp Nou nowadays because we are more culturally aware.)*

Of course being wrong has a down side: my firm belief that Silvio Maric would prove to be the new Robert Lee, that the Labour Government would herald a golden age of fairness and that *The Blair Witch Project* might not be a piece of

shit film and an entire waste of two hours of my life, are scars that refuse to heal. Only last week I made my way to the gym (in another attempt to attain the abs of Brad Pitt and the arms of Vin Diesel in the half hour before another feast of Guinness and pies and chips) safe in the knowledge that there could not be a more sickening self-satisfied single on present release than Ms Jennifer Lopez's "I'm still (I'm still) Jenny from the block" bollocks. There are music videos in the gym.
Oh dear.

Was I ever wronger? S Club Juniors have done a cover version of the truly repulsive Donnie Osmond song *Puppy Love* wherein the ghastly little pampered monsters mime their hearts out and embrace one another with hearty Christmas sincerity to the strain of a tune that was an atrocious and embarrassing pile of puke 30 years ago. I leant against a rowing machine for support, mouth flapping open like Phillip Neville in a strong wind and tried not to retch as, at the end of the performance, the message "Remember a puppy is for life, not just for Christmas" came on the screen as the happy cherubs enjoyed one last communal hug before being whisked off to their separate trailers for parties with crack and gin-soaked hookers (probably).
If I were a puppy and I saw this grotesque spectacle I would insist that you put me in a sack and drowned me immediately.
"What's that got to do with football?" you ask.
Nothing at all, but you need to know that if that song gets to Number 1 in the charts no wait… if I ever, ever hear that fucking song again…. I won't be here in the New Year – I will have gone off to join Al-Qaeda with the express intent of bringing Western Civilisation to its knees. Jesus Christ himself would offer no redemption to a society that allowed such an abomination to be broadcast.

If there is one thing on the planet guaranteed to wind people up it is pig-headed knuckle-scrapers refusing to admit that they are wrong. Like sunderland fans insisting 7th in the league is something to show off about (name me another team who finished 7th off the top of your head – right now – you can't, that's because no one cares. Idiots.) and Newcastle fans thinking Laurent Robert is a luxury we can't afford. I'm sick to death of the latter argument – it's like playing a child's video game on "easy" and winning and then being expected to do it again every fuckin' month for two years. But, as the dismal fuckwits won't shut up neither will I. In the pro-Robert corner is Sir Bobby Robson and the sensible people (and me). In the anti-corner, led by the *Evening Chronicle's* Alan Oliver are the sheep-brained arse-heads who would rather our players ran around tackling clumsily for 90 minutes. Whose side are you on? And more importantly who do you want to be right?

Seriously I want to know, because some fans seem to simply shut up and ignore the games Robert has won for us and then instantly get all gobby again when he has a less effective match. Ignoring that his considerable threat alone stretches and disrupts the opposition.

Yes, he has games where we would want more from him but do you think you are going to get it by screaming at him and questioning his loyalty? For fucksake, you sometimes wonder about people's motives. The rush to decide Bramble was no good after he had played three games for us was worrying enough but the virtual lynch mob that went after Bellamy for getting sent off against Inter Milan was plain staggering – what's wrong with you people? The kid fucked up but nobody died and surely he's got enough in the good-will bank with his goals against sunderland and Feynoord alone for us to be a little more forgiving. Alan Shearer could have been sent off in the same game, would people have been as quick to tell him to grow up and show some discipline, I doubt it. Basically are we are all in this together or are there some of you who would rather lose and be proved right?

Happy fucking Christmas.

While Shola Ameobi still oscillates wildly between "fuckin' awesome" and "fuckin' atrocious" from one minute to the next, Titus Bramble is at present in the employ of sunderland which is a relief because, while capable of playing very well, he remains a daft liability-bomb waiting to explode all over his own team's face. The important difference being that at least now it's funny.

Chapter 43

February 2003

Bullshit Detectors

I have worked with some lads from Middlesbrough and most of them have been brilliant. The best among them are hilarious, insightful and fascinatingly strange. For example I told one of them, Nathan, that I had quoted him in The Mag regarding Sam Allardyce and thanked him for the term "hippo-headed bastard", to which he replied, "I actually said hippo-headed cunt and it wasn't me who came up with that, it was my mum."

I have allowed them through the carefully guarded checkpoint between colleagues and friends and as a consequence would have found it hard to keep up a level of vitriol towards The Boro with any degree of honesty if it wasn't for the fact that they hate their football team more than anybody else. Then on Real/Century Radio there was always Boro spokesman and gobshite, Bernie Slaven, but he died after being hit in the head with a speed boat.

Middlesbrough FC are a puffed up collection of holier-than-thou piss-drips and in February 2003 they excelled themselves when they called a game off against Newcastle the day before it was due to happen. I rang Andy, another of my contacts-on-Tees before I wrote this, asking him what the weather was like. "Six feet of snow," he lied, "I can't get my front door open or see out of the window." Then he laughed.

I write this on Saturday morning. It's 11 o'clock and I should be on the brink of a day of beer, football and being stuck on a bus for hours longer than necessary because of the Cleveland Constabulary. Instead I fear I will have to face up to a host of long put off menial chores. I am not pleased.

We football fans are a sceptical and suspicious breed. This is understandable as we are peppered with bullshit as if it were buckshot from Grandpa's blunderbuss on a daily basis. Conspiracies are afoot and real truths are guarded from us.

Games being postponed are natural breeding grounds for rumour and perceived skulduggery so I must proceed with caution.

Twice in the last ten years Newcastle United, in form and flying, have been due to play at West Ham when our hosts, depleted through injury and suspension, were forced to call the game off due to bad weather. The fact that the ice on Dot Cotton's bird bath would have cracked under the weight of a malnourished cockney sparrow and that (on at least one occasion) Dagenham fulfilled their own home fixture despite being a mere badly placed Billy Bonds header away from Upton Park, fuelled our paranoia. Newcastle lost both rearranged games. So when our game at The Riverside was postponed 27 hours before the game was due to take place our inbuilt Bullshit Detectors buzzed into life. The pitch was fine it seems but the access roads were dangerous.

The facts: Boro, without centre half pairing of Ehiogu and Southgate and at least three other first choice players and with Boateng apparently looking rusty in his first game back after a long injury lay off, conceded five goals at home to Aston Villa on the previous Tuesday. To put this into context Villa had only managed four away goals all season up to that point. The following day Newcastle kept a third clean sheet in a row whilst winning at Spurs and went second in the League. The form did not point to a home victory. Boro fans I work with and whom I had much earlier in the season nervously arranged to meet for a pre-match pint were so sure of a painful Newcastle victory that none of them were prepared to go to the game at all.

My first witness is Sir Robert Robson: "I don't think there was much will on behalf of Boro to get the game played. We asked for the game to be played on Tuesday night but nobody seems to be interested in that idea."

Three days clearly wouldn't be long enough for Boro's injured players to get their feet back under the table. Presumably this is the same table that Boro owner Steve Gibson wasn't hiding under on Friday resplendent in Corporal Jones helmet screaming, "Don't panic, don't panic! The Geordies are coming, the Geordies are coming! Don't panic!"

The plot thickened by Friday tea-time as caller after caller from Middlesbrough rang up *The Legends* bloody awful Century Radio programme to say that the approaches to the Riverside were hardly likely to trouble the ghosts of Ernest Shackleton and Captain Scott. One fan claimed to have been in touch with Middlesbrough Council, who told him they have a contract to clear the snow and ice in and around the ground and that the football club hadn't been in contact with them.

Boro are habitual offenders of course and were docked three points after they didn't turn up at Blackburn Rovers a couple of years back because one or two of their boys were feeling a bit peaky. They kicked up a right old stink but the lost points were not returned and they were relegated for the lack of them. A repeat conviction is unlikely because they postponed the game on advice of safety officials, the police and a Premiership referee. Evidence good enough for The Premier League and most of the media but let's have a closer look, shall we? That will be Middlesbrough safety officials who work for the club would it? OK. Middlesbrough Police? Remember the grotty old away section at Ayresome Park, how if you stood on the left hand side of it you couldn't see much of the pitch? 1991; promotion-chasing Leeds went there and white shirted away fans, squashed together and struggling to see, kept popping out of the crowd like bursting spots – where they were dragged away by the constabulary for invading the pitch. Leeds United complained on their supporters' behalf. Boro said they would investigate the police, the police said they would investigate Boro and both exonerated each other and said it was the Leeds fans' fault. But they did agree to half the capacity of away supporters in time for their game against.....? That's right, Newcastle United.

The relevance being that the two parties clearly have a cosy relationship. And this of course will be the same police who deliberately cause Newcastle fans to miss the kick-off every fucking year, will it? And The Premiership referee wouldn't happen to be Boro supporting Jeff Winter, would it? Oh it would. How fuckin' strange.

Middlesbrough Football Club you stand accused of "Cowardice in the Face of the Enemy" and unless some lily-livered, politically correct commie-pinko bastard has changed the law since 1918 – you can be bloody well shot for that. How do you plead?

Get out from under that table and answer me you craven bastards!

The game was rearranged for the 5th of March, four days after Newcastle played Chelsea and six days before a Champions League match away to Inter Milan. Middlesbrough won 1-0. That's playing Middlesbrough and being in The

Champions League -you can only hazard a guess as to which of those events we will live to see next.

Another of my friends from Middlesbrough, Brian, said of the original date; "Playing the match was dangerous. There was a real danger that you were going to give us a right twatting." It has also been pointed out to me that Bernie Slaven didn't die after being hit in the head with a speed boat, that was Kirsty MacColl. Which hardly seems fair.

Chapter 44

April 2003

sunderland 0 v Newcastle United 1

Three games from the end of the 2002/03 season sunderland were already assured of the lowest points total in the history of any League, anywhere in the world (or something) – we in Newcastle were keen to gloat but our own Champions League qualification hung in the balance.

So we were finally proved right.
Newcastle fans have been telling anyone who cared to listen (and plenty who didn't) for years that sunderland are shit and finally the world can see it. Worst Premiership Team Ever. They should be awarded some kind of trophy, perhaps on live TV before next year's Charity Shield, and they should be forced to stitch the words "Worst Premiership Team in History" into all their shirts until some other bunch of talentless fools betters their monumental crapness and ineptitude.

sunderland fans, as is their nature, have been trying to rewrite history with their habitual blinkered and lopsided view of the world. Explaining the facts sensibly to them is like discussing theology with a hill-billy who has an air horn.
Papers and phone-in shows have been swamped with nit-wit mackems bemoaning their last two seasons as under-achievement when the simple truth is that the two seasons before that when they finished 7th were actually massive over-achievement. And it seems to be particularly difficult for them to get into their thick heads that 7th really isn't that great. They also bemoan the loss of quality players but who was the last player to leave sunderland who did anything of note afterwards? They were at their very, very best with a squad of mediocre players working hard and kicking people (how quickly they gloss over the fact the two 7th place finishes were during seasons where they had the worst

disciplinary record in The Premiership) .

Bottom line: they can't even live up to their own average standards without bully-boy tactics and Niall Quinn's peculiar brand of non-footballing football. Yet they still want it both ways as well – they demand to be seen and treated as equals with Newcastle but also want all the nice stuff that comes with being the plucky underdog. Mick McCarthy has been the perfect manger for sunderland coming, as he does, from the same school of deluded gas-bags as Glenn Hoddle and David O'Leary. Within seconds of us packing up the three points to haul back to civilisation manager and fans were rewriting the story of the game into some sort of moral victory for sunderland with only corrupt refereeing robbing Mick's feisty young terriers of the rewards their brave performance merited.

Mick McCarthy you are in fact Foghorn Leghorn and I claim my five pounds. We had 60% of the possession, the shot count was 10-19 and we won the game. And got all the points. Which makes six on the season, which is as many as it is possible to get and we can't stand for any of that crap about it being a narrow win when 1-0 is exactly the same width as 2-1 and they've been banging on about that for years. And therein lies the final and unavoidable truth; that deep down the mackems actually acknowledge their inferiority because a win for them is massive and a win for us is merely expected.

We were discussing this in the pub before we got the buses: for some of our fans the stakes are just too high, with potential loss bringing harder pain than potential victory brings excitement (one lad was so nervous he admitted to drinking a can of beer in the shower at 7.30 am); they want sunderland down dead and never likely to darken our door again.

I am in the minority who like the derbies and while it goes without saying that if sunderland lost every game they played for the next twenty years I would laugh until I passed out, I love the drama, the noise, the fear and the high stakes. Because in the end it doesn't matter one jot (or even half a jot – whatever a jot is) what I or any other Newcastle fan wants sunderland to do. Our opinion is actually of no practical relevance so if we have to play them we may as well get on with it and no amount of pre-game pant-wetting is going to help.

True, it would be embarrassing to lose to "The Worst Team in Premiership History" but all their pre-match boasting about stopping us getting into The Champions League was more nonsensical honking because in beating and drawing with Liverpool this season sunderland have actually done more than most teams to help us finish ahead of them. The one thing we all agreed on was that Newcastle United would decide who won the day. If we played to even a fraction of our potential we would win no matter what sunderland did. We then got on with the business of drinking as much as feasibly possible bearing in mind the short hop down to the home of the inbred ratshaggers can actually take a bladder-stretching hour and a half when in a 40 bus convoy.

Credit at this point to those people who made an extra effort for this (possibly) last ever league game against sunderland. True Faith fanzine for the hundreds of "Ha ha" banners and the people responsible for amending all the brown and white road signs to say "Stadium of Shite" for which you can apparently get five years at Her Majesty's pleasure. Splendid work.

1831 was the year of sunderland's most significant gift to the country. In 1831 sunderland gave the nation cholera. An epidemic that wiped out over 15,000 people country-wide began on Wearside, presumably because of their inability to wash themselves. That's 172 years - ample reason to shovel the whole sorry shit-hole into the sea and little has happened in the meantime to change the mind of any right thinking person. The place in an abomination on God's good earth and the inhabitants who scurry about dressed as trampy clowns should be given as wide a berth as their forefathers who were responsible for so much death.

That's not a tin shed on an allotment, that's someone's house. These people live like animals and why do they take to the streets in such numbers to gawp at us? All these modern self-assembly kit grounds must come with the same free CD to blast out before kick-off: Blur's *Song 2*; that Gallic instrumental nonsense and all the other stuff you hear at Bolton and Boro. At St James' Park this season we have had The Ramones, The Clash and The Transplants (coolest band on the planet right now – get to Steel Wheels) damn but we rock! So we provided our own soundtrack: "Have you ever seen a mackem in Milan? Have Ya FUCK!".

Years ago we hated playing in home shirts and white shorts – we lost at places like Oxford and Watford but now we barely care and Shearer, sporting what has become known as his sunderland hat (pink bandage), led our beautiful boys out into a cauldron of hate. And you can feel your heart beating and you have to concentrate on your breathing and the butterflies in your stomach won't calm down and the anxious itching in your brain is unbearable and you can physically feel the home crowd's spite and fear. And we soak it all up gleefully and spit it back and wave our "Ha Ha" banners and jingle our keys and laugh in their hateful faces. It's intoxicating and you won't get this at Portsmouth next season. 45,000 roar as they try to win the game through sheer force of will in the first minute and in the second minute Solano crosses and Shearer scores with his bandaged head. What a start.

Disallowed.

Kieron Dyer was flattened on the edge of the area after a darting run but for some reason Viana took the free kick quickly and Kieron's resulting cross was headed behind. Viana for us and Williams for them both got booked after Williams ran the length of the pitch to get involved after Viana had tripped the lumbering Kevin Kyle. Our hosts were undoubtedly pumped up and were kicking higher than war time can-can dancers. Proctor had two go-gos at Woodgate before Kyle broke Andy O'Brien's nose. And in the time it took us to get Caldwell on and sorted Given had to get down sharp to keep out Bellion.

Shearer with stitches in his head, a broken knuckle and creaking knees had his misery compounded by a reckless Thornton tackle that broke his ankle and he limped out of the action as the stupid mackems cheered. This is Shola Ameobi, ya knuckleheads – he scored in the Camp Nou and you fuckers are not Barcelona. Shola had only been on the field three minutes when he skipped past a couple of tackles and shot just wide. Having already seen Bellamy miss when clean through and Solano put a free header wide you start to worry. It was suddenly heart in the mouth time as Griffin headed against his own bar and Woodgate nearly scored an own goal tidying up after a good save from Given.

Twice a Newcastle player was tripped on the edge of the sunderland area and both Bellamy then Dyer looked up astonished from the floor to see the ref waving play on – the hidden laws of football suggest we get the next one and when Kilbane tripped Bellamy with the ball long gone we had ourselves a nailed-on penalty. Not a controversial penalty, mind. There was no controversy, the ref got it right.

Nobby Solano stepped up and because he is cool and because he was having his best game in ages we had little doubt.

Sorensen went the wrong way and the net at the opposite end billowed and the world was instantly euphoric.

Could we hold on until half-time without shooting ourselves in the head? Bollocks to that it seemed and Newcastle had their best five minutes of the match and sunderland were reeling. Bellamy again went clean through and again Sorensen denied him. Craigy-boy was also crudely hacked down by the already booked Williams in this period but the mackems' ignorant bluster about the ref favouring Newcastle overlooked that incident as well.

For 35 minutes of the second half Woody kept the defence tight and cool, Jenas held the midfield and we created enough chances to win comfortably – a second goal would have killed them and we would have got a bucketful – but Bellamy couldn't beat Sorensen and Nobby blazed another good chance over the bar.

Shola broke clean through but was pulled back; you know if that had been Van Nistlerooy or Henry they would have gone straight down and the last defender would have been off – game won. Likewise Bellamy skipped past Williams in the box and stayed up after getting his trailing leg clipped. Ashley Cole or Beckham would have been spitting a mouthful of grass at the referee.

With ten minutes left, sunderland started to give a final heave – a goal now would feel like a disaster to us and like a win to them...... so naturally the home fans started to leave in their hundreds. Given made a smart save from a Thornton free kick who then put a similar opportunity wide.

The remaining home fans desperately urged their team on and, not for the first time this season, we Newcastle fans found ourselves watching intently but silent. Perhaps we think we have got too sophisticated with all this European travel but for a few minutes we were quieter than was good for us. Our boys seemed unconcerned and spent a confident four or five minutes in and around the sunderland penalty area in which time Bellamy was again denied by Sorensen. We were back in control and with 89 minutes on the clock.... but...

a high ball was lofted hopefully into our area, Flo clattered into Given and Kyle headed into the Newcastle net. The unwashed exploded all around us. For a second it looked as if the ref had given it and was pointing back towards the centre circle. Numb disbelief – they can't allow that – they allowed that Phillips goal for them down here and he was a league offside. Oh bollocks.

But what's this, what's this? sunderland players swarming round the ref. No goal. For years Newcastle fans have wondered why the hell sunderland fans spend so much of a derby match looking at us instead of at the pitch. Yes yes, we look way cooler than you slack-jawed, monkey-faced, deck chair wearing, slope-browed, knuckle-dragging ninnies – but there is a game going on here for Christ sake. So can I just report for those of you not in attendance that for a good 30 seconds after we realised the goal had been chalked off, with some sunderland fans running onto the pitch and with others jumping up and down sticking their fingers up at us, they were still screaming and punching the air. Seriously, the image will live with me for a long time because it was very, very funny.

Slowly the realisation spread through them and that reaction was even funnier. Clutching their heads, open mouthed, twisted faces, shocked and disbelieving. Oh how we laughed.

The final two minutes dragged horribly but fortunately Jonathan Woodgate has got more bottle than me and he snuffed out all remaining danger calmly and the final whistle blew.

Not the thrashing they so richly deserve and have sneakily avoided over recent years from us but as we waved nicely and sang "We'll meet again, don't know where, don't know when" they filed out shouting abuse and making hand gestures for our further amusement. Some stayed to gawp at us for ten minutes, others went outside to look at us as the buses pulled away. Strange people.

Half past six by the time we crashed into The Hotspur on Percy Street like returning warriors, sunderland vanquished, scrummy beer, a pub full of happy Mags – what could be finer. The five and a half hour wait for the three minutes of highlights on TV flew over.

So that's it, people. Ding dong the witch is dead, we've beaten them twice and sent them on their way and sunderland should be dead to us so don't ask me to "stand up if you hate sunderland" next season because I can't be fucking bothered and I can barely remember who they are. We need to set our sights higher than this sorry bunch, we should be looking to pick a fight with somebody from a higher weight division. Oi, Inter Milan you cheating bastards – what the fuck are you looking at? Do you want some?

2010/11 and we are back to squabbling over who can finish furthest from the relegation places with our neighbours – like eunuchs fighting over the Viagra it is and it's boring.

Chapter 45

May 2003

Twenty Two Months of Uninterrupted Football

In my not very humble opinion this was the exact point when it all started to go wrong.

This month's 'Billy Furious' is brought to you in conjunction with 'The Flying Scotsman' public house, Forest Hall, Newcastle-upon-Tyne. 'The Flying Scotsman', where Kevin and Carol will warmly welcome you to sample their cool drinks and hot food (served daily) in a friendly atmosphere.
Ha ha, sponsorship at last – now I've really fucking made it.

It was twenty two months ago that this cavalcade of football came charging towards us like a pack of mad dogs and we've barely had a chance to breathe since. Intertoto Cup qualifiers, great season, World Cup, Champions League, great season, mackems down, more Champions League qualification (ahead of whingey scousers) and beautiful new shirts to flounce around in on our holidays. We dived into a vat-full of the drug of our choice: it's been more addictive than crack, more expensive than cocaine and probably as good for our health as a heroine/ecstasy/speed rocket up the jacksie. But who cares – we survived and what a blast!
I watched the FA Cup Final in 'The Flying Scotsman' (Is that enough now Carol, can I have my wife back?) and when it finished I breathed out a sigh of relief. Partly because the pig-awful match was over but mostly because that was it. We'd seen it out to the end. From competitive matches in July, through drinking beer at 9 in the morning for a month watching the World Cup, spectacular wins, crushing defeats and all within the haywire mental head rush of life as a Newcastle United fan with Bobby Robson at the helm. Terrifying, thrilling and in the end, exhausting.

"Bollocks to the lot of you, I want a rest."
I said this in the pub and some people looked at me as if I was mental. Mad football junkies talking about getting tickets for England's under 21 game in sunderland because Shola might be playing. Leave me alone you crazy bastards.

I'm having nothing to do with football for three months. I don't care what happens, I'm not fucking interested...

One day later. One day. Kevin Phillips says he won't sign for Newcastle and my mind is spinning into a fantasy world where Mr Phillips is discussing the move with Freddie Shepherd:
KP: "You seem to have a lot of good strikers here. Where do you see me fitting in?"
FS: "We see you 'fitting in' to a sack with some unwanted puppies and some rocks – which we intend to throw into the river."
KP: "I beg your pardon?"
FS: "Only joking. We wouldn't be so inhumane. Of course we wouldn't put puppies in a sack. It will be just you and the rocks."
KP: (nervous laugh) "Seriously though, I see myself in a floating role behind Shearer and Bellamy."
FS: I see you more in a non-floating role. In a sack full of rocks, disappearing into the Tyne. You have to understand Kevin, we are buying you to drown you. We intend to sell tickets. That offside goal you scored against us three years ago still really bothers me and I feel you haven't been punished enough, despite two seasons of utter, and I mean utter, humiliation. You have a straight choice between drowning or signing for Middlesbrough."
KP: "Oh that's a tough choice, can I get back to you on that?"

I decided to give myself another chance to concentrate on more worthwhile matters than three months of transfer tittle-tattle. Catch up with missed films, play *Grand Theft Auto – Vice City* on the Playstation for 12 weeks or burn the fuckin' *Big Brother* house to the bastard ground and dance on the ashes. No rumour, no matter what, would I give the time of day to, at least until August. Then Newcastle's interest in Lee Bowyer exploded out of *The Sun* like an unwelcome cack-bomb and all bets were off. Sky Sports claimed a five year deal was imminent. The good folk at nufc.com claimed everybody was jumping the gun and later Radio 5 reported that Bowyer's agent had been "in talks with several clubs".

By the time you read this it might all turn out to be hokum but for the record… I don't want that poisonous little fucking shit-bag at our club, in our colours, under our flag. I don't like the fucker and you can't fucking make me. I detest him and his lily-livered apologists. His signing will damage our club horrifically. He has yet to come out and say he is not a racist (unlike Woodgate) despite countless opportunities and his refusal to do so has made him a mascot for the extreme right. He is serving a six game European ban for stamping on an opponent's head. He also stood in front of me and all the other Newcastle fans at Elland Road a couple of years back and shouted "Cunts Cunts Cunts!" after scoring against us. Do you want to pay that bastard's wages?

Honestly the second you turn your back on this football habit – it bites you on the arse.

Have a good one.

Lee Bowyer later did insist that he is not a racist but in buying him, and only him, that summer Newcastle effectively slammed the brakes on their own progress and everything from that point started going wonky to the point that eight years later we are nowhere near where we were.

Chapter 46

2002/03 postscript – A Distorted View

This season opened in Sarajevo with Newcastle playing Zeljeznicar in a Champions League qualifier. What was the score and who scored? Go on, go on, go on, – quickly, and what happened in the return leg?

Obviously we got through because we remember playing Inter Milan and Barcelona later but what was the score in Sarajevo?

Like I could fucking remember without nufc.com.

There were too many games in this season for a normal person to take in, never mind an abnormal person who sees Newcastle United taking to a football field as the perfect excuse to get mind bendingly pissed. We played 14 European games so it was a good job we got dumped straight out of both domestic cups or the remains of our livers and wallets would have dribbled out through the bottom of our trousers.

A giddy headrush your Champions League and, especially for those of us not generally invited, it is all too easy to get carried away. Having flattened West Ham 4-0 on the opening day of the domestic season, Newcastle failed to win any of the next four games and were 19th in the League. Then, oh cruel fate, we had an away game in Kiev, (which we also lost) before sunderland at home. Fortunately sunderland were woeful and two first half (Leazes End) goals from Bellamy and Shearer sealed the easiest derby game we had played in years. "Youse weren't very good, mind," said a mackem at work. "We've been to the other side of Russia and back this week, what's your bloody excuse?"

I try not to be petty and parochial about these things normally but sunderland's shitness throughout the season was too delicious to ignore. Peter Reid had built a hard-working physical team that twice over-achieved within a strict budget but having finished one place above relegation the previous season he seemed to panic and start throwing money around; Marcus Stewart, Tore Andre Flo and some other garbage I can't be bothered to remember, so obviously they remained woeful. They only won four and drew seven games all season but amazingly one of the wins and one of the draws were against Liverpool who were one of our main rivals for a Champions League spot.

Newcastle fans had little time to savour their derby victory because four days later we were getting beaten at home by Feyenoord. Then we went down 0-2 at Juventus to have a Champions League group stage record that read played three, lost three. Which was pretty embarrassing to tell the truth. But not as embarrassing as losing 2-5 at Blackburn.

A couple of scrappy wins either side of the Juve games had dragged us up the table but we were beaten within seconds of late fans (*) getting through the gates of Ewood Park because Nicos Dabizas got sent off for handling the ball on the line. Blackburn scored again half a second later and it looked like being a long afternoon but Shearer pulled one back from the spot and got another early in the second half to make it 2-2. Nobody would have blamed us if we hung on to that but we tried to win and the outcome was catastrophic. You know when people say, "it is better to have a go and concede five" – not when you concede five it isn't.

But then we beat Juve and Charlton and Kiev and Middlesbrough one after the other and things were looking up so we didn't need losing after extra time and penalties to Everton in the League Cup before a trip to Arsenal, which we also lost.

Then followed a terrible quandary with Joe Strummer and the Mescaleros playing in Newcastle the same week as our football team was away to Feyenoord in the Champions League qualifying decider.

Shamefully I did neither. I drove a seven and a half tonne vehicle to Birmingham listening to the radio, wracked with guilt. I only mention it now in the highly unlikely event that anybody reading this was on the A38 on the 13th of November 2002 and wondered why a big red van was veering wildly between the lanes with a screaming driver looking like he was driving the fiery road to hell. With minutes remaining at 2-2 a draw put us in the UEFA Cup, a loss put us out all together but a winner put us through in The Champions League. After agonisingly and impotently shouting "attack" then "for fucksake defend" at the radio, Craig Bellamy made it 3-2 in the 90th minute. And I might have spent a moment driving without due care and attention.

At this point we pause and listen to *Johnny Appleseed* – cos Joe was dead within 6 weeks.

(Cuffs away manly tear.)

A-hem, anyway. Newcastle qualified for a second group stage (because they really used to drag the competition out then) and by the New Year we had lost to Inter Milan and Barcelona. On the other hand, a series of odd goal wins, including a Robert missile of a free kick against Liverpool, had us up to fourth in the League.

After shuffling quietly out of the FA Cup at Wolves, because we had better things to do, a five game unbeaten but largely forgettable (in that I had entirely forgotten all of it) run took us to third.

Bayer Leverkusen were beaten home and away to give us an outside chance in the Champions League. These games were either side of a 3-0 win at Leeds where Kieron Dyer was astonishing and unplayable. Quick, clever and skilful he dominated the whole game with a display that is heartbreaking considering the amount of time he has spent injured or underperforming.

Speaking of which; then we signed Johnny Woodgate.

We beat Chelsea and got mugged by Boro before going to Milan in our thousands.

Howard Wilkinson took over from Peter Reid at sunderland while we prepared for a game in the San Siro. A magical game that we deserved to win but earned a creditable 2-2 draw as Newcastle United peaked higher then ever before. If only we had bought the ineligible Woodgate sooner, if we had got the penalty when Bellamy was wiped out in the area, if only we could have got at the Milanese bastards who never seemed to stop throwing stuff down on us? Actually scratch that last one because it would have been a blood bath and we would have got the blame for shaming English football.

As it was, we exited the Champions League with our heads up and we still had an outside chance of the title until Man Utd came to St James' and battered us 2-6.

We stumbled on to finish third because Liverpool and Chelsea kept falling over each other and Hugo Viana scored in both our last two games, against

Birmingham and West Brom, to earn us an extra four points. You probably forgot that, as well as that it was 1-0 (Dyer) against Zeljeznicar.

* The reason I was late was because I won a game of "Killer" on a pool table two miles away from Ewood Park. Oh yes, I can remember that.

Player of the Season: Alan Shearer; goals from Milan to Birmingham. Special mention to Gary Speed who was majestic and hasn't been mentioned enough.

Goal of the Season: Jenas at home to Manchester United; a 25 yard scorcher which for 10 minutes had us in the lead of a game we lost 2-6.

Chapter 47

August 2003

Ferret Racing

I went to the ferret racing in Scorton.

Those amongst you who have memorised all the road signs on the A1, through the simple act of driving up and down the rotten bastard a thousand times, will know that Scorton is just south of Scotch Corner.

It's a charming village that has a "Feast" every year and although I've yet to witness any manner of public banquet on my irregular visits, they do have many events, shows and rural activities. For example, my Uncle Richard (a Scortonian and life-long Newcastle fan) has deemed himself too long in the tooth for the 'Chariot Race' around the vast and raised green (humans pull other humans round in wheeled Roman style carts and all have to run and then drink beer and then run some more – not sure if the winner is the first to finish or the last to vomit) and this year he won many prizes for the quality and enormity of his dahlias and onions.

Naturally there is a funfair and an alarmingly competitive fancy-dress parade but my personal highlight of this year's Scorton Feast was the inaugural 'Ferret Racing'.

Quite frankly if the whole event isn't heavily sponsored and televised live on Sky Television next year, someone hasn't been doing their job properly.

Obviously, being a city dweller, I assumed that the ferrets would have little mouse or hamster jockeys, dressed in tiny silks, affixed to their backs and would have to leap through fiery hoops whilst not being distracted by the opportunity to rush up somebody's trouser leg. A friendly and patient old fellow assured me that the sight of mount devouring rider would alarm even sturdy, country bred, children and that in 70 years on the planet he had not once witnessed a ferret run up anybody's trouser leg, let alone take a hearty bite out of a scrotum. Dispensing with my cycle clips I approached the racing arena with caution. There was a painfully long delay between races but the thrill made the wait worthwhile with competitors (with names like Trixie and Bandit) popped into boxes and released into clear tubes. The ferrets speed along the pipes, which had a nasty bend and a small hill in them to test the rodents' agility (ferrets are apparently rodents and not, as I imagined, small bears) and the first ferret to get the tip of its tail clear of the course is deemed the winner. There were heats and a thrilling final.

I find myself waffling on about sport other than football because the league programme has already been interrupted by a pointless England match. A poor second to the Scorton Ferret Racing was the "friendly international" live from the expertly manicured pitch of Ipswich Town's Portman Road. (Why, Mr Robson, do we not consider a bid for the groundsman next time we are rounding up Ipswich's best young players given that our own playing surface has been such a hindrance in recent years?)

The nation yawned and flicked round the channels in search of something more interesting than well grown grass. In the studio Alan Shearer tried to brighten up proceedings by turning up in a suit he had presumably borrowed from Ronald McDonald's dad but it was hopeless.

England won 3-1 but the media weren't happy and not because nobody needed this pointless interruption so early in a new season. Why, who cares? The important, yet unreported, thing about this game was that revolting children blowing tuneless horns for 90 minutes has to fuckin' stop. Since the FA and press wet their pants about a few chaps running on the pitch when England played at sunderland *(where the locals are allowed to run on the pitch normally)*, the next game at Middlesbrough was held up as a shining example of how fans are supposed to behave. Wherein people didn't run onto the pitch but neither did they sing or support their team in any way, except by letting their horrid children honk like wounded geese long enough to give a dead man a migraine. The people selling the horns should be treated like they were selling hard drugs. They should be locked up after "falling down the stairs" at the nearest police station. Some bastard at Ipswich had a bell and they were allowed to ring it like they were the fucking village idiot for the duration of the entire match. Can you imagine being sat in front of the bastard.

Beware! There is a small proportion of our own crowd who like to copy what they have seen on the telly, (jester hats, the "shall we sing a song for you" song, writing shit messages on their mum's best sheets etc). So be vigilant, be responsible and if you see some painted-faced, flag wearing fan walking towards St James' Park with a fucking bell take it off them and stick it up their arse. 50,000 people will buy you a pint.

The pitch at St James' now looks comparatively brilliant all season and we rarely mention it. And yet the standard of the football played on it has lowered. Make of that what you will.

Chapter 48

November 2003

When I Grow Up

Parents are being too nice to their children and it's bad for them. It's true; I heard it on the radio. Radio 5 Live to be precise, the presenters were very concerned. Molly-coddled children, it seems, do nothing for themselves and nothing without an attendant adult close by with car keys in their hands. They reach adulthood with no street smarts, no idea how the world works and can't even cross the road properly. They will scamper around in the street like startled pheasants and rush into the clutches of the first sweaty palmed paedophile who offers them a Mars bar the second they let go of the family's apron strings.

Is it true, I don't know? I have no interest in children beyond the fact that you are no longer allowed to cuff the unruly ones about the ears, which is a shame. What is left to look forward to in retirement if you can't stalk the streets with a silver handled cane boxing naughty urchins' lug-holes; "G'wan you rascals, I know where you live!" etc.

I was lucky enough to be born in a time where the express intention of parents was to teach their offspring the ability to walk, specifically so they could bugger off and give them some peace. The vast majority of us have reached something resembling adulthood capable of walking the streets of Benwell or Brooklyn without being run over or abducted and molested by predatory perverts.

I suppose we live in a time when crime is down but the media driven "fear of crime" is at an all time high, so it's not surprising that parents get concerned. Whatever, I don't really care. What I do care about is when these darling cherubs with their "I want, expect and demand that" attitude start turning out for football teams that we pay to watch.

We pay to watch men play football. "It's a man's game" sounds like awful chauvinism but hands up who has paid to watch ladies play football. I will fight to the last breath in your body for the right of women to play, watch and be involved with football to whatever level they wish BUT I pay to see men play football. And the men playing football seem to be getting older and fewer. Unfortunately, many of the people getting paid to perform in our professional game at the moment aren't men at all, they are pampered whimpering little ninnies.

Look at Ronaldo at Manchester United with his ballet dancer's feet and his theatrical falls and his pouty face crying up at the ref. He's never been slapped round the back of the head for not putting Johnny Cash's *Live At Folsom Prison* album back in its sleeve properly, the little bastard. Robert Pires anybody? How can his dad watch him play with any pride? "Get off the floor and play properly or you won't get any tea!" Materazzi at Inter Milan pretends to be a man but he regularly cries like a little girl.

The rules now protect the snivelling, the cowards and the liars. Whatever you think of Roy Keane, the man, the player, the psychopath – he plays the game like a man. Alan Shearer, it goes without saying plays the game and is "A Man". Isn't it pathetic that being "a man" is now seen as a compliment when it should be a given.

Claude Makelele, former Real Madrid "enforcer" now aboard the Chelsea pirate ship, complained last week about the Premiership being too rough. Really? It's never been so soft and the game is poorer because of it.

Proof?

I'll give you proof; when David Batty picked Nicky Butt up by the throat (and twisted) in our 5-0 win over Man Utd it was as exciting as any of the goals. He would have been sent off for that now. The recent Arsenal v Manchester United "outrage" where the players all started getting stuck into one another was the only thing that lifted the game above "very boring". The television viewer, half asleep, leapt to full concentration: "Oh hello, this is more like it." And don't think those hypocrites in the press box didn't do exactly the same thing.

I miss David McCreery style tackles like a best friend who has gone to live on the other side of the planet; ball in stand, opponent on face, mud stains the length of Davie Mac's back. Now if you dive in and miss the ball you get booked. No one should want to see thugs prosper and good players get injured but we demand a bit of violence damn it. Force the players to play like men.

Use video replays to punish divers and liars: for example, if you claim to have played the ball and you didn't, three match ban and forced to eat soap. Tuck your

shirt in, pull your pants up, get a proper haircut, you call that music? Now see what you've done. I've turned into my grandfather.
Bah!

At this point in the argument some conceited bloody rugby fan will pipe up about rugby players behaving like proper men – like to be a proper man you have to rake your studs down another chap's face after you have given his testicles a good squeeze – oh, and rugby is rubbish.

Chapter 49

January 2004

Will This Bloody Game Never End?

I've made a terrible mistake. I have got nobody to blame but myself and I can only hope that you don't judge me too harshly. I've chosen the path I walk and I walk it alone, all I can do is urge you not to follow. What can I say except I am very sorry.

It was during the dead zone between Christmas and New Year, there was no football to look forward to on New Year's Day and the world seemed lifeless. It's that period where you have drank so much that a state of hazy confusion feels like sober and no amount of alcohol seems to do anything except make your eyes sore and your head pound. Every morning you wake up with a dry, fat smelly camel's tongue instead of your own, walking down the stairs is exhausting and "Damn it, I can't do up the top button of my jeans anymore."

"Fuck it, I don't need this, I'm knocking this drinking thing on the head!" I proclaim.

Wifey looks sceptical at most of my proclamations but before she could scoff I was up a ladder wedging crates of beer, bottles of wine and Jack Daniels into the darkest corners of the loft where they couldn't tempt me. "I'm going for a run." Ha ha, clean living. Well for January at least.

It seemed like a good idea but I think I have been a little bit hasty. You only have sober for a couple of days to remind you why you drink in the first place.

There is an episode of *Father Ted* where Father Jack sobers up, looks around himself and says, "Oh God, am I still on that fekkin island?" – life seems like that. It's all too horrible and confusing, people are ugly and nasty and mean-spirited. Drunk or hungover, you filter out a lot of the shit, you ignore dangerous idiots, stupid shoppers and you don't lay awake half the night wondering how mobile phones actually work.

And, "going for a run".

Going for a run?

Staggering around in the street wheezing, bright purple and with no feeling in your fingers can't be good for you, can it? 80 year old men are scampering past me shouting "Morning! Lovely day isn't it?" and I haven't even got the strength to tell them to "bugger off" as I'm too busy clinging to some railings, whimpering and weeping silent tears that are freezing to my ice-cold skin.

Yes, yes I'm actually on time for work, I'm more productive, and I spend less time thinking about sleep but what good does that do me? It's all still pointless and demoralising and I can't even look forward to a beer afterwards. In fact my whole rewards system is ruined; surely getting through a day at work or a trip to the supermarket without throttling some ignorant fucker is worthy of a beer or two.

Worst of all, I can tell I'm an idiot. Usually if I trip over my own feet, forget the name of somebody I've known for years or say something stupid, crass and inappropriate I let myself off because I'm pissed. I haven't had a drink in ten days and I still do all those things. I'm actually like that, bloody hell! Drunk and I think I'm rock hard, cool and hilarious. Sober and I'm fuckin' useless. It's all too hideous.

And so to the football. Football minus beer is just silly. For a start, why would I want to travel all the way down to Southampton drinking and laughing like a fool when I can sit sensibly on a sofa with a bottle of mineral water for a fraction of the cost? Let me tell you, I shook with nerves for 90 minutes. I know it was Southampton away and we have let in some horrible late goals down there but 90 minutes were up and we were playing brilliantly, leading 3-0 and Southampton virtually had their coats on and I'm still thinking, "get it away, get it away, will this bloody game never end?"

Leeds at home on Wednesday and my match crew are quaffing ales and taking the piss out of each other before gulping down a last delicious pint and wobbling up to the ground. Vibrating with Red Bull (apparently you can get it without vodka in it) I'm actually in my seat before the kick-off. Too self-conscious to sing, I'm silently mouthing the words to the songs and wondering if it's always this cold. I'm freezing and I can't remember being cold at the match since the Simod Cup game against Shrewsbury, when fist-sized hailstones blew in a 100 mile an hour wind and Mirandinha scored for no other reason than he couldn't stand the idea of extra time.

The second half went on for ages, everybody around was spouting silly drunken nonsense and the comforting knowledge that at least we can all go and have a drink afterwards was denied me.

Back in the pub for more Red Bull and Uncle Bobby comes on the TV. The sound is turned up and a reverential hush falls over the celebrating throng. Bobby is asked one question and he's off; jabbering away to himself, asking and answering his own supplementary questions and waving his arms feverishly. It's like watching Gollum talking to himself in *The Lord of the Rings*; normally I cheer and laugh but tonight I'm more than a little worried. It goes on because instead of a little nightcap (treble Jack, no ice) that knocks me out solid until the cruel alarm clock of another working day, I'm still fizzing off the Red Bull. I'm worrying if our manager's a crackpot and why the Queen Mary cruise liner doesn't fall over and sink?

I've got away games at Old Trafford and Anfield to come. It's going to be a long fuckin' month.

An underrated gauge of respect Newcastle fans have for their manager is the hush or lack of hush that falls over a noisy pub when he speaks. Some managers always brought an urgent round of fevered shushing, some you thought, "Oh this should be good" while preparing to shout "liar!" at the screen. It is proof that a manager still has some way to go to convince fans of his suitability if supporters choose to carry on their own conversation instead of listening to why it was the ref's fault that we lost.

Chapter 50

April 2004

The True Meaning of Easter

An underestimated holiday, your Easter, in many ways better than Christmas – for a start you aren't expected to haemorrhage cash for a month, bestowing thoughtful gifts on people who buy you pointless shit in return. Also the pubs aren't stuffed with amateurs who can't handle more than a couple of Cherry Bs without vomiting over each other's trousers; there is a distinct lack of Slade and the weather's nicer.

Obviously, like Christmas, the whole deal was hijacked by sanctimonious Christians whose basic message appears to be, "Hey Jesus was killed and rose from the dead to prove that if you are nice to people you can live forever in the kingdom of heaven with smug gits like me." Which makes you immediately want to rush out into the street and punch a stranger in the face, basically. Why would anybody want to spend eternity wearing knitted sweaters and singing 'Kum-by-ya' and who do I have to kill to get a thousand year lock-in with Oliver Reed and Keith Moon?

Obviously the whole rabbits and eggs malarkey is a crude pagan euphemism for humping each other's brains out to celebrate the coming of spring. However, the true meaning of Easter is football, and lots of it.

It's a bit hard to stomach, Arsene Wenger moaning away about how many games his team has to play, what with being in the Champions League, the FA Cup and racing away with the title when he has nobody but himself to blame. A bit more rank incompetence at Highbury and less of the free-flowing super-football and they wouldn't have to worry about playing too many games. Serves them right for being so good, it's the Newcastle players I feel sorry for – because despite being generally rubbish and stupid, the games keep stacking up. The amount of effort our team have made to ensure they play the least possible number of games this year (giving the ball away, running around aimlessly etc.) and yet here we are with a fixture backlog.

What that nice Mr Wenger fails to appreciate is that in the absence of football a vacuum is created that threatens great peril – honest hard-working people will die.

Easter is a boom time for the evil DIY trade and many will perish at its fiendish (self-assembly) blade. As I have mentioned before, half a million people a year die or are seriously injured as a direct result of DIY accidents. Across the country people are drilling into electric cables, falling off ladders, hitting each other with hammers and sawing one another's limbs off doing those 'little jobs' that they have been putting off for months.

Seriously, families are statistically less likely to get hurt if they all took heroin and started firing crossbows at each other. Two people a year die taking, what I believe our young folks call, Es and whole campaigns are set up to warn us of their danger. Can you imagine the uproar that would be caused if a drug were killing or injuring half a million people every year? And what is being done to stop these fuckers at B&Q, Wickes and Homebase peddling death?

Nothing.

At least B&Q employ a lot of deranged loonies in orange aprons so that you can never actually find what you are looking for in their ten acre superstores BUT fantastic looking, double-handed power tools are still on open sale for any fumble-fisted halfwit to buy and kill himself with. I say "himself" deliberately here – women don't daydream about being Hans Solo the second they pick up a shiny new drill. Ever.

Sound and beautiful relationships are destroyed by DIY: "Hold that straight!"; "No, pull the other end!"; "You're putting too much on!"; "I thought you fucking well measured it!"; "I'm going to the pub, I'll be back in about ten years you dumb cock-eyed bastard!" None of this would happen if people didn't attempt "doing it themselves". *The Mag's* own Alan Harrison once told me, "If you can't fix it with a hammer, get a man in." Alan is a generally contented man with a beautiful family as a direct result of this simple philosophy.

DIY is fundamentally evil if you think about it and follow it to its natural conclusions. By performing it you are tearing at the very fabric of society, if we all started doing other people's jobs for ourselves – nobody would have a job. Society works because we give other people money to do things for us. If you strip that away we will soon all be living in caves and dragging each other around by the hair.

No Arsene, we will not stay at home and destroy civilisation – we must go to the football and drink lots of beer to save the world. It is a divine mission and we undertake it with a stern fortitude.

We must burn Ikea to the ground and go to the match. HOORAH!

Happy Easter.

Chapter 51

June 2004

Behind Enemy Lines

Somewhat disappointingly for some Newcastle fans sunderland had not spiralled in a smoking ruin down the Leagues like a doomed Stuka following their record breakingly bad relegation, in fact they were on course for the play-offs in a bid to get promoted back to where they clearly didn't belong. I got an unlikely opportunity for a bit of re-con work.

In the midst of a cold dark winter I got a text from a lad who I hadn't seen in about 15 years. He is one of those splendid and hilarious fellows who drift out of your life through no fault on either part.

His name is Tony and he with Julie, his wife, was among 3,000 Norwich fans with tickets for City's game at sunderland. Norwich were in fine form at the time while sunderland had a fixture backlog that was beginning to take its toll – on the phone Tony was already buzzing with anticipated victory.

They flew up in a blizzard on a Friday night, delayed five hours they arrived very late and very tired but they spoke very highly of the Newcastle fans, who guided them, in a shared taxi, to their Wallsend hotel. I expressed surprise: not at the friendliness of our natives, we always heartily greet the enemies of our enemies, but at there being a hotel in Wallsend.

9.30 the next day and the game was called off because of the snow. With the flight home not until the Sunday Tony and Julie had little to do but sit around Newcastle as the snow turned to grey slush and the wind lashed rain along Percy Street. I met them early in the evening keen to introduce them to the delights of The Three Bulls Heads only to discover that they had spent most of the afternoon in there. There were a lot of very fucked off Norwich fans in town that night and the shared opinion was that "the pitch was fine, sunderland fuckin' bottled it!" I was keen to encourage this opinion obviously but also explained that was what we in Newcastle call "doing a Middlesbrough" in an attempt to get the phrase adopted into the national vernacular. I also told them that while the whole weekend may have seemed like a pointless waste of time and money on their behalf, the fact that there were now 3,000 more people in the world who disliked and distrusted sunderland was actually a big plus from where I was sitting. This didn't seem to cheer him up much, likewise some of Newcastle's finest bars also failed to drag either of them out of their weary funk, so Wifey and I shoved them into a taxi and ran off into a night that ended some time after clumsy and ill-advised dancing in my new boots.

You may or may not recall that the fixture was rearranged for a mid-week match after Norwich's promotion was assured. In fact the First Division Championship was virtually in the bag; West Brom needed to win their last two games and Norwich had to lose at both sunderland and Crewe, to go up second.

Julie couldn't come so Tony brought a mate, JB, to our house – a huge beer monster with a loud laugh and a "couldn't give a fuck mate" lust for life that seems to sit comfortably with many Norfolk folk. Along with my offer of accommodation I had rashly demanded any spare ticket that might be going which meant I got Julie's ticket, next to Tony.

Part of my responsibility as host, I felt, was to get them to Wearside in time for the kick-off but getting them out of the pub in Newcastle was harder work than I expected so Norwich hitting the woodwork twice in the first five minutes was something we only heard about later.

Getting to, and being in, the Stadium of Empty Seats without a mass of cops was weird enough but Norwich's crowd was like nothing I'd seen before in an away end. Big family groups, with young children and jolly fat ladies in big scarves. Elderly couples, groups of girls and not a Burberry cap to be seen. They all seemed to know each other and they sang 'On The Ball City' in an impenetrable accent.

When Norwich were last in the Premiership 'On The Ball City' had to be the most awful dirge in football and remains unique in having the words 'steady on' in the chorus. The 21st century version rattles along at a fair old lick and I couldn't tell you one word of the first part – I did join in with the 'steady ons' though.

Suffice to say the daft mackem fans spent most of the game struggling to stay on their hind legs, staring at the away supporters and singing anti-Newcastle songs at them. Infuriatingly, Norwich barely tried at all. Halfway through the second half sunderland were 1-0 up but West Brom were 3-1 down. "Will you tell your team to fucking try, Tony?"

"It doesn't matter, we've won the league!"

"Well it matters to me," I pouted as the mackems started a Mexican wave – and the Norwich fans gleefully joined in. This is madness I thought and jingled my house keys frantically in a one man show of defiance.

"We are the sunland" etc "We are the loyalest football supporters the world has ever had." They never used to sing that, did they?

"Filthy little thieves," I hissed.

"Stoke have scored a fourth," Tony happily barks, ignoring me. "Delia, Delia, give us a wave" and everybody started applauding the nice lady from the telly and Norwich fans were thrilled about getting into the Premiership promised land, where the sun shines warmer and where they hand out cash in municipal skips. A place where Andy Gray puts that extra bit of gravel in his voice when one of your players does something remarkable.

It hardly seemed the time to point out that these happy people will be paying the fat end of forty fucking quid to get into shit-holes like St Andrews, that Chelsea will have your bloody eyes out for a seat that doesn't actually afford you a view of the pitch and that they will be patronised to death by October.

Norwich had lost but the team were happy and dancing on the pitch with a home-made Bacofoil representation of a cup as the home team looked on, play-offs awaiting. This cheered up the daft mackems whose team were utterly, utterly rubbish. The whole club is like a rotting, re-animated corpse going through the clumsy motions. They were never easy on the eye but now they are nothing but a dirty team playing ugly zombie football. You can't really blame the fans who continue to stay away in their thousands – the whole place stinks of death, their play-off place was a savage indictment of the state of the Nationwide League.

Outside, people in red and white shirts shook hands with the fans coming out of the away end, wishing them a hearty "Good Luck".

"You don't want to be wishing me good luck," I growl at a confused looking monkey man before marching off in search of the Metro back to civilisation.

Chapter 52

2003/04 postscript - A Distorted View

The decline began a full year before Newcastle United parted company with Sir Bobby Robson. There are two elements to successfully managing a Premiership team: 1. is (somewhat unsurprisingly) coaching; 2. is bringing in better players than the ones you have already got. 2. helps with 1. but if you stop doing 2. altogether 1. gets difficult. And improving the team gets harder the higher you get as the amount of available players who would improve your team becomes fewer.
In the summer of 2003 Newcastle bought Lee Bowyer.

In June 2003 Newcastle were a better football team than Chelsea. We can take a minute to think about that if you want, especially in view of them winning a League and Cup double in 2010 while Newcastle were in the Championship. In 2003 Newcastle were better than Chelsea; we had just finished third to their fourth, the year before we were fourth to their sixth. Not only that but Chelsea were about to implode; Ken Bates (not normally a reliable witness to anything but on this we'll take him at his word) claims Chelsea were two weeks away from bankruptcy when he sold the club to Roman Abramovich. A Chelsea implosion would have made what happened at Leeds look like an unfortunate blip, because Leeds have got 35,000 fans who refuse to stop going no matter how many time their team gets relegated, while Chelsea's crowd traditionally evaporates to virtually nothing in hard times. If nature had been allowed to take its course Chelsea would be playing Gateshead this week with the Gateshead fans mocking the Blues' meagre away following.
Chelsea should have been a salutary lesson as to what happens when white trash live beyond their means by purchasing luxury goods with money they haven't got. The yard sale outside Stamford Bridge should have been the warning the

World needed about unsustainable borrowing. Because they effectively won the lottery, but pretended they were getting by on hard work and merit, the lesson wasn't learned and whole nations went bankrupt. In short Chelsea are responsible for the World-wide banking crash.

There, I've said it. And don't say they're not because they are.

With Newcastle's qualification to the Champions League in his back pocket, Captain Bobby should have been able to stroll through the wreckage of where Chelsea used to be with impunity. He could have been sipping a large brandy and puffing on a fat cigar whilst pointing at inexpensive international footballers desperate to reprove their worth. Instead Abramovich took over and Chelsea added another £100 million of talent to what was already a decent squad. Newcastle bought Lee Bowyer.

In June 2003 Newcastle were better than Chelsea. By November Chelsea were beating Newcastle 5-0 (£42 to get in, thank you very much) with a team that had Terry, Gallas, Veron, Crespo, Lampard, Mutu and Makalele. With Joe Cole and Eider Gudjohnsen on the bench. Newcastle's players for the day included O'Brien (who got sent off), Bramble, Bowyer, a Caldwell and Shola Ameobi up front on his own.

This is not to say that Newcastle had gone to shit, in fact the great frustration of the 2003/04 staff was that it was capable of being brilliant. Arsenal's self appointed "Invincibles" were played to a standstill in a thrilling 0-0 draw at St James' where only the Gunners well-honed gamesmanship stopped them being all vincibled.

But too many of Robson's young guns had been allowed to think they were Billy Bigbollocks and by Christmas my mate Spugsy was suggesting we take player's mothers hostage to make them start applying themselves to the job in hand. "Punch their mother in the face in front of the little bastards, and shout, 'Get yer fuckin' finger out or I'll do it again' (smack) 'too late', the cunts."

As I wrote in *And They Wonder Why We Drink:* "the 2003/04 season was fuckin' awful, with spineless performances, long balls being lumped at Shearer, misplaced passing, players being picked week after week despite poor form or fitness....

... away from home the story was even worse: two wins; a comeback after a terrible start at Fulham and a hilariously ill-deserved victory at Middlesbrough. There were the gutless surrenders at Bolton and Manchester City where we barely strayed into opposition territory after half-time and we also conceded late equalisers trying to hold onto what were fortunate leads at Birmingham, Portsmouth, and Blackburn. Newcastle didn't beat any of the bottom nine teams away from home who were all bollocks."

But the actual moment it really started going wrong was the Champions League qualifier against Partizan Belgrade, in fact I can hear an audible snap whenever I think about that game. With a 1-0 away win already in the bank we managed to lose 0-1 at home, playing bewildering tactics we were eventually eliminated on penalties. In one horrible, grindingly frustrating match we destroyed the previous season's hard work and brilliance. We did qualify for the UEFA Cup where we played some of our best football, finally losing to the pace and power of a Didier Drogba inspired Marseille in the semi-final.

Drogba left Marseille at the end of that season. Perhaps he was never going to partner Shearer at Newcastle but can you imagine him at Arsenal with Henry? No, he went to fucking Chelsea who the next year would win the League.

Yes I'm bitter about it.

Leeds United were relegated, Middlesbrough beat Bolton to win the League Cup but nobody outside Middlesbrough or Bolton cares anymore.

Player of the Season: Laurent Robert; 12 goals from midfield and more assists than you could care to count.

Goal of the Season: Laurent Robert; home to Fulham. The most underrated goal of all time because idiots thought it was a fluke. Upside-down in mid-bicycle kick Robert saw he was going to miss the ball and twisted in the air like a dropped cat to back-heel the ball over his own head and into the Gallowgate net.

Chapter 53

January 2005

New Year Resolutions

If you think about it, not making a New Year resolution is a bit rubbish. What you are saying is either A: "I am a perfectly evolved creature. I am the great white shark of land dwelling mammals. Everything about me is fantastic and as best as it could possibly be. No one thing could make me a better specimen of a 20th century human being." Or B: "I've given up. There was a time when I gave a fuck but that time has passed and quite frankly I can't be fucking bothered any more. I've tried making New Year resolutions before and, well, by January 2nd I lost the will to live. What you see is what you get and if what you see is a fat smelly idiot, that's just about fine by me."

None of us think we fall into either category, certainly not "B", so we make an effort, which is the only reason most gyms stay in business. There aren't enough doormen in the town to keep all our gyms operating at a profit and most only get by on the two or three hundred quid they get every January from well-meaning lazy people who, by March, only have gnawing guilt where their Brad Pitt/Angelina Jolie stomach should be.

But we try, which is good. Unfortunately we have too high a level of our own expectations. For example, two years ago I decided that I would, as a New Year resolution, be from January 1st a black/Italian kung fu expert. You may scoff but, compared to last year's attempt to give up the drink, it went very well. At no point during my quest to be a black/Italian kung fu expert did I wish I was dead and hate every living creature on God's good earth. Aiming too high is the problem but like I said, we must all continue to try or we may as well start digging our own graves.

"What, pray tell," you ask, "has this got to do with football?" Well, during Newcastle United's recent encounter with West Brom and again with Yeading in the FA Cup at Loftus Road I was struck with an idea that would make a perfectly feasible New Year's resolution that would be both attainable and a potential money spinner. Reader, as you are my witness, within the year 2005 I will struggle, with my every waking hour, to complete the following task: I will, before the year is out, literally hit a cow's arse with a banjo. Having done so, I will set up a school that will specialise in cows, banjos and the bringing together of the arse from the former and the heavy end of the latter. The text book will retail at twenty of your English pounds and will feature diagrams and a point-by-point procedure that will afford even the most inexperienced banjo wielder the expertise required to bring said instrument satisfactorily onto the rump of the bovine quadruped of their choice.

Fig 1: Locate A: "banjo"
Fig 2: Locate B: "cow"
Fig 3: Work out which end of B is the "head" and which end is the "arse"
Fig 4: Hit the end that is not the "head" of B (cow) with aforementioned A (banjo)

I don't know anybody who has actually hit a cow's arse with a banjo, but popular culture would have it that the task is the easiest thing in the world. However, it is seemingly beyond many at our football club and if a community school class, run by me (at an extravagant profit), will stop Lee Bowyer booting the ball half a mile over the bar every time he gets a chance from more than half an inch out, I guess we will all be better off for it. We can work on players in black and white shirts actually passing the ball TO THE BASTARD FEET!! of other players in black and white shirts next year. During which time the more advanced pupils can work out what in the name of hell Darren Ambrose is any use for. Is it just drunken spite on my part that made him look out of his depth against bloody Yeading?
I was asked last month, within the pages of this very publication, if I though Graeme Souness has "lost the plot" yet. Well I'm yet to be convinced that our new manager is aware of the existence of any "plot", never mind of its whereabouts. But as to the sneaking insinuation that we were better off under

Bobby Robson I give you exhibit A: Nobby Solano and exhibit B: (his Robson bought replacement) Mr Darren Ambrose. Make your own fucking mind up. Happy New Year.

Suffice to say my attempt to strike a cow on the arse with a banjo went about as well as Graeme Souness' attempt to discover any kind of plot.

Chapter 54

2004/05 – 2005/06 postscripts – A Distorted View

I already dealt with these seasons in hilarious and minute detail in *And they Wonder Why We Drink* – what, you think I should go through it again for you? So every writer has to produce all their previous work on a subject, whenever that subject comes up do they? And I end up quacking out the same routine just because you can't be bothered to pick up….. I mean ring me up, email me, I'm on Twitter (billyfurious1st), I'm not hiding. I'll send a copy to your bloody house and won't even charge you for the postage. Yes, I'm that keen not to delve back into these two wretched bloody seasons.

Oh, did you see what I did there, despite having written an entire book on the subject, I fell into the same trap as everybody else does. Thinking Graeme Souness came in after Mr Robson was sacked and everything went instantly to dog eggs. It didn't.

If Bobby Robson had been eased aside or better, to a different role within Newcastle United in the summer of 2004, Newcastle would have been behaving like a top of the table team recognising the need for a new approach. After all, Liverpool replaced Gerard Houllier who had finished fourth and won trophies for the club and very few people slagged them off. As it was, Newcastle's board of directors spent months looking like they were trying to undermine their own manager, in the hope he would resign. Problem being he didn't even notice, so they sacked him gracelessly after the season had already started and they looked liked incompetent baboons in the process. Then they confounded their idiocy by employing Graeme Souness. However, we scored 85 goals that season and won 24 games, lost 16, made it to the FA Cup semi-final and the UEFA Cup quarter-final before cruel fate kicked our legs out from under us. 2-0 up against Sporting

Lisbon the injuries kept wracking up and Souness (having already packed Bellamy off to Celtic) had a pointless hissy fit with Laurent Robert (over comments he had made weeks beforehand) and dropped our best crosser and dead-ball specialist for one of our most important games in the last decade. No, it took Souness at least a few months to get his instructions all wrong. Some of Newcastle's players had clearly become terribly flaky and ill-disciplined and they were starting to get on our nerves but Graeme mistook the need to "bring them into line" with "sell anybody who looks at you funny, even if they are really good". So we lost Robert and Bellamy for relative buttons and gambled the entire farm, next door's farm and any farms we were ever likely to visit for the next ten years on Michael Owen and Albert Luque. To his credit, Souness also brought Nobby Solano back and bought Emre and Scott Parker. Some Newcastle fans didn't take to Parker; the day I write this he has just been named Sports Writers' Player of the Year despite playing for a terrible West Ham team. In the last act of fairness Souness is ever going to get from me, Emre with his skill and vision and Owen with his predatory instincts would have scored bucket loads of goals if they had stayed fit.

They didn't.

Souness later admitted he knew it was over for him when Owen got injured at Spurs in December 2005 – yet he and his army of lickspittles clung on until the start of February 2006. Incidentally, Manager of the Month for February 2006, anybody? Alan Pardew, West Ham United.

Glenn Roeder came in, despite objections from all over the place due to his lack of qualifications, and with a wilful naughtiness we galloped up the table to finish 7th. This charge into Europe included wins at sunderland and Middlesbrough and a last day victory over Chelsea, who were Champions. Thrilling stuff actually, you should read a book about it.

Sunderland went down with 15 points which beat their previous record for being the worst team in the History of the World. Or something.

April 2011: Their very own manager Steve Bruce has just pointed out that sunderland have only finished in the top half of the top division twice in the last 55 years. I didn't know that, I thought they were a massive club, equal if not bigger than Newcastle United. Funny that.

2004/05
Player of the Season: Shay Given.

Goal of the Season: Kluivert v Chelsea in the FA Cup. From a Robert cross, a goal of great and largely forgotten beauty. Fuck the haters.

2005/06
Player of the Season: Scott Parker.

Goal of the Season: Emre v sunderland.

Chapter 55

August 2006

The Optimistic Anarchist

Going in to the 2006/07season, Newcastle were being managed by Glenn Roeder despite his not having the relevant qualifications. Over excited by my club's wilful disobedience I fear I may have allowed pre-season excitement to get the better of me.

Football in this country has been going down the toilet for years. Last season was garbage, the League was won by September and 82.65% of games were tedious and insignificant pig excrement. There are too many snouts in the trough with a vested interest to allow the truth out but football is being destroyed by the twin evils of: Chelsea, with their juggernaut full of roubles; and managers who think "fit" and "organised" are the first and last words in coaching the modern game. Things look to be getting worse, with Chelsea throwing so much money at their squad that Man U and Arsenal are starting to look small-time, and the arrival of Watford. Watford are managed by Adrian Boothroyd who is the most qualified manager ever, The League Managers Association's golden child, their anti-Roeder if you will. The trouble being that Watford will make deadly-dull and functional Bolton look like a cross between Holland (1978) and The Sex Pistols. Things look grim and we haven't even got sunderland to cheer everybody else up with their hilarious buffoonery.

However, unlikely heroes have appeared on the horizon and all is not lost, and when I say "unlikely" I understate the fact. Ken Bates, the potty old pirate, is the least heroic figure in football, having unleashed Abramovich on the Premier League as well as leaving his grubby finger prints all over the Wembley fiasco. But if Ken can prove that Chelsea illegally nicked a couple of kids from Leeds Utd, as he claims, they could face a points deduction and the points handicap system the League needs will be unwittingly introduced. Chelsea obviously dealt with the Jon Obi Mikel situation *(who had agreed to join Manchester United before Chelsea backed a truck full of money up to his house)* by brazenly throwing money in Man Utd's face like Alex Ferguson was some kind of disgruntled pole dancer but Ken won't be bought off so easily. He will want his pound of flesh, his moment in the spotlight and his subsequent disappearance will bring Chelsea down. The fall back is another unlikely saviour in the shape of Michael Ballack and his monstrous ego. Ballack will, at some point this season, upset everybody in the League, especially Frank Lampard; they both play in the same position and they are both used to playing in every game. It will all start out chummy but by Christmas they will be scratching each other's eyes out, which is exactly the same amount of time Mourinho needs to start turning up to games dressed in a toga, making his horse head-scout, talking about invading the sea and declaring himself a God.

The least likely saviours of football are referees but they are the real reason the new season is going to be entertaining. You see, over these last few years the rules of the game have been gradually mutating to the point where nobody really knows what they are anymore. And without rules we will have chaos, unmitigated anarchy.

All the things we thought we knew are now wrong. How many times during the World Cup did you think, "That wasn't even a booking" when a player was sent off? There is no such thing as "ball to hand" anymore, even if shots are blasted against players' arms from an inch away and you have to be some sort of multi-science genius to understand the offside law. I keep thinking I've got it, then they either change it again or the dizzy bastard of a linesman seems to be making up as he goes along. So we have arrived at a stage where refs can do pretty much what they want. And what they seem to want is none of this over-organised 11 against 11 rubbish. So Liverpool, Watford, Everton, Bolton and all those other dreary teams of Cybermen can spend as long as they like planning games with advanced computer systems but the refs seem hell bent on sending five players off in the first half, so it will all have been for nothing.

Wayne Rooney won't complete 90 minutes all season.

We should run a sweepstake on the exact moment that Sheffield United manager, and serial whinger, Neil Warnock's head actually explodes. (If you could get a double up, with the 100th time Radio 5's Alan Greene says, "This is a nonsense. Can't we go back to the time when offside meant offside" you would be rich enough to never have to work again).

So where does this leave Newcastle United? Well I'm very much of the opinion that while the World Cup was the gateway to this new chaotic era, the research was completed last year, with Newcastle in the role of white mice. We had seven players sent off last season, despite not being a physical team. All but one of those sendings off was, by any normal rules, wrong (the exception was Jean Alain Boumsong being dismissed for gross indecency, you remember....no, you will have no doubt been mentally scarred, by the grotesque image of our French international trying to cover up missing a basic clearance by trying to mount Peter Crouch roughly from behind – anarchy or not, we can't have people trying to bugger Peter Crouch in front of our young folk). So we at Newcastle are used to turmoil and unfairness, we exist in a chaotic environment where nothing is ever normal, yet Glenn Roeder remains calm. It is his great strength and while lesser men will lose their heads and wail he will calmly assess the situation and reorganise. Obviously not to the point where we actually win anything but it wouldn't be a crime to go along for the ride and actually enjoy ourselves at the football, would it?

Manchester United won the League and Chelsea's decline was so steep and severe that they won a League and Cup double in 2010 with a squad containing both Lampard and Ballack. Jose Mourinho went Caligula style mental to the point that he won the Italian League, Cup and Champions League with Inter Milan the same year. Wayne Rooney didn't get sent off at all that season, by the end of Roeder's tenure Newcastle were insipid (13th) but most disappointingly, Neil Warnock's head didn't explode even once.

Chapter 56

September 2006

I Am Your Spokesman (sorry about that)

I have been speaking on your behalf, I hate it when people do that to me so I feel I should apologise and explain myself. Some of us at *The Mag* have discussed this matter at length in our secret underground bunker in the past because the media often come to us for your opinions. You may not like this, but if we don't do it they will find a balloon-head who will be outside the club shop on a Wednesday morning. Some unemployable, toothless cross-eyed, half-wit with a jester hat shouting, "We'll win the League now, nee botha, TOON ARMY!" and the nation will cringe, roll its eyes and think, "That's what people are like in Newcastle."

Anyway, Radio Five Live rang on the day of the transfer window closing saying, "we are looking for fans to comment on their club's new signings."

Oh hello, thought I, is there a sniff of something exciting in the air? And the moment got the better of me and I said yes, the problem being that they wanted me to comment after midnight and I now had all day to think about what I was going to say. Don't freeze up, don't say anything stupid and don't call anybody a twat.

Above all don't, like so many other people, start talking in clichés. Excuse the diversion here but there is a new one that boils my piss and you won't thank me for pointing it out because it will boil yours too when you notice how often it turns up. It's asking and answering your own question within the same sentence, in a smug fashion. For example; "He's got the one thing that defenders hate" (leaving a slight profound pause at this point, like everybody doesn't know exactly what you are going to say) "and that's pace".

Or; "If there is one thing that defenders are afraid of, it's people running at them with (pause) pace." Fuck off! Apart from there being other words in the language to describe a fleet-footed velocipede, I long to hear "If there is one thing defenders are afraid of it's (pause) ghosts. Ghosts who shove frogs down the underpants of the living, they are especially afraid of that, oh yes."

"If there is one thing that defenders hate it's (pause) house guests farting or wiping bogeys under their sofa when they think no one is looking. House guests who point and laugh obnoxiously when the defender's dog licks its own testicles and who shout "Oi Mavis, you she-ape, put the fucking kettle on" at the defender's wife."

As a group, defenders must hate lots of things more than pace: queuing, going to the dentist and that advert for loans where the man ends up on an expensive and enormous lawn mower despite having a tiny garden. Diversion over.

The other thing to bear in mind is that you have only got a few seconds to make a point so multi-layered arguments are a big no no. I had this idea about saying, "Jonathan Woodgate signing for Boro is like seeing a much loved ex-girlfriend shacking up with a drooling, fat, smelly simpleton. You are disappointed for yourself obviously but more so for her, wasting her life with some unworthy arse who takes himself too seriously. Woody will be up to his elbows in ASBOs and shitty nappies and probably on drugs, when we would have treated him like a princess…" but that would have made me sound like somebody with issues so I simply blamed Dot for Newcastle's lack of activity in the transfer market. Dot was reading out the sports headlines and all she had come up with for me by 11.38pm was Antoine Sibierski which, quite frankly, wasn't good enough. To her lasting credit and despite being irredeemably Welsh, Dot apologised. Which I in turn must do to you, for gibbering on national radio when I was your representative.

Just be grateful that I didn't adopt the voice of Old Man Steptoe to start describing how Roeder and Shepherd are like the parents of Hansel and Gretel regarding poor James Milner: "We loved 'im, so we did but we couldn't afford to keep 'im so we sent 'im to Martin O'Neill's gingerbread house but he came back 'ome, so he did cos he'd left a trail of breadcrumbs y'see."

I'd have got the entire North East sectioned.

What we didn't understand at the time was the reason Newcastle only bought Antoine Sibierski was that Freddie Shepherd had spent all our money, and much of our future money. We still owed money on players who no longer played for us and were owed little or nothing by other clubs for players we had sold. We didn't have a pot to piss in and would have been pissing potless for years if the club hadn't been sold so it was a surprise to discover that Antoine Sibierski was actually rather good.

Chapter 57

October 2006

New York City Mags

"Look! A bear on a motorised skateboard."

"What?"

It's 10 a.m. outside the Art Institute Of Chicago, the warm September sun has already burnt the haze off Lake Michigan and a seven foot, brown furred creature with mad goggly eyes and a manic grin is weaving swiftly along the sidewalk. He brakes violently, puts his paw round a girl and punches the air for someone quick enough to get their camera out, then with a rev and a buzz he is gone. Wifey and I go back to looking at our phones which remain stubbornly passive. "Nothing, from anybody," despite the fact that it should be half-time at the Boleyn.

Chicago's U.S. style football team kick off at 12, the cheapest tickets are 60 dollars and the game takes all day so we're not going to that. Sitting in a sports arena feeling bewildered by the proceedings is the kind of thing one goes on holiday from. We assumed that by this time Newcastle will have lost at West Ham, our team's generous nature surely means that if Tevez and Mascherano are ever going to click it will be against us, we are just waiting for confirmation. But as we always say, "people who don't go to the match know fuck all" – a flurry of texts arrive later, 2-0 to the Toon, Duff and Martins.

Going to Chicago has been a longtime dream, while renowned as the home of the planet's coolest Blues bars, to grizzly old punkers it's more important as the birthplace of Big Black, Ministry, Alkaline Trio and Rise Against. Big Black in fact reformed to play their first show in over 15 years the week before, missing it so narrowly is a scar I will boast when most others are forgotten. Along with Public Enemy, Big Black are the most important band the world has seen in the last 25 years and I can prove it given time, their *Songs About Fucking* album will still bloody the nose of all comers even though it doesn't have their best song,

Kerosene, on it. (Musical History lesson over).

So, we are already in the best imaginable mood, news from the UK has just the one downside, it is impossible for Obafemi's first goal for us to be anywhere near as good as the one I am imagining over icy cold beer in Rossi's Bar. The Bears are destroying Detroit on the TV and the jukebox is rocking under the stewardship of a drunken nurse who claims, "I would like to fucking marry Jack Daniels." Despite the urge to wed dead distillers the locals are magnificently friendly throughout our stay.

Our friend Shaun is a massive Blues fan and we have promised to steal him a beer mat from Buddy Guy's Legends bar in return for him taping *The Sopranos* for us (Sky Plus is still considered the Devil's work in our house). Ever the optimist, I fully expect to return with a T-shirt signed by Mr Guy himself and have Shaun hate me forever so peering through the locked door of an establishment that is clearly closed was obviously not part of my dastardly scheme. "The pool tables are blue," I say, oblivious to the ominous looking men lurking in the shadows. The "L" train rattles overhead as we wander through the night and all we need is a hooker with one leg and a sailor with a flick-knife to have found ourselves in a Tom Waites song. Brilliant.

It is during this part of the evening that we discover a bar promising to show Liverpool v Newcastle in two days' time. This is largely useless information because by that point we are winding through the mountains of West Virginia in a purple Chevrolet with no hope of a phone signal, never mind a TV showing foreign sports.

We race through eight states and a thousand miles in three days but we don't stop at any point to fire high calibre firearms because apparently I'm "not bloody Hunter S Thompson", which is a shame.

We dump the Chevy in Philli and get the train to New York City, where we arrive at what feels like the Earth's capital and where you, dear reader, finally arrive at the point of all this nonsense. Ladies And Gentlemen I give you: "The New York City Mags".

They meet for matches at Nevada Smith's which is on Third Avenue between 11th and 12th, the game kicks off at 11 a.m. so we have got a drink in our hands by 10.30 which turns out to be very bad. There are TVs all around the bar showing games from all over the world. A couple of Hearts fans are at the bar watching them beat Aberdeen and a group of Roma fans are chattering in Italian and keeping a half-eye on Inter v Parma whilst waiting for their game against Chievo to kick off.

We've only been in touch with one of the Newcastle fans, Rhod, but he is on his honeymoon in Jamaica so we have gone in blind and unexpected, assuming because they are Newcastle fans that they will be canny. But "canny" doesn't do them justice, they were fucking crazy fantastic bastards the lot of 'em; from the second Duncan came in banging a great big bloody drum we knew the early start wasn't going to be a hindrance to these people. They hung flags, sang non-stop throughout the match and jumped about with beer and fevered enthusiasm only pausing occasionally to good-naturedly abuse the two Everton fans in attendance. You couldn't help getting swept up in the infectious madness; I claimed, "At least half of Shola's toe was onside" as Everton tried one of those sneaky little mass-scurry-outs and Ameobi walloped us 1 up. With spirits high despite a disappointing 1-1 scoreline and abandoning Nevada's to the Barca fans, we found ourselves outside a pub in Greenwich Village where anyone passing was in danger of being dragged into hilarious drunken lunacy. Never unpleasant or obnoxious they charmed all who came upon us, ladies, gents and at one point a group of sailors. Then some damn fool started waxing lyrical about Irn-Bru and vodka and before we could stop him a great tray of the stuff had been delivered. From then on, things got terribly messy and I fear I may have irreparably damaged myself. Wifey hasn't been able to look a drink in the eye since and I can only hope we didn't horribly offend anybody.

The pictures show that at some point it got very dark and that there was more Irn-Bru. Smiling barmaids from places I don't remember are mixed among photos of our hosts with wild eyes and boundless energy. We flicked back through them, in a somewhat fragile state in the 10 hour gap between checking out of the hotel and getting onto a delayed plane.

So if you are going to find yourself in New York and you are not some idiot who is going to show me up, you should drop by and see the NYC arm of our family. Apparently you are welcome to join them, they have a web-site http://www.toonarmynyc.com/

At the start of 2011 the NYC crew had moved out of Nevada's to a bar called Legends – you can check out the details on the website.

Chapter 58

October 2006

Two Forgotten Games

Mid-week matches of any description are wonderful. Dark, cold, wet and in Newcastle, they are unforgettable. One from Europe, one from the League Cup. And when I say "unforgettable" I mean in the "I don't remember that at all" sense... But the point is there were no medals given out for going to these games, no significant steps were made towards success, it was just football for the sake of football and it was great.

Newcastle United 1 v Fenerbahce 0 (H)

Is Turkey in Europe? I don't mean to be insolent, I only ask. They are not in the European Community because of their awful record on human rights and being on nodding terms with bad people, which is odd because Romania got in despite openly harbouring vampires. UEFA's moveable boundaries are another matter altogether of course, stretching right over to Israel and this is a good thing. More of the world's waifs and strays should be hoovered up, I positively look forward to Newcastle playing teams in Greenland, Venezuela and Cuba. This, of course, is assuming that we can expect to be in Europe ever again – at present our whole club stinks of death and the path ahead looks to be descending.

In our ongoing enfeebled state Glenn Roeder should be applauded for his lateral thinking; adopting the attitude of the clever but malnourished weakling when arriving at a new school, where one takes on the role of erratic and dangerous lunatic to avoid being bullied by the boys who have been shaving since they were four.

It worked as well, Fenerbahce seemed utterly baffled by us as we did the equivalent of throwing chairs at people and jumping out of second storey windows, by playing Duff at left back and Antoine Sibierski at all. So lacking in pace, control and ability was Mr Sib that a wise person might hope that his early injury in this game would mean a swift withdrawal from proceedings. But he hobbled back into action and for the most part watched the game ebb and flow around him. Of course the wonderful thing about football, and Newcastle in particular, is that it makes no sense, so despite playing the game like he had won the opportunity in a raffle, Antoine would occasionally show a flash of brilliance and only went and won us the bloody thing. So Newcastle have got a ten million pound striker on the bench (Luque) who we need to play to stand a chance of getting a quarter of our money back and this free bloke is playing instead? OK. It does however make absolute sense because while Glenn and Freddie conspire to provide us with the tiniest team of wee folk in this club's history, anyone who can make contact with a ball passing at over seven feet off the ground must be treated as some sort of God.

Nothing happened in the first half.

But oh what joy a half empty ground affords those of us too daft to cancel our direct debits. People started wandering around, The Leazes End was all but abandoned as we hopeful fools migrated to join those in the Gallowgate in search of a close view of a mythical Magpie goal. Or failing that, a mid tier view near to an exit for a swift getaway seemed the very best of ideas.

As Mr Zico's team dithered, Mr Roeder's swelled in confidence but it was a slow process. Ramage and Taylor at centre half have a combined age of about 11, Duff was itching to run off at the first sign of trouble and after a wretched display against Bolton no one of sane disposition was trusting Carr. Emre was clearly injured, Parker had caught a dose of the hopeless from mixing with the England boys, Milner looked to be sulking and Martins is so desperate to please that he is lashing the ball violently goalwards with his every second touch. Which means all our hopes rested on Charles N'Zogbia so (gawd bless 'im) Roeder did the equivalent of eating the contents of the teacher's big pencil sharpener and washing it down with red paint by taking him off. Solano came on and was dreadful, Shola warmed up. Now presumably down to 20% fit, his introduction would at least put Sibierski out of his misery – but no – Martins got hooked and all forward mobility was sacrificed. By now Emre had also limped from the fray, replaced by Butt who looks to have recently turned 50.

Solano came to take a corner from near my new seat. I rose from the plastic normally warmed by the rear of one I Hudson to encourage our lovely Peruvian and blow me if he didn't put in a decent ball at last. Rustu, a magnificent pirate of a keeper, unaccountably flapped and who should be on hand to smack in the rebound but Antoine Sibierski who launched himself into the Gallowgate by way of celebration.

The traditional way to proceed after taking the lead in these parts is to collectively soil ourselves and never attack again. This also proved perplexing to our guests who apart from missing a dolly of a sitter barely darkened our penalty box thereafter – which didn't stop the fevered whistles from the young and the frightened.

Our next game in this competition is Palermo, now how the hell does a skint chap with no holidays left get to Sicily at short notice? Still it could be worse, Kap Farvel, Caracas or Havana would cost a fortune.

Newcastle United 3 v Portsmouth 0

Ha ha, proper fucking old school this. Newcastle, midweek, lashing rain, 25,000 hardcore and the game not on the telly for the idle, the mollycoddled and the impoverished. You had to be there to see it - but why would you want to be? Twenty quid a ticket with weather that should be charged by the cops on account of it being so intent on beating you up. There was hardly a dry seat in the house, in The Leazes, even half way up, the rain was somehow thrashing against the back of your head.

But we live for this shit, it's what we've done most of our lives and it's exhilarating.

The game was a cracker as well, ignore the mewling of the pathetic babies in the press box who tried to suggest that the game should not have been played just because they got damp bottoms and splashes on their lap-tops. Bollocks to them, this game was not for them, it was too primeval, too far beyond their ken, those of us with football in our souls longed to be playing in such a game, never mind watching it.

With enough water on the pitch to either stop a ball dead or send it skimming away there was potential chaos with every kick. As soon as it became apparent that any player sliding on his arse could travel faster than it was possible to run, SJP soon became STC (Slide Tackle Central), and how much fun is that?

Credit to both sides for trying to play football and not looking to use the conditions as an excuse to be malicious. Newcastle had little choice but to slide the ball around with Rossi and Martins up front, while Portsmouth's front two of Toon old boys, Andy Cole and Lua Lua were also keener to ply their trade on the grass. No matter how much splashing that involved.

Guiseppe Rossi *(on loan from Manchester United)* looks a cracking little player, he spent the entire second half at Boro warming up and itching to be on and tonight Roeder let him off the leash. That he works so hard is no surprise, along with a decent first touch that is the least that is expected at Old Trafford, but his movement and attitude are a joy to watch.

Even in July the Gallowgate End was dark and chilly but assured of its dryness, not to mention its proximity to the nearest Metro, I set off to visit friends there again. Unfortunately some fluorescent coated Nazi was having none of it. "Health and Safety", he bleated at the four of us looking to take up one each of the hundreds of empty seats before us. God help us all if four people changing ends at half-time is going to tip the whole fucking ground into the river.

Stephen Taylor has many qualities; acting is not one of them and his theatrics are getting a trifle embarrassing, he may have been fouled in the area but Ginola would have blushed at the way he went up and down. It did cause enough of a distraction for Rossi to bring the ball down and bend it into the net however.

Five minutes later a deep cross from Duff on the left was met with a thumping header at the far post by Nobby Solano who also got the third. It looked like an own goal and the tannoy gave it to Rossi but apparently one Pompey player kicked it against another and Solano poked in.

It was nice to see Dyer back for the last half hour, full of swift running and mischief, we could all benefit from his continued presence but you've heard that prayer before.

3-0 to Newcastle, with happy Mags jumping around in the rain. Like I said; proper fucking old school.

I understand that it is no longer possible for a game, at any level, to be "not on the telly" should you want to see it.

Chapter 59

November 2006

And Out Come The Wolves

It was around Guy Fawkes night that the media reported that a young man in sunderland put a firework in his bottom and lit the fuse.

From within a group of people behaving in a peculiar way, the behaviour doesn't feel peculiar at all.

Hundreds of years ago I had the misfortune to spend a (thankfully brief) period of time as a pupil at a Darlington primary school. At lunchtime the collective behaviour was the sort of thing that David Attenborough could whisper excitedly about on *Planet Earth*, as hundreds of children rushed silently into the dining area, sat down, grabbed the nearest spoon and stuffed it into their mouths. Odd? Not if you were there and seven years old.

The silence was because the head dinner lady was a witch-eyed fucking harridan with a shush that could crack glass. A spiteful hag who, if she heard you speak, would send you to Mr Hardy who was a P.E. teacher and thus a fearsome bully who would explode into a scarlet rage if you ducked a header from a four stone, leather football and considered a child telling the new boy that, "you aren't allowed to talk at lunchtime" akin to pooing in the Queen's best hat.

A minority of the spoons were old and had D.E.A. stamped onto the handles. This stood for "Darlington Education Authority" but was believed by all pupils to mean "Dirty Eating Animal" and consuming your prunes and custard with such an implement was a humiliation likely to cause even the toughest child to wet themselves with shame. Frantic grabbing, stealing and intimidation was required to hold onto a spoon that didn't carry this damning mark. The best way to be confident of not having your spoon snatched was to publicly lick it or stick it in your mouth. To witness this behaviour as an outsider was like accidentally stumbling into Bedlam. At my next school ALL the children did "Traditional Country Dancing" on a Monday afternoon but that's a whole different nest of repressed neuroses.

Which brings me to the communal air of panic and depression hanging over our football club's supporters. Even Alan Shearer is joining in: "It's going to be a long hard season" he groaned during *Match of the Day* (11th of November), oh thanks Al. And what do you think we should all do for Christmas, kill ourselves? Oh and we hate all our players as well by the way; lazy, rubbish bastards that they are, who would or should leave the second the transfer window opens. Glenn's a nice chap but hopelessly out of his depth and the chairman wasn't at the ground for the Sheffield United game because he was round your house nicking your kids' bikes. Probably.

The rest of the season is going to be played out to a Joy Division soundtrack, we will wring every ounce of misery and self pity out of our inevitable relegation. If anyone dares suggest any of the players are playing well they will be shouted down as liars and if you even think about saying Roeder's substitutions at Man City (that turned the team from being utter garbage into Brazil) was anything other than a happy accident we will burn you as a heretic.

When did we turn into these people? These moaning fucking bores, intent on fulfilling our own worst prophecies? It lacks spine, dignity and worst of all, our enemies love it.

I hooked up with a sizeable percentage of my match crew to see Rancid at a sold out Carling Academy this week along with more punks, beautiful freaks and mashed up bastards than you could shake a stick at. No one does a joyful ska-tastic, thrashabout better than Rancid and halfway through *Fall Back Down* with the entire place gleefully hollering, "If I fall back down, you're gonna help me back up again, if I fall back down, you're gonna be my friend" I thought, "fuck this negative fuckin' bullshit, I'm not going out like that". I've started saying to doom mongers "You think we're going to get relegated? OK, ten pounds a point, every point we finish below fourth bottom I'll give you ten pounds, but every point we finish above third bottom you give me ten pounds, with no limit. Do you want some?" As yet no takers.

Obviously ignoring the humiliating thumping Arsenal are going to administer tomorrow, because they are playing really well and are due to give someone a public humping, I'm coming out swinging. Unless you or someone close to you has died, been diagnosed with cancer or (worst of all) has realised they are Vernon Kay, I don't want to hear about it. How can the world be anything less than fantastic when mackems are haemorrhaging the blood vessels in their arses by sticking rockets up their own jacksies and lighting the fuse for our amusement? And what a crime that this was reported in a negative way by the local media – if they had announced that firework induced anal damage was the fast-track to a lifetime of Incapacity Benefit the feckless' feeble-minded twats could easily have been convinced to line up along the Tyne Bridge with Catherine Wheels nailed to their sphincters to see in a wonderful new year.

I may be wrong but fuck me with the Rag-man's trumpet, it won't be the first time and I'll be having more fun than some of you miserable buggers. While I'm feeling positive, I bet that miserable canteen witch died a slow and painful death and I wonder if Mr Hardy is still alive? I would hate to have missed the opportunity to kick him in the leathery old bollocks.

Fall Back Down appears on the *Indestructible* album.

The phrase' "Fuck me with the Rag-man's trumpet!" appears courtesy of Lord Flynn of Jarrow who said I could have it.

Newcastle finished 13th. Five points clear of relegation.

Chapter 60

January 2007

Boooooooo!

Spurs have a brown away kit. Brown? They mostly wear it in Europe when we have our own matters to attend to (like beating a Palermo team clad in salmon pink – what a world we live in), so I have rarely seen it. What joy to discover that the group of Tottenham fans in my pre-match pub had amongst their number a lad sporting a replica shirt of this exotic "autumnal" hue. I'm afraid I may have given our guest quite the wrong idea about what to expect from a trip to the North East of England by stroking it above the badge and emitting a less than masculine "Oooooo", before we had been formally introduced. The look in his startled eyes, at having his bosom interfered with by a grinning, drunken halfwit may have been the seed of my idea to enthusiastically cheer every touch of the ball made by Cristiano Ronaldo on New Year's Day.

It has been said that Cristiano has been playing well *because* of the abuse he has been getting this season, that he has actually been fuelling what has been an extraordinary run of form with the negative energy of opposition supporters. Which is very clever of him, but I thought, "Why the hell would we want that, much better to cheer him enthusiastically surely?" It would at least do his silly little head in. I put the idea to my pre-match crew who agreed in principle, obviously after three or four pints "cheer him enthusiastically" had mutated through waving, winking and smiling, to what could only be described as being aggressively homosexual. Getting some of the larger, wobbly-bellied boys in our crowd to try and put their hands down his underpants at corners and some other suggestions I don't think our younger readers should be exposed to yet. While this would certainly have the required result of "putting him off a bit", I doubt the relevant authorities would approve of crowds sexually molesting footballers, not when they are on the pitch anyway.

What I was most keen to avoid was a boring and ineffective, half-hearted hatred. Hate with the searing heat of super-nova or don't hate at all, especially at a football match, otherwise you end up that low-level drone of ill-content that emanates permanently from Goodison Park.

Unfortunately I lack the gravitas or the self belief to attempt to mould the crowd to my will, so only Ken, the gentlemen of advancing years to my right could be convinced to join in. Wifey rolled her eyes at me and pretended we were complete strangers. But oh how Ken and I laughed as Ronaldo hit his first shot of the game a full 35 yards wide and out for a throw in.

Why are we supposed to be booing Ronaldo anyway – can anybody actually remember? We apparently now lack the stamina for a 90 minute wall of noise anyway. I know I start to cough and wheeze violently after a sustained period of booing, last time we played against Chelsea I thought I was in danger of booing up a lung.

Half-hearted hatred isn't going to put anybody off anyway, fifty thousand people constantly chanting, "Your house is on fire!" would no doubt distract a player. But much better to fake (or release depending on your orientation) gay attraction.

And don't deepen your voice and get all homophobic on me, we already qualified for the Campest Crowd in the World Finals during that pre-season game at Bradford when Brian Pinas played his only game of note for us. Singing "Stand up if you love Pinas" and "We love you Pinas we do" was fun and you know it. We should be confident enough in ourselves to use other people's phobias against them. For example; if we should discover an opposition player is afraid of spiders we should constantly scream "Look out, there's a tarantula in your hair!" at him. I have it on good authority that Thierry Henry is averse to snakes so the obvious thing to do is hiss his every touch on April the 9th.

Next time we are due to cross swords with boastful Christian El Hadj Diouf, I shall be taking a collection for a 50 foot banner with the legend "Even Jesus Thinks You're A Twat!" written on it. In blood.

It hasn't got to be us all pretending to be John Inman but football is homophobic to the point of being backward. So upset with the suggestion that he might enjoy life on the other side of the rainbow was Ashley Cole that he forced the Sun to apologise publicly. The Mag can hardly afford the ramifications of me pointing out that getting cross at being called gay is a sure sign that Ashley Cole is actually very lovely (obscured for legal reasons). So I won't be doing that, but ask yourself "how far am I prepared to go to help this club win a football match?" If it's just joining in with some low level booing then that really doesn't help at all. One of the only songs we can all still remember the words to has the words, "we are mental and we are mad" in it. What I'm saying here is that we should start living up to this boast and if that means barking like dogs at Steven Gerrard or whispering "We're gonna get you, we're gonna get you" at Jonathan Woodgate then that is what we should do.

That said, I was disappointed to find out that the Ghaly who plays for Tottenham is not, as I understood to be the case, the nephew of the former Secretary General of the United Nations Boutros Boutros, because I intended giving him a jolly good booing for his uncle not having acted to prevent the genocide in Rwanda in 1994.

Newcastle drew the game 2-2 thanks to goals from James Milner and David Edgar. Cristiano Ronaldo, clearly distracted by a small number of Newcastle fans cheering him, failed to score. Paul Scholes, who would never be distracted by thinking a crowd was gay for him, scored both goals for The Salford Mob. Newcastle introduced a singing section that breathed some much needed life into the SJP atmosphere but they were often rude about Mike Ashley and in 2011 it is being done away with.

Chapter 61

March 2007

All Hail The Intertoto Cup

Four years ago I made a bet with my friend Guy. I had made a statement, "We have to come to terms with the fact that we are never going to win anything." "We are going to win something, one day," said Guy.
"Don't be silly," I said.
Guy was smiling a big confident, annoying smile, "How much do you want to bet?"
"A hundred pounds!" I snapped. That should shut the silly sod up, I thought. Wrongly.
"OK".
"Hang on, when do I get paid?" Come the apocalypse was I expected to go to Guy's house for my money or would I have to wait outside the gates of Hell with my hand out? What will a hundred pounds buy you in Hell and could I drag him in by the wing before he could fly upward for more milk and honey with smug Americans?
A span of five years was agreed upon, we have one season left after this one before he has to give me a hundred pounds. It's obviously a bet I long to lose.
But a complication has arisen, Guy thinks the Intertoto Cup counts. Most of our conversations take place with one or both of us drunk but I am sure we specified which trophies counted just in case we added to that glass thing Robert Lee held up in Ireland, after a flurry of goals from Jon Dahl Tomasson in 1997. But to be on the safe side I have been actively poo-pooing the Intertoto Cup whenever I am in Guy's earshot.
Obviously our enemies have been doing the same thing and I don't want to be on their side so at the Liverpool game it was decided that the Intertoto Cup did not count towards our bet. So.....

Right you fuckers, let's fucking go!
The Intertoto Cup is an amazing thing to win and anyone who doesn't agree is a blithering idiot. Either that, or a treacherous lying lizard with quisling eyes and webbed feet. Probably. Think about what we had to do to win it; the qualification alone took 38 games (all of last season in fact). To get the required points we had to beat Arsenal and Chelsea and we had to win at sunderland and Middlesbrough. That is a dream cup run for any Newcastle fan and we should celebrate long into the night (oh hang on, we did, didn't we?)
Our progress in the competition has involved us starting the season a month early and winning away to Palermo (who were second in Serie A at the time) as well as beating sides with the European pedigree of Fenerbache and Celta Vigo. So damn right The Intertoto Cup is something we should he happy to win. Order the open top bus, shine the Lord Mayor's Mr T necklace and sacrifice something. So where the bloody hell is it? Many in the media complimented Newcastle for getting over 30,000 for the SV Zulte Waregem match when it was all but over from the first leg and was on the telly. I don't know about the rest of you but (apart from the fact that the club keep sending me tickets before I'm even aware games are due to take place, or against whom thanks to this accursed direct debit I'm too lazy to cancel) I for one bolted out of work early to be drunk and up the ground sharpish to see our splendid new trophy.
I fear the delay in its presentation has been due to the self-conscious shyness on the part of our club in the face of unseemly sniggering from our many detractors. And not, as Guy suggested, that the Intertoto Cup is actually the size of a semi-detached house and that we need four army Chinook Helicopters to lower it into the stadium.
The suggestion that no one knows where it is because no one can remember who had it last is a slanderous slur on this prestigious award.
You will remember that Kevin Keegan told us years ago that the first trophy was going to be the hardest to win. Maybe I believe him and like the teenage boy who believes that his first shag will be but a doorway to a world of endless debauchery, so The Intertoto Cup will be but the first step on a road made of shiny solid silver for Newcastle United.
Or maybe, having stood amongst the awesome support of 5,000 fans at Wigan, seemingly making no difference to the fact that our players were staring cluelessly into the mouth of yet another gift horse I have simply gone back to

daydreaming. Daydreaming about what to spend Guy's money on, something he would disapprove of obviously like drugs, a big bouquet of flowers delivered to Cherie Blair or drinks for sunderland supporters. Basically we should make the most of The Intertoto Cup because my money's safe.

Chapter 62

2006/07 postscript – A Distorted View

Newcastle played some bloody odd teams in some bloody odd places in 2006/07: FK Ventspils, Levadia Tallinn, Zulte Waregem, Middlesbrough. We had some good players on the payroll as well: Shay Given, Scotty Parker, Emre, Charlie N'Zogbia, James Milner, Obafemi Martins, Nicky Butt, Kieron Dyer, Michael Owen; players of ability and reputation, but none of them tall and none of them defenders and most of them missing for part, or in the case of Owen virtually all, of the season.

To win the Intertoto Cup a team has to qualify for it in the first place in its domestic league which a matter of some precision because too many points will put you straight into the UEFA Cup. Intertoto qualifying teams compete with each other for the right to progress to the UEFA Cup. The last Intertoto qualifier standing in the UEFA Cup wins the Intertoto Cup. Winning The League Cup is a breeze comparatively yet Newcastle United accepted the trophy like they had been awarded third place in the village fancy dress competition when they were only wearing their normal clothes. We played 60 games in total and they became a blur of tedium. American comic Doug Stanhope says, "Boredom is a disease worse than cancer" and Newcastle's season died of cancer of the enthusiasm.

There were over 20,000 empty seats in St James' Park by the time we played Zulte Waregem in the UEFA Cup in February, and in the next round only 28,452 turned up to see us beat AZ Alkmaar 4-2. Which was a shame because we played some of our best football in the first half of that game and led 4-1 at the break with Obafemi Martins unplayable and scoring twice. More people needed to witness how good Alkmaar were despite having no players most Newcastle fans had ever heard of. So few people were paying attention when Alkmaar beat us 2-0 and knocked us out in the away leg, that their coach Louis van Gaal, wasn't even mentioned in the betting when Glenn Roeder resigned as Newcastle manager. If ever I needed reminding of my pathetic influence over opinion in this town, my utter failure in even getting van Gaal mentioned was humbling. The Premier League carried on for the most part without Newcastle United; while we dithered around in mid table of little interest even to ourselves, cracking games were being played elsewhere; teams at the bottom of the League would leap back to life, even Everton were worth watching, Reading finished eighth and played some scintillating football with a group of players who shouldn't have been able to get in the Newcastle United team. Newcastle won one of their last 11 League games and finished 13th. Man Utd won the League, Bolton qualified for Europe.

Nicky Butt said after the last game of the season (a 1-1 draw at Watford after Roeder had resigned), "It needs to be put out that not every player playing in Newcastle colours this season has played for the shirt or played for everybody connected with the club. The majority of lads in the dressing-room are good lads and good professionals, but there are a few who don't want to play for the club." (nufc.com)

Things at Newcastle needed shaking up radically. Sam Allardyce was appointed manager, then Mike Ashley bought the club. Which turned out to be a bit more radical than we were prepared for.

Player of the Season: James Milner for his professionalism and refusal to hide even on bad days.

Goal of the Season: Obafemi Martins in an ill-deserved victory at Spurs. A rocket into the top corner and the best of his 17 goals in his first year in English football, playing in an inconsistent team that didn't make enough chances for him.

Chapter 63

August 2007

The March Into Darkness (continued)

The last chapter of And They Wonder Why We Drink was called "The March into Darkness" – this is what happened next.

The story so far – 1993 Newcastle United came out of the old First Division like a missile and hit the year-old Premiership in an explosion of colour and passion. Fearless, they grew stronger, flair and power, home and away, all seemed possible ….(faster please)…everybody's second favourite team…twelve point lead…lots of money spent….Toon Army….. successive managers… you know the rest….. bored now.

2006/07: personality crisis; other fans call us deluded, fair enough, how could we not be anything else? There is such a gap between the club we can be and the club we actually are, how could we not be confused? And what better face for that confusion than amiable Glenn Roeder trying to keep everybody happy, while his shoelaces are tied together. Lovely Glenn doing his best while the club is an utter frustrating shambles and greedy men are lining their own pockets at our expense. Glenn, horribly doomed and cursed by misfortune, walks away.

This essentially, if my imagination is a reliable witness, is what happened next: it is night time in Leazes Park; a mysterious black-clad stranger turns up with fire where his eyes should be and says, "Have you ever considered not wanting to be everybody's second favourite team? Have you considered a different path?" Behind the stranger from trees shrouded in fog, a figure menacing, huge and dark glides towards us.

Fire erupts from the ground, lighting a large familiar face.

"Have you ever considered, Sam Allardyce?" In the distance a wolf howls, the shadows behind Sam appear to become tangible, like great filthy wings they seem to stretch up and out, then fold neatly into the back of Sam's coat. He smiles.

"No, not him," we cry, "he's the man who made Bolton. Ugly, awful Bolton the anti-football team who all true football fans despise, why if he were given control of Newcastle United we would become.....monstrous."

At this point any of us could have walked away.

Most of us didn't. We signed the cheque and handed it to the man with the fiery eyes and for a moment we could have sworn that our own eyes flickered with flame.

We woke up. Nothing seemed to be different.

Then, whoosh, a mysterious stranger buys out the Hall family and they are gone. Freddie Shepherd, perceived as an unlovable bungler but street fighter tough and always of rude health, is suddenly struck down with a strange debilitating illness. He can be seen clutching his chest at Lord Allardyce's inauguration. Too weak to resist he sells to the mysterious stranger, who brings in a man called Mort. The word Mort, with its various different spellings, means 'death' in more languages than we care to list but no one seems to notice.

Mort peruses the state of the club, has Shepherd unceremoniously thrown out into the street and says, coldly, "There is work to be done here."

On the pitch our shirts have transformed from mostly white with gold trimming to mostly black. Our captain Scott Parker, a blond, bright-eyed decent man with a pure heart vanishes to be replaced by Joey Barton, dark, brooding and a notorious bad-bastard. Our bungling clowns in defence, who have brought joy to millions, are replaced by cold-eyed men from Eastern Europe with unpronounceable names.

Our support, darker because of the new shirts, now has a meaner element – Dyer is hounded from his home of eight years – this is no longer a place for redemption. You play, we pay, you work, we pay, you fight, we pay. You don't work and fight – we kill you. It's not fair and it's not nice but it seems we don't do fair and nice anymore.

We all need to know whose side we are on because this new season looks like being one hell of a battle. The old top four are all strong, but crucially all the dead wood and the mid-table sludge look to have come to life. Villa, Blackburn, Man City, Portsmouth, Everton, Spurs and West Ham seem to have been invigorated. If Reading and Bolton continue to punch above their weight we will have 13 teams other than Newcastle who will be hoping to finish in the top six. They will all take points off each other but crucially they will take points off Arsenal, Man Utd, Liverpool and Chelsea. One of Derby, Fulham, Wigan or Birmingham could start well so providing somebody doesn't win their first 20 games (and Man Utd's squad looks formidable) we could be in for the most competitive Premiership season since its inception.

Which leaves our regional squabbles: here the issue is polarised, you could have walked away this summer. The fact that you are reading this means you didn't. We are the ones standing behind Dark Lord Allardyce under the black (mostly) and white banner. So no bickering and bitching with each other, ignore the pathetic mewlings of old women in the local press and let's unleash hell.

(One more thing – if you are thinking of watching *Ghost Rider* with Nic Cage, don't, it's rubbish.)

Chapter 64

November 2007

You Don't Know What You're Doing

England failed to qualify for the European Championships after losing to Croatia, while Steve McClaren watched from beneath his brolly. Closer to home, Newcastle United's fans were growing impatient with Sam Allardyce – losing 0 to Liverpool's 3 didn't help but we did take the time to pass judgement on one of England's "Golden Generation".

The stupid 12.45 kick-off meant that this was the first Premiership game after the England debacle against Croatia. Usually mid-season England games are nothing but an annoyance to us in Newcastle and only worth mentioning in relation to how badly injured Michael Owen got – but the relevance, fall-out and parallels from Wembley splashed all over this game like nephew-sick in my spare bedroom. (That'll teach him to try and match drinks with Wifey – but he is only ten) (19, he's 19 alright?)

There has obviously been fevered debate on what went wrong and the state of the game. Too many foreigners, players don't try hard enough – blughh – in the late 70's England never qualified for anything and there was no such thing as foreigners then (except for the black man in *Love Thy Neighbour* obviously) and the worst thing about the England performance against Croatia was that they were trying really hard.

The truth is straightforward – the coaching system in this country is bollocks and therefore all managers produced by that system will be bollocks. Who was the best qualified manager in the Premiership last season? That would be Aidy Boothroyd at Watford – and they were good weren't they? *(They finished bottom.)*

Foreign coaches, often with inferior players, take the piss out of their English counterparts; witness Van Gaal v Roeder and Bilic v McClaren. It is claimed that

English coaches are not given a chance at the top level – that's because those clubs want to stay at the top level and don't want to entrust their multi-million pound empires to the bastard sons of Howard Wilkinson.

Everything McClaren accidentally learnt during the qualifying campaign was ignored or forgotten for the last game – the tactics were predictable and pathetic and the players didn't really stand a chance. So it seemed a little harsh that the SJP crowd took to booing Steve Gerrard from the start of this game. It would have been a much better idea to unnerve him by singing songs about his house getting robbed, as thieves seem to be through the windows of at least one Liverpool player's house every time they play away from home and it's bound to be Gerrard's turn soon. *(oops – 13th of December 2007.)*

Of course the press assumed we were booing Stevie G because of England's failure but the press assumed a lot from this game that wasn't true. Personally I was booing Gerrard for his obvious dislike of NUFC and the fact that the celebrity status that sees him and that shark in a wig he married plastered all over magazines for thick people also affords him privilege from every ref in the country. Him and John Terry, BOOOOOO!

Like England, Newcastle have enough quality players to give anybody a game providing they can match that quality with urgency and belief. It's not about effort and sweat – England and Newcastle players can and do run round and round and round for hours – it's belief in what they are doing that matters. McClaren was hopelessly out of his depth, the job was too big for him and he was cruelly exposed.

So what of our own English coach? Having avoided being shot at dawn for the rank cowardice in the face of the enemy by going to sunderland and playing for a draw Sam Allardyce sent the players out for this game with the tactical game plan equivalent of having their shorts round their ankles.

What followed from then on was extraordinary. You really had to be there, despite the fact that many of those in attendance really wished they weren't. Too much of what has been written has been done so by people who were not there and the *Match of the Day* highlights were a re-writing of Stalanistic proportions. Newcastle started with five across the back with Geremi and N'Zogbia as wing-backs and Rozehnal between Beye and Enrique. Emre appeared to be the holding midfielder a lot of the time, which meant Nicky Butt kept turning up on the right wing. Alan Smith was possibly supposed to be doing the same on the left but he would often vanish from sight for long periods of time, so it was difficult to tell. The forwards were Viduka and Martins but they were so far away from the rest of the team that they were virtually irrelevant and don't need to be mentioned in relation to this game again.

It was a horrible shambles from the start, Sam claims we were trying to "contain" Liverpool but it looked more like we were bending over and handing them the lubricant.

After half an hour of disorganised buffoonery Liverpool got a free-kick. Gerrard was still twisting his face at the ref about nowt when it was tapped towards him. Our players bolted out to block and in a fair world would have spirited the ball upfield while Stevie G complained some more - instead he noticed what had happened and smashed the ball into the Gallowgate end net. The twat.

Alan Smith was moved to the right to stop Geremi getting tortured quite so bad and His Blondeness remarkably, given the amount of times we dared to tippy-toe into the Liverpool half, nearly equalised with a dipping shot that bounced inches wide.

The fact that we were still in with a sniff but went down with barely a whimper means you couldn't even have a decent whinge about how refs treat Liverpool players like Royalty. Less than one minute into the second half Beye was shoved in the back seeing out a straightforward ball and the ref gave a corner. Imagine if that had been Carragher who had been shoved – there would have been stray dogs barking the length of Bensham Bank such would have been the pitch and volume of the Scouse whining (and how come Carragher was absolved of England blame - didn't he go AWOL?) The corner hit Kuyt on the leg an inch out, the ball bobbled into our net and the game was over as a contest.

The game was not, however, over as a spectacle. The simmering distrust for Sam Allardyce and his tactics felt by a sizeable part of the crowd went thermonuclear. Spontaneous and open rebellion erupted around the ground. Sub James Milner was demanded by the home support but Sam instead replaced Emre with Barton and the half-time jeers were repeated. When he did introduce Milner it was for N'Zogbia and not His Blondeness and the volume of the displeasure made you giddy. *Match of the Day* showed a couple of fans clearly shouting, "You don't know what you're doing" when the truth was that it was the loudest song all day and it rang round the ground as our manager gnawed on his gum, wide-eyed. "Big Sam for England" offered the Liverpool fans to generous applause.

On the pitch, the brilliant Torres was thwarted again and again by Shay Given to stop things getting seriously horrible score-wise. But the action off the pitch was even more interesting; people were leaving and sarcasm was rampant from those that stayed as Newcastle passes were cheered. "One shot, we've only had one shot" rose from the Gallowgate then as if to underline the fact that they were turning on the manager and not the team or the club there was sporadic supportive singing. It was remarkable, and in an "oh look, my arms have fallen off" sort of way, grotesquely amusing.

When Gerrard was booed off and Peter Crouch was cheered on you could tell the mob was drunk on its own wilful naughtiness and a state of anarchy had briefly been declared. The only home player booed at any volume was Stephen Carr on his introduction in the 78th minute. There was more booing when the Man of the Match was awarded to Alan Smith, which was surely chosen by somebody out of pixyish badness because His Blondeness had a shocker.

In the post match interview Allardyce looked in a state of shock, his mouth was making the right noises but he looked drenched in sweat and his eyes appeared to be on the lookout for men with guns. At the time you thought "he is so fucked" -

we've turned on managers before but never so early and so damn hard.

Our next manager is going to have to be foreign – no one in this country would be mad enough to come here. Sam says he should be judged after 38 games not 14 and we'll hold him to that because, like England, we should bribe or kill people to get the right man and, like England, we can afford to wait.

It is a source of constant bewilderment in Castle Furious when Allardyce, Souness, Gullit or McClaren turn up on TV as "experts" when they have been so horribly and publicly exposed as nothing of the sort.

In the interests of balance I should say that not all Newcastle fans turned on Allardyce. My splendid friend Bront made a spirited defence of Big Sam and as we both like an argument and are both as stubborn as fuck we eventually had to shy away from the subject for fear that we might come to blows. When I say blows it would have been the briefest of conflict between his hand, my head and a wall.

Chapter 65

January 2008

"Just Who The Hell Do You Think You Are?" – Stewie Griffin (Family Guy)

Sam Allardyce was sacked, Newcastle tried and failed to get Harry Redknapp. The world queued up to slag us off.

Sam Allardyce was given far too long at Newcastle United. Nobody sensible wanted him here in the first place and it was obvious from very early on that the relationship was a bad idea. If at some point during the last eight months he had deliberately driven his car into the Gallowgate statue of Jackie Milburn whilst wearing a sunderland bobble hat it couldn't have been more obvious.

It sounds ridiculously simplistic but Newcastle fans love football. A pox on your trophies. Score goals, win games, try and play some decent football and we can (with the aid of a pint or two) just about stomach the idea of work on Monday. Allardyce seemed obsessed with stopping any actual football breaking out, especially away from home. The first rule seemed to be "no football" – football fans don't want to get up in the dead of night and spend hundreds of pounds travelling the country to see "no football".

Why is that so bloody difficult to understand?

Newcastle fans would rather their team die on their feet than live on their knees – ideally we would all like to live on our feet – Sam had us dying on our knees. At Wigan.

No one doubts that, given time, Allardyce could repeat his success at Bolton – which translates to: after five years of playing mechanical anti-football Newcastle United could have looked forward to finishing eighth.

Yummy.

The striking thing about Sam's dismissal has been that nobody outside Newcastle seems to have a fucking clue what they are talking about but that sure as hell isn't going to stop them having an opinion. Allardyce's departure has been met with the almost universal disapproval of people who haven't had to watch all Newcastle United's games this season and haven't been expected to believe some of the piffle he has spouted.

Football fans from all over the country have been launching themselves at every available media outlet demanding to know who the hell the Geordie fans think they are. Professional chin-strokers have been queuing up to tell us that Newcastle United are not as big a club as their fans think. OK, but if we are so irrelevant why have we been over the papers and TV all week and how come you lot care enough to pass comment on us? Trust me, if football clubs in Nottingham, Southend, London, Manchester and Liverpool were being run by dancing gibbons Newcastle fans wouldn't be ringing up Victoria Derbyshire at 11 o'clock in the morning at Radio 5 Live to decry the insanity.

The 6-0 at Manchester United seems to be being thought of as us getting what we deserve because we were beastly to Sam. Like Man U are suddenly some kind of sword of righteousness? Their breakthrough goal was after a dive from a serial cheat, we had a good goal disallowed, goal two was from a stupid mistake, goals 4 and 5 were offside and goal six wasn't actually a goal because the ball didn't cross the line – that makes it 1-1 in my book, well done everybody.

Manchester United of course are used as an example of patience with a manager paying off. Here's why that argument is bollocks; by March of the Italian season in 2005 AS Roma were onto their fourth manager of that campaign. By the 2006/07 season they were playing the best football in Europe, scoring buckets full of goals they finished second in the League and won the Italian Cup, having spent hardly any money. This "you can't expect to turn things around straight away" thing we are being beaten with is nonsense, has nobody seen a League table recently? Manchester City, anybody?

This assumption that we all want Shearer is starting to get on my onions as well. Alan Shearer is (according to nufc.com) still not qualified to be a coach, has no scouting network, has friends in the current squad and no experience.

If Shearer is half the local hero we think he is he shouldn't be playing golf with Freddie Shepherd in Barbados – unless by "playing golf" you mean smacking our ex-chairman in the back of the head with a nine iron.

The eye-opening factor about owner Mike Ashley's courtship of Harry Redknapp was just how much money he was reportedly prepared to shell out to get the man he wanted. For that kind of money you could surely get anyone? The imagination fair soars.

So which lucky manager is going to sup next from the "poison chalice"? A job that after doing for even the briefest time means you will never work again but will be able to afford not to have to.

Note to every manager worth a damn across Europe; now is a good time to ask for a pay rise, a bigger transfer kitty and a golden hat for the wife.

What makes us Newcastle fans think we are a big club? Well this week it was announced that Newcastle is the 13th richest football club on the planet, which is pretty big, but it's not the size that matters. Big Jack Charlton was run out of Toon in 1985 because the fans didn't like his style of football and the fact that he preferred the likes of George Reilly and Gary Megson to Chris Waddle. St James's Park averaged about 27,000 at the time so the rebellion was hardly the nouveau riche having a hissy fit.

Rest assured we know exactly who we fucking are thank you very much.

Harry Redknapp, having turned the Newcastle job down, took over at Spurs when they were bottom of the League and in the 2011 season they reached the latter stages of the Champions League – suggesting Mike Ashley's Plan A wasn't that daft. Certainly in retrospect, hiring Redknapp would have made more sense than trying to reanimate Kevin Keegan.

Chapter 66

January 2008

Keegan, Keegan

Two weeks ago a friend working in a respected Tyneside school gave a pupil detention for saying Kevin Keegan should be the next manager of Newcastle United. The boy was only allowed to leave after promising to stop being so silly. Appointing Keegan made no sense; a backward step, too long out of the game and the uncomfortable feeling that he looked a lesser version of himself at Fulham, England and Manchester City.

However, the name Keegan put 10,000 on the gate at St James' Park for the FA Cup replay against Stoke City. The man did nothing more than sit himself down on Wednesday but not since Rosa Parks has this simple action caused such a reaction. Despite being down to ten men for most of the game the team played better than it has in years. With freedom and verve and an obvious esprit de corps – cynical, gnarly people in the crowd were cuffing tears of joy away as the intoxicating euphoria of their younger selves swept over them and children, unborn when the man last arrived, were berserk with excitement

The next day the city was still smiling, naysayers on Tyneside were hard to find and they all sounded like drab, dreary people lacking the lust for life that makes Newcastle special, a feeling that Kevin Keegan inspires and magnifies.

Keegan is our Pirate King with an appetite for adventure and mischief. Priorities, trophies and points can be talked of and dreamed about but it's the giddy thrill, the indomitable madness that makes you want to climb the rigging and scream defiantly at the other ships in the Premiership sea. No we won't do as we are told and lower our hopes, no we won't be sensible and no we won't be upset by the sniping from those keen to mock our every failure.

Ah failure. Keegan failed at Newcastle before, we are constantly reminded. He took Newcastle from near-relegation into the Third Division to third in the Premiership in two and a quarter seasons, then was only thwarted in winning the

League two years later by the unquestionable brilliance of a Cantona-inspired Manchester United. Offer that kind of failure to Norwich City or Queens Park Rangers today and see them turn it down.

Things have changed since the last time Keegan was in Toon. Indeed, this time Newcastle have already got some decent players and this time they have got a billionaire owner. Mike Ashley in a matter of months has turfed the embarrassing oaf Freddie Shepherd out of his chairman's seat, has seen off Sam Allardyce, who had no business here in the first place, and has paid off the £100 million debt. Those who choose to question his choice of seat and attire do so from a position of ignorance and a lack of understanding of how Newcastle United infects the blood.

If you choose to jump on board don't expect to leave with your sanity or, in fact, at all. The top four in the Premiership have too many guns for us to take on at the moment or in the immediate future but they will know that we are out there. We may well burn or sink but we will have lived. Now hang on, because it's about to get a little rough.

Original draft for *The Sunday Times.*

In the pub before the above mentioned Stoke City match Bront and I were again in agreement. Kevin Keegan was a ridiculous choice for manager. In fact everybody at our table in The Old George was saying the same thing, "this is just stupid" – there were six of us. However, everybody else in the packed bar was jumping up and down singing "Walking in a Keegan wonderland." So we just laughed and got on with it.

Chapter 67

January 2008

Hippo-headed Twat

Kevin Keegan's first game in charge was a 0-0 draw at home with Bolton Wanderers.

I tell you what, these dignified silences don't come easy to us drunken gobshites. I didn't want Sam Allardyce here, I have long disliked him and everything he stands for but for the sake of unity I've tried to look on the bright side. Who wouldn't want a team of super-fit killer cyborgs? However it has been clear since we played sunderland, when our manager appeared to be screaming at his players to defend a 1-1 draw against clearly inferior opposition, that he was dead in the water. Allardyce going was like having a stone taken out of your boot, the stinking corpse of an albatross cut from round your neck and being cured of asthma in one beautiful moment.

Yes, we should have given Sam the full season but for a reason that I've not seen amidst the prattling of the clueless and misinformed who still backed him: I wanted him to know he'd failed. I wanted the hippo-headed twat hounded out of town in May humiliated and having to publicly admit the Newcastle job was too much for him. Unlikely I know, given the pig-headed nature of the man and now he can stride into another job, with the kind of misplaced idiot-arrogance that usually only bent coppers have the gall for, with his excuses all nice and lined up. Interesting to see where he ends up n'all – most other fans think we should have kept him here – see how many actually want him in charge of their club.

Newcastle United's fans have been brilliant through this, the instinctive spontaneous reaction to cowardly tactics against Liverpool was impressive enough but the response to more of the same at Wigan was even better. "We're shit and we're sick of it!" – we should be being treated like heroes for standing up and saying, "We are not fucking well having this!" in an age when supporters are expected to pay up, dress up and be grateful for being allowed into a football ground. But no, other team's fans have been squealing at us like cross little piggies and we have become pariahs.

The arrival of Mr Keegan only raised the stakes – we now seem universally disliked for having principles and refusing to be bullied into silence. Good. (*)

"There was an explosion in Newcastle on Saturday night. It was the sound of the bubble bursting," said some smug cunt on a phone in. Why don't you fuck off and worry about your own dismal existence?

The game was poor, but thanks to having three players suspended, four in Africa and having had to play for over an hour on the previous Wednesday with ten men thanks to obnoxious show-off referee, Uriah Rennie, that wasn't such a shock. Yet this game, rather than being banished to that shadowy area of the brain that seems set to delete dull games from the memory within a month (I can never remember what we did against Everton for example, not ever), should be kept on video or Sky + for a long time. Then whenever someone says, "we should have given Allardyce more time", we can strap them to a chair and make them watch the full 90 minutes again and again until they beg for mercy. At which point we can scream in their faces, "Really, more time, are you sure? Because that, that (at this point we can jab at the Bolton players on the screen with our pointy righteous fingers) that is what he would have spent five years turning us into. A pathetic excuse for a football team, a functional, well-drilled group of big blokes stretching the laws of the game to the limit – intent on doing nothing except stopping the other side playing and nicking it. Bumping into people off the ball, wasting time, jostling and man-handling and cheating for the entire game. Hoping to bore the opposition into a mistake then nicking it with a set piece and thinking that it's OK to charge people money to see it. See him, that's Gavin McCann, he's not a footballer; see him, that barrel chested oaf is Kevin Davis. He will work his way down the leagues cheating and complaining and wasting people's time. He will die and be forgotten. Is that what you wanted here? Answer me, stop bleeding out your ears and answer me you fucker!!!!"

(*) not all other fans have been against the sacking of Allardyce. I would like to thank my friend Nat Splendid from th'Boro who said, "I see you got rid of that hippo-headed twat then". Nat's name isn't actually Splendid but his real name doesn't do him justice so I changed it and if he doesn't like it he should be grateful that I didn't follow my initial instinct to kiss him on the mouth. As you can see, I am looking to bring his phrase "hippo-headed twat" into common usage. A man has to have goals.

Less than two years later Kevin Davis got picked for England.

Chapter 68

February 2008

A Despicable Institution

Newcastle played at home to Manchester United and with Keegan in charge our famous 5-0 victory over them was dug up, again. Could the same thing happen? Keegan said no. He was right; the teams shared six goals, with Manchester United taking more than their fair share. They are good, your Manchester United, but people don't like them. Here are some reasons why.

Amidst all the whistles, gumdrops and hoop-la of the 50th anniversary of the Munich air crash much went unsaid, it is often the case when the nation is browbeaten into mass sentimentality. For example, nobody pointed out that at the time her death, Princess Di not only wasn't a princess anymore but was also guilty of one of the two remaining offences that incurred the death penalty in this country. I understand that this delightfully gruesome loophole has been subsequently de-looped but these lynching crimes were; piracy on the high seas and a Royal spouse getting gigetty-gigetty-giggetty with folk behind the future king's back. Queen of Hearts? The woman was the scourge of the seven seas – no hang on that's not right............

For a start, no one questioned the importance of Manchester's City and United removing their sponsor's names from their shirts when they played each other recently. It said – "normally we can just about stomach the stench of filthy commercialism but today is about respect." "Oh really," the clubs' sponsors didn't say, "is that what you think of our brand, is it? A filthy smear on your sensibilities – give us our bloody money back!"

More importantly, why was it assumed that Man City fans couldn't shut up for the minute's silence with people barking, "it's a disgrace" (people always say things are a disgrace) before the event?

Newcastle fans had an immaculate minute's silence for Bob Stokoe who despite having played for us is better remembered for looking like a tramp having a fit when managing sunderland and for making vaguely racist remarks about Ossie Ardiles. Fans are usually pretty good about marks of respect, which brings us to the actual elephant in the room nobody wants to talk about. The day of the actual anniversary England played and the FA weren't going to have a minute's silence because they didn't trust the fans to observe it – at the risk of pretending to be a 70's hippy-student poster - WHY? Why is it so accepted that people dislike Manchester United so much that they will openly disrespect the dead to express that feeling?

I'll tell you why, because Manchester United is a despicable institution, that's why.

So despicable that even the club's treatment of their own fans is deplorable; compulsory Direct Debit for season ticket holders for tickets for all cup games (even for games they can't get to like midweek against Coventry in The League Cup with Ferguson playing his reserves). Old Trafford on a match day is run like a military junta with fans having their season tickets removed for standing; then Ferguson slags his own people off because of the lack of atmosphere when a large proportion of proper fans have been deliberately replaced with goggle-eyed tourists.

Against Premiership rules, Alex Ferguson refuses to do press after games presumably because he doesn't like people asking awkward questions. Dissenting voices are bullied or removed and because Manchester United have been getting away with it, others can follow and we reach the present situation where the "Big Four" expect, and get, privilege off and on the field. Alan Smith got sent off for Newcastle at Old Trafford for swearing at an official – a straight red. Two weeks later (if my lip reading skills are up to scratch) Wayne Rooney screamed, "You fucking cheating prick" in a referee's face and got nothing. What the hell did Smith say that was an entire red card worse than that?

Ferguson came out against the 39th game – not for any of the stand up moral reasons but because he hadn't been asked personally about it. This level of fucking arrogance carries over to Rio Ferdinand & Vidic being virtually unbookable, Ronaldo and Nani constantly diving and the aforementioned Rooney being the most obnoxiously spoilt little cry-baby in football.

This is a problem because when he comes up against refs with backbone, when playing in Europe or international football, he consistently lets himself and his team down.

Domestically he is indulged when for his own good he needs to be sent off and sent off and sent off until he realises that he should just shut the fuck up and play football.

Manchester United don't need the level of privilege they demand, because they are really good at football. Not just that they have brilliant players (the amount of time and money they have had under a good manager it would be criminally negligent of them not to have brilliant players), it's the way those players work. Everything is done at speed, the first touch is good, the work rate is phenomenal and that's the basics for them. That's the least that is expected. They especially don't need refs licking their faces and stroking their hair when up against teams of sackless, disorganised little girls who've had their spines confiscated for weeing themselves in public. So it didn't really matter that Ferdinand fouled Owen in the area after 25 minutes (from behind, played man before ball – learn the rules Mark Lawrenson or get off my fucking telly) because the first time something goes wrong Newcastle United do the footballing equivalent of bursting into tears then setting themselves on fire. So no big shock that a second later Ronaldo crossed and Rooney ran past a static N'Zogbia to make it 1-0.

From then on our worst fears were realised with the pitch constantly looking like there were eight red shirts in each half and clocks and watches at an apparent stand still. We nearly made it to half-time but Carrick picked up a shabby Barton pass and was instantly twenty yards away from our England international before putting in Ronaldo who beat Given. This was Shay's last act – turns out he was injured again so, like at Villa, a much needed sub couldn't be used because he declared himself fit and wasn't.

Ten minutes into the second half, Ronaldo fell over, Faye gratefully spirited the ball away then gave it straight to the nearest red shirt. Ronaldo got it back, Taylor brilliantly managed to nip through the gap between Ronaldo and the ball and it was 3-0 with the twinkle of shiny toes. Useless fucking rabble.

We had an hour left – and it was horrible. Gnawing silence from the home crowd while the smug red swine in level 7 gloated noisily.

In the 79th minute Faye smashed in from close range at a corner which provoked

Man U to go up half a gear and score two more. Rooney bending in from the corner of the area after a weak Smith clearance and Saha dollying in a fifth in injury time.

Finally, if I may respectfully return to the only air crash where anyone ever died, could I ask the court to also consider the entire Torino team killed in 1949 and the South American rugby team who had to eat each other after crashing in the Andes in 1972.

You doubt we would have had to stomach the "Flowers Of Manchester" nonsense if Bobby Charlton had been found gnawing on Duncan Edwards' leg.

8.3.08: Emergency post script: Did you see the level of hysteria when Ronaldo didn't get a penalty when nudged over in the area against Portsmouth? Ferguson wanted Keith Hackett's head, Queiroz wanted the ref sent off and darling Cristiano said he felt "scared to play with my skills". Anyone fancy arguing with me on this "demand for privilege" point?

Thought not.

Chapter 69

March 2008

Kevin Keegan and Zombie Jesus

Newcastle United have never played Real Madrid and I have been blaming Temuri Ketsbaia for years. This is harsh on Temuri who (if the meanderings of my imagination can now be used as hard evidence) now lives in a windmill made entirely of dog hair in a forest of shadows. But it's a harsh world, a world where Vinnie Jones has been put to death for ruining the X-Men film franchise... (what do you mean he's still alive? - I left specific instructions!)

It was 1998 when we played Partizan Belgrade in The Cup Winners Cup, a competition Newcastle United, of all teams, had little business being in but once again we had found the key for the cat-flap into Europe because the actual cup-winners had more important matters to attend to.

Newcastle lost on away goals and Ketsbaia missed a dolly of a sitter (I was going to add the word "inexplicably" to that sentence but it was Ketsbaia so all the explanation was on hand) and we lost a game we should have won.

Five years later we played Partizan again in what turned out to be the single most disastrous match in our recent history. One game between Newcastle United and the group stages of the Champions League and we had won the first leg in Belgrade 1-0 (Solano). At SJP Bobby Robson's team and the crowd were unaccountably cautious and nervous, Woodgate made a rare mistake, and Partizan won 1-0 and beat us on penalties. Partizan went on to play Real Madrid in a group that, owing to the complexities of The Champions League seeding system, Newcastle probably wouldn't have been in anyway. But I have always felt we all missed out.

If only Ketsbaia had smashed that chance into the net in '88 they would have been more nervous of us than we were of them and our entire recent history would have been different. I told you it was harsh of me but I was still shaking a mental fist at the shiny-domed loon as I witnessed Roma fans wandering around Spain's capital last week instead of beautiful boys and girls in black and white.

EasyJet fly to Madrid from Edinburgh so after a couple of hours swearing at the car radio where, among other things, the recently sacked Lawrie Sanchez was making pathetic excuses for himself and Allardyce (You were both found out – now go and manage in the Championship where you belong), Wifey and I were queuing up with a mob of Celtic fans taking a less than direct route to Barcelona. Doing as you are told, minding your own business and drinking a lot are the keys to happy flying in our experience so we woke up in a hotel room with two balconies, a power shower and nufc.com where the news was bad – that oaf Shepherd and that third nipple of a man, Douglas Hall, were paying themselves how fucking much to bankrupt our club? And voices in the media are saying Ashley and Mort are responsible for our present crisis when Shepherd has spiked their guns to the tune of 75 million bloody quid. (Calm down, you are on holiday).

We have chosen now to visit Madrid because Real are due to play Roma but we haven't got tickets. You could buy them on the internet but the Real official website is worse than Newcastle United's and the other on-line sources are ridiculous. All touts have to do in this day and age is call their tickets "Hospitality Packages" and they can demand unicorn teeth and diamond encrusted underpants for the damn things. £185 each? Sod that! Wifey even tried to get tickets for the Roma end which would have been fine provided we didn't mind popping by the club shop in Rome to pick them up. A.S. Roma are understandably cautious of who they give tickets to given their fans' somewhat anti-social habit of stabbing folk.

The Real ticket office didn't open until 5 p.m. which seemed a bit odd but these people think nothing of having their main meal at midnight and eating bulls bollocks when they do, so odd is what we have to adapt to.

Madrid is an impressive city and time gets gobbled up exploring it. Wide pavements, vast roads, grand buildings - you are constantly reminded that space isn't a problem so there is room to be lavish. Parks and fountains and palaces sprawl unselfconsciously, then a side road will suddenly have you in a labyrinth of back streets with bars, restaurants and shops where (certainly in the area we staying in) the young men were so happy to be alive that they were holding hands and kissing each other on the face.

In our search for paintings by Caravaggio and Hieronymus Bosch we came across one of the few statues in the world of Satan/Lucifer (Angel Caido – fallen angel - which is an angel crashing in a park and is brilliant), more Picassos than anyone needs in a lifetime, a 15th century painting of Kevin Keegan and a depiction of the resurrection of Christ that looks like it was commissioned by zombie-film specialist George Romero.

The Santiago Bernabeu stadium has seven vast tiers but must sink deep into the ground because on the outside it's not much bigger than th'Boro's Riverside. You can get there, like everywhere else in the city, for a single euro on their Metro system. A euro that seems entirely optional because when the ticket machines don't work the guards simply wave you through onto sparkling new trains.

Roma beat Real Madrid in the first leg 2-1 so with the game thrillingly poised it wasn't a shock to find out that the return leg was sold out. With the delicate boy on reception at our hotel also unable to find us tickets, our options had dwindled to the point of forgetting about the football and going in search of cerveza and Rioja to emborra charse (get drunk). Although I swear I had only had a couple when what looked like Gabby Heinze came by our table to use the cigarette machine. Camels he bought.

I perfected the phrase "lo siento no hablo espanol" (I'm sorry I don't speak Spanish) which along with my natural skill at pointing seemed enough to me but it was constantly met with babbled and complicated spitty/lispy questions from barmen and waitresses – some of whom seemed very nice. As to the rest; I told you I don't speak your language, what do you want, me to open a vein or something? I can tell you to fuck off in lots of languages – entender, cabron? (understand, bastard?)

The day of the game, after visiting the Americas Museum (piles of stuff they nicked), we hit Finbar's, the bar in Madrid nominated by nufc.com's "Global Mags" page as the place to watch Toon games on the telly. The friendly barman was unaware of this honour and worse still could get one ticket for the match.

Wifey and I eyed each other suspiciously for a second – it was her credit card that got us here (a somewhat more imaginative Christmas present than the Toon scarf I got her) so I couldn't go and there was no way I was leaving her unattended in the vicinity of Roma's Daniele De Rossi, even with 80,000 chaperones. More for his sake than hers.

The last option was to go to the stadium and see what we could pick up. With our poor grasp of the lingo and the fact that the people selling weren't likely to be the most honest of fellows there was an obvious element of risk. I could all too easily imagine Wifey going home penniless leaving me married to a fat Spanish bin man with a big moustache and unusual sexual appetites. Again.

After sleeping off a generously proportioned Mexican lunch we awoke to news of disturbances at the stadium so back to Finbar's was the decision. Obviously we could have stayed in Newcastle or our hotel room and watched the game on TV but the Finbar's option was excellent. Three TVs service the few tables by the door, the narrow bar and the small room at the back where we found a table to pile drinks on. By my reckoning we had two hundred euros of ticket money to get through.

Roma have been an idle distraction for Wifey and I in the 17 years since we first went to their Olympic stadium. More so recently and not just because obsessing about Newcastle United 24 hours a day has got so depressing and irritating. Roma don't have the best players in Serie A but their system under Luciano Spalletti has developed over these last two years into a distinctly un-Italian style that other Italian teams can't seem to cope with. They play fast for a start, really fast, to feet and with urgency. Francesco Totti's natural position is behind the strikers, which is where he plays except Roma don't play with any strikers. Despite this they score loads of goals and Totti won the golden boot last season, Roma finished second and they won the cup. They are stronger again this season and have been a joy to watch. They defend in numbers but when they get the chance they don't so much break as swarm.

In the previous chapter I call Manchester United a despicable institution, which I stand by, but that doesn't leave me anywhere to go in my opinion of Real Madrid who make the Salford Mob look like a temple of Buddhist monks. Give me another six pages and I can blame Real for the ransacking of the Incas and the Aztecs, bullfighting, the Inquisition, the rise of Franco and Spanish fascism and the fact that I can't have my tea until two hours after bed time. Suffice to say like most decent people I delight in the all too rare occasions when a matador is gored and favour Barcelona.

How quickly we have grown accustomed to smoke-free bars; not in Spain, where you are still free to mask the stench of sweat, manky carpets and urinal cakes with a thick cloud of tab-fog.

By kick-off Finbar's is tense, smoky and full of a heady mix of Irishmen, excitable young Spaniards and more bloody Celtic fans which means we are keeping our thoughts to ourselves despite paying an apparent English tax on our beer. By law any group of Celtic fans must have one happy drunk, one smiley lass and at least one spotty rat-eyed little bastard that you have to watch out for. The game, despite a picky ref, is thrilling, Madrid are good but the mental strength Roma show under extreme pressure is brilliant (and completely alien to us) and the speed and confidence of their breaks is devastating. Both sides hit the bar before Roma score first (Taddei). A young lad in an Italia top jumps up to cheer – Wifey and I raise a conspiratorial eyebrow. Real equalise (Raul –offside), the lad in the Italia top jumps up with nearly everybody else. Real get a player sent off but keep attacking – at the death Vucinic scores for Roma making it 2-1 on the night and 4-2 on the tie. The lad in the Italia top doesn't move but Wifey and I after several pints of bravery clench our fists and smile.

As we wobble off to bed Mr & Mrs Madrid tuck into their starters and we can all hear sirens in the distance.

It would have been nice to come here with several thousand other Newcastle United fans, the city certainly has enough bars to cope, but any chance of that is some way off unless we get Athletico Madrid in some Intertoto qualifier. (Oh the unbridled optimism). But the itch has been scratched to some degree for now and Ketsbaia doesn't have to worry about me turning up at his windmill in the night anymore.

Madrid? (shrug) It's alright.

Chapter 70

April 2008

Newcastle 2 v sunderland 0

Featuring Michael Owen's finest Newcastle hour.

I like Roy Keane. There, I've said it. I like the way he goes through life looking like he hates everybody. And he's much more fun to have around the Premier League than most lower placed managers, an interchangeable mob of dreary bullshitters droning on about poor decisions and "plugging away". Keane doesn't seem to care what people think about him and seems to dislike the same things about football that proper fans do; corporate spectators, spoiled players, people not trying, managers moaning about refs – I would go so far as to say that if Roy promised to make Ashley Cole eat his own shit at gunpoint he would be the most popular manager in the country. Keane was also complimentary about Kevin Keegan recently when it was very unfashionable to be so.

Roy Keane could give sunderland a whole new dynamic – where they actually have some self-respect and don't live their lives fussing about what they do in comparison to Newcastle ahead of anything else – but he won't. He won't because of the mentality of the snaggle-toothed, semi-evolved pigfuckers following his team. Turning up here dressed in off-white and inflammation-red, like mobile acne with a silly accent, one collective thought in their filthy skulls; that a point at Newcastle will make sunderland better than Newcastle, a better place with identity, transport links, culture and decent gigs. A place where the highlight of their non-football lives isn't Mickey Rooney driving around their grotty little bottle shop in Chitty Chitty Bang Bang.

Another good thing about Roy Keane is he's not really doing very well. He's spent £40 million and what has he got to show for it, a half decent 'keeper and Kenwyn Jones? Jones seems to be a grotesque hybrid of Shola Ameobi and Tigger (bouncing all over the place with a disarming smile and little idea or interest in direction or purpose) and he represented sunderland's only realistic threat. The rest of the team seems to be made up of the same kind of faceless grafters and hackers we've been annoyed by then forgotten for a hundred years. For the 48 hours going up to this game Newcastle fans all seemed to be saying the same thing: "The only thing that worries me about this game is that I'm not worried, which worries me."

As we hopped up the steps into the Leazes End (determined not to look up and right) I shivered briefly. Was it the unseasonable chill, nerves, excitement or the giddy thrill of DJ Rob playing The Ruts "Staring At The Rude Boys"? Who cares? We live for this shit and as "a voice in the crowd" shouts, "We'll Never Surrender!"

The atmosphere was brilliantly cranked up by the club putting out black and white cards which turned the ground into a sea of beautiful stripes and by Graeme Danby singing The Blaydon Races. This seemed like a damn silly idea but worked a charm – opera singers at football overdress and overdo it but Graeme was just a big bloke in a Toon top with a flag on a pole. Albeit a big bloke in a Toon top with a flag on a pole who can sing like a Viking God. Three verses, three chorus – the last of which was performed with the flag held rampant in front of the unwashed before stamping off with some "TOON TOON"'s leaving the, by now, fevered home fans to shake Valhalla with the "Black and White Army"'s.

Our blood was up and cluster bombs of exhilaration shook into one apocalyptic roar and instead of tailing off on the whistle as all too often in recent years it went on. McShane took out Owen within seconds and the volume hit eleven with demands for justice. Two minutes in, far too early to ever score in a derby, Geremi bent a ball in from the right of centre and Owen was suddenly behind the last defender and heading the ball expertly into the Gallowgate End net. There was a pause of about a tenth of a second while we took in the enormity of what we were watching then the crowd went thermo-nuclear.

After this the game took on a pattern all too familiar; Newcastle try to play some football while sunderland hurtle around diving into challenges, kicking people spitefully then lying about playing the ball, closing down space then (and they have done this at least twice in every game they have ever played, I swear it) one of their players will have the ball at his feet with a moment to compose himself, he'll look up, set himself – and kick the ball into the crowd - "Wa-hey!" we cheer, because like when the Harlem Globetrotters throw the bucket of paper, you never tire of the classics.

McShane, distinguishable from the rest cos of his pasty skin and sandy thatch, had a nightmare. On ten minutes he headed a Newcastle corner into his own net that the ref seemed to disallow because he had had second thoughts about the award of the corner the goal came from because there was no foul in there. The ref was Mike Dean and he did well, he tried to let the game flow and didn't try to even up the bookings which after persistent handballs and late tackles sunderland won 5-0. "Hasn't he already been booked?" we kept asking each other because you couldn't tell the useless fuckers apart.

Our lack of pace through the midfield was a problem especially as it was five against three in there. Afterwards the mackems would moan that Keane should have played two up front – but you are only allowed 11 on the pitch you bloody idiots and without the five in there Geremi, Butt and Barton would have taken the piss. All three played well especially Nicky Butt who was composed and masterful but sheer weight of numbers forced them all into mistakes.

But not as many mistakes as McShane was making. He was useless. A shame then that Oba had a bit of an off day. Martins twice got in behind his hapless marker in the first half, firstly he shot from an angle with Owen unmarked and secondly was blatantly flattened. When the chief of refs publicly apologised to Keane in the week leading up to this match you feared this would happen, obvious penalties waved away.

Yet, on half-time Owen played into Viduka whose cheeky flick put Owen back in. Some jug-eared goon dived in as Owen tried to nip the ball past him and it hit jug-lugs on the hand. And up we all went.

Penalty.

Barton seemed to want it. Owen took the ball – we all remembered him taking some rotten penalties when at Liverpool. And this was a rotten penalty.

It took so long to squeeze under Gordon and make its way into the net that a large proportion of the ground thought it saved. But the explosion of arms and noise from the Gallowgate was instantly reflected in the Leazes.

A good time to score but as the half-time whistle went we were looking for a third.

The second half was long and poor as our technical players struggled for air amidst studs and sweat. In retrospect and on repeat viewing we were comfortable, our only risk being in our own galloping imaginations. All our defenders played well *(Beye, Faye, Taylor, Enrique)* as did Harper. Jones was nullified and sunderland had nothing else except effort and the erratic unpredictability of the stupid. Kieron Richardson (as well as having an annoying cousin) has an England cap or two – he came on and instantly vanished.

The best chance of the half came when Jose Enrique Sanchez Diaz cut out a ball and eased it to Geremi who hit a 50 yard pass to Martins. Martins brought it down, twisted away and hit the advancing Owen who instantly put Oba in one on one with Gordon. Owen and Viduka were square but Martins blasted his shot straight at the keeper and Keegan was so cross he took Oba straight off. Duff came on and we went 4-4-2.

After a splendidly insipid free-kick from the edge of our area by them, Viduka made way for Andy Carroll who wasn't far off with a chance crossed on the run by Owen. By now Owen was Man of the Match by a mile. Even without his goals he was two classes above anything they had. As if to underline that fact, in the 80th minute, Chops came on – I couldn't bring myself to boo him. He isn't good enough for us – he is good enough for them – I like that fact but I did join in with "4-1, even Chopra scored".

By this point the mind is a battlefield. Don't think we've won. They haven't got time to score three. They are rubbish. Clear that ball. Bastard! Ref man. Don't think we've won. They haven't got time to score two. Would one hurt? Yes it fucking would, give them nothing. Don't look at their fans. We are going to win – this is great. If they get one we'll panic. I'm panicking now. Oh God this is going on forever. That clock has been on 86 for ten minutes. Run away. Stay and fight. Sing you bastard. This means everything so give everything. This is no time to be shy. Newcass –erl Newcass-erl Newcastle. Newcastle Newcastle Newcastle.

And as one we are on our feet and the ground is shaking and we are cheering everything and they are dead. Finally I glance up and right at level 7 and the acne are flat and fucked and we've won and they know it and they can't leave. This is so cool.

The whistle blows to end it and we are up and embracing, almost tearful. We shake hands and smile and slap each other on the back.

Outside is all black and white laughter and the city is already buzzing and the bars are crowded.......... this is going to get messy.

Chapter 71

2007/08 postscript – A Distorted View

The victory over sunderland put a gloss on a catastrophic season. Sam Allardyce's apologists claimed Newcastle had had a good start under him which on results alone might have been a good point except that we carried a lot of luck (90th minute winners against Everton, Birmingham and Fulham, 87th minute equaliser against Derby). Also the fixtures were a bit wonky so we played a lot of what should have been easier games early on. For example, Derby County broke sunderland's record for the lowest ever points total. They got 11 points and won only one game and ended with a goal difference of -69. Four of those points and that win came from playing Allardyce's Newcastle United. Likes a stat does Sam, not heard him mention that one.

To be fair, we started well and looked impressive in a 3-1 win at Bolton on the opening day. When Newcastle beat West Ham 3-1 in late September Wifey and I had spent the morning sand-boarding just outside Swakopmund in Namibia and in the bar we watched the game in the drinks worked out at about 80p a pint. As a consequence we might have got a little overexcited. The rugby World Cup was on 19 of the 20 TVs in a beautiful wooden beamed sports bar, with the last one showing a disappointingly (for us) sunny St James' Park. Because the two of us were making so much noise the locals came to see what we were shouting about and many were caught up in our excitement, cheering and jumping up and down with us, when N'Zogbia added to Viduka's two goals. That was the high point.

By November things had got horrible, a 1-4 home battering by Portsmouth, mutilated by Liverpool and abject surrender at Blackburn.

The loss at Wigan broke Allardyce with the away support singing "we're shit and we're sick of it" – losses to Chelsea and Man City were Big Sam's last two games.

The next game was a 6-0 loss at Old Trafford where four of Man U's goals shouldn't have been given as goals at all and Alan Smith was sent off for swearing. Manchester United (whose players are allowed to swear at officials) with 31 goals from Ronaldo went on to win the League, Chelsea were runners up

Kevin Keegan came in and had to endure seven games without a win, while the nation mocked, including batterings off Liverpool, Man U and Aston Villa. A spirited draw at Birmingham provided the sliver of light Keegan needed to work with. Joey Barton had come back from injury and Martins, Viduka and Owen all played up front. We won four and drew two of the next six including a brilliant 4-1 win at Spurs where Obafemi Martins scored another cracker to go with the one he rocketed in there the season before and Newcastle finished 12th. That's 12th; ahead of both our regional rivals who had apparently not suffered the same "catastrophic season" we had endured. Relegated Reading and Birmingham were three and four points respectively behind sunderland. Middlesbrough were 13th.

Despite finishing the season with a -20 goal difference we thought things were looking up – we were wrong. In January 2008 the club made three non-playing appointments as well as Kevin Keegan: Dennis Wise was appointed Executive Director (Football) alongside Tony Jimenez as Vice President (Player Recruitment) and Jeff Vetere as Technical Co-ordinator. They seemed barely relevant at the time but a time bomb had been planted.

Player of the Season: Habib Beye.

Goal of the Season: N'Zogbia curled one in at Boro and a Martins bicycle kick at Bolton wrestle with Owen heading in against sunderland. Don't make me decide, I've got a hangover.

One can sand-board by either A: standing on a board similar to a snow board, on which the rider weaves carefully back and forth down a sanded slope which is bloody difficult or you can B: just throw yourself face first down a dune on a waxed up sheet of hardboard. Which is easy but as you can hit speeds of up to 55 kph it is also exhilarating to the point of being fucking terrifying. If you ever get the chance to do it don't waste time with A because there are no chairlifts in sand-boarding. The lager to drink in Namibia is Windhoek and ostrich makes for good eating.

Chapter 72

September 2008

A Question Of Trust

In June 2008 Chris Mort had stepped down as chairman and was replaced by Derek Llambias. Mort was arguably the most popular and trusted chairman Newcastle fans could remember, although his tenure was brief. He spoke positively for the Ashley Empire and seemed to be enjoying his involvement with the club. The season began with an unlikely draw at Old Trafford, a 1-0 home win over Bolton and a spectacular performance at Coventry in the League Cup. The next day James Milner, man of the match at Coventry, was sold to Aston Villa. Newcastle lost their next game 3-0 at Arsenal where the loudest cheer from Newcastle fans watching the game on TV was for Mike Ashley draining a pint straight down in the away end.
Then following the arrival of Ignacio Gonzalez and Xisco, Kevin Keegan walked out. Tyneside went instantly insane;. Keegan seemed to go into hiding and so did Mike Ashley and Llambias. If nature hates a vacuum the press around Newcastle hates one more. Wild rumours were allowed to run unchecked and calm informed assessment was utterly absent lost amidst the mule- like braying of the hysterical.
Here is me trying and failing to get my silly head round it all.

The 1994-95 season is 14 years ago but therein nests one of my most vivid footballing memories: I had just started a new job, an executive position with much in the way of serious responsibilities but I was still within earshot of a radio. Not my radio obviously because this one was tuned into Metro FM who announced that Andrew Cole had been sold to Manchester United. The instant shock of nausea and disbelief was so jarring that I nearly dropped my mop. Splitting up the dynamic Beardsley/Cole forward line was bad enough but giving half of it to the team we were trying to finish ahead of in the League was clearly the act of a mad man. Then, as now, angry people went to St James' Park where, unlike now, someone listened to them.

That someone was Kevin Keegan who was months later wearing the widest of smiles as we all saw Les Ferdinand in magnificent stripes for the first time and, if asked, we would all have said, "Andy who?"

I was endlessly retelling myself that story while contemplating the unmitigated fucking lunacy of selling James Milner to Aston Villa and sitting in front of Sky Sports News as the transfer window was closing. Xisco? Gonzalez? – never heard of 'em but if Kevin wants them they must be good.

It turns out that Kevin hadn't heard of them either – bugger.

A couple of people tried to tell me that £12 million for Milner was a good deal for us – like shit it is. If Spurs had offered us a straight swap for Robbie Keane no one would have thought that was a good idea because while Keane can run around for days like a daft dog he can't be trusted to kick a football in a straight line without falling over his own feet. And Liverpool just paid £20 million for Keane (we'll ignore the fact that Benitez is a tubby, mincing little ninny who has a hissy-fit if he can't constantly throw tens of millions of pounds of other people's money around, piling up footballers who are no better than the ones he has already got.) Milner (22) playing off the front this season, linking play with intelligent running and passing, was a reason to be optimistic, without him we were back to a witless and rigid 4-4-2. Keegan knew that, hence the "James Milner is the last player Newcastle United should be selling" comment days before Milner was whisked out the door.

Somebody must have blowing some serious smoke up Keegan's arse for him to come out and promise us all everything was going to be fine. He claims he was let down so he walked. We never have that option.

So we find ourselves in this revolting fucking predicament. It's like being beaten up in broad daylight in front of everybody you ever knew. Kicked around the street by people who are supposed to be your friends while mortal enemies beg them to stop. The pain and the confusion is bad enough but the humiliation is beyond endurance. Steve Cram was on Radio 5 saying, "I genuinely feel sorry for Newcastle fans" – don't you pity us you bastard, we've still got an airport!

It's funny because when Keegan came back in January nobody outside

Newcastle thought it was a good idea, since then there has been little national reporting that hasn't involved scoffing and belittling; now he's gone it's been reported like it's the end of the sodding world. To us it has felt like it because we saw Keegan as holding the whole club together – fending off the evil works of the quisling Dennis Wise, keeping the players happy and generally being the only person with our interests at heart. To consider any other point of view puts you on the side of Dennis Wise. We have long despised Wise and could only tolerate him on the payroll as some kind of glorified scout providing we never had to look at his stupid and eminently smackable face.

Now we feel that Wise is only here to destroy us from within. But is that really likely? I doubt anybody has written more hateful and insulting things about Dennis Wise over the years than me and only this week considered his severed head on a spike on Gallowgate the only way I was ever going to get a decent night's sleep again – but – what if we are all wrong?

What if the information leaking out of Newcastle United is correct? What if Keegan, on being told he had £12m to spend, did ask for Beckham, Henry and Lampard?

What if it was Tony Jimenez and Wise who got in Gutiérrez and Coloccini ? What if Gonzalez and Xisco turn out to be as good? What if the mistake was getting Keegan back in the first place? (Remember Andy Cole was still scoring goals for Manchester United when both Keegan and Ferdinand had long gone). What if oft-cited potential purchaser Anil Ambani buys the club, reinstates Keegan and our "Messiah" tries to sign Champion The Wonder Horse with some magic beans?

Even if all this is true, nobody up here is going to believe it because people from within the club have been falling over themselves to say Keegan had the last word on transfers and now we are being told that Keegan was told from the start that wasn't the case. So is it so surprising that now their main problem is that we won't believe them?

Meanwhile public opinion is being gathered from foolish children who were barely born in 1994 who are bursting with impotent rage and have access to clean sheets and a paint pot but not to a dictionary.

Newcastle man – it does your fucking head in.

On the 13th of September Newcastle lost 2-1 at home to Hull City in an ugly hate-filled St James' Park. Noisy protests before, after and during the match were obviously a huge distraction to events on the field. Hull maintained their organisation while everybody in black and white seemed confused by a heady cocktail of misinformation, spite and excitable people keen to see themselves on TV.

A reportedly shocked Mike Ashley put the club up for sale. His drinking in the away end at Arsenal was now, apparently, a disgrace.

Chapter 73

October 2008

The Black Eagles of Besiktas

Joe Kinnear arrived as Newcastle manager and started shouting at a journalist.

The Royal Albert Hall, that hive of British culture, has had excitable crowds buzzing through its many doors for decades, the sheer weight of its size and reputation is as oppressive as it is impressive. Inside, stage front is the floor where you may have seen the toffs standing singing Land Of Hope And Glory during The Last Night of the Proms. Going up from there, opening out in warm red, are layers of soft seats and plush carpets until at the very top you find the Gallery where we stand leaning over the highest balcony. It's like peering into the world's biggest vagina.

The Bunnymen are doing a 25th anniversary performance of the *Ocean Rain* album with half an orchestra and even up in the clouds the sound is immaculate. They do a 'best of' set then there's a break where only the swiftest and thirstiest punters could get a drink in the ridiculously crowded bars before doing the album in question track by track. If *The Killing Moon* ever sounded better than here with a battalion of strings attached, people will have died of joy and….

Right that's got rid of casual readers – culture, vaginas and Ian Mac's velvety voice will cut straight through to the hard core – we can get to the real point because there are some things you can only say amongst friends: like; if as many people died at football in Newcastle as have done at The Great North Run they would have closed St James' down years ago. It's bloody dangerous and there are perverts in the bushes watching ladies going to the toilet. Ban it.

That sort of thing.

Right then – get this (and remember we are a family and we love each other) but we must still whisper; at home (cough) Newcastle fans are not the best fans in the world.

(Cough) who said that?

Oh we used to be and like old heavyweight boxers we will always think we can be again and if anybody outside the family says it we'll laugh in their faces but right now? Forget it.

This present situation isn't about tribal passion, it's about hysteria. As the train to Kings Cross glided over the Tyne I felt I was escaping a fucking lunatic asylum where not only had the lunatics taken over but they were about to start eating strangers alive. David Craig, that nice chap from Sky Sports News, now does much of his reporting from what looks like a bunker, presumably because he dare not venture outside owing to the fact that he smells of twat-nip. Like all clubs we have always had an element of dingleberries but suddenly, like badly dressed wasps, there are swarms of the fuckers and David can't stop them pestering him. And anyone who thinks we are going to come out of this bullshit looking like anything other than snotty-faced, idiotic little simpletons needs to sober up for a minute.

Newcastle is no place for Londoners eh? – Les Ferdinand, Gavin Peacock and Robert Lee – I'd go on but the argument is too fucking stupid.

Some of us have been behaving like the most pathetic of battered wives over Keegan: "Ee but I luv'im", "we used to 'av such a laugh" – give yourself a shake woman – he keeps walking out on you, next time he turns up tell him to fuck off. I don't doubt that Mike Ashley has fucked up but I bet he thinks his fundamental mistake was bringing Keegan back in the first place.

A lad next to me at the Bunnymen gig was complaining to his mate during the break. "I can't believe the Man City game isn't on TV this week, Channel 5 are showing three UEFA games but not ours."

Furious brain – "keep quiet this is nothing to do with you." Furious mouth – "I think it's on Sky."

"Really, are you sure?"

"Pretty much. I might have got your hopes up only for them to be cruelly dashed but that's football eh?"

"Tell me about it, I'm a Man City fan."

Furious Brain – "don't say a fucking word." Furious mouth – "Newcastle."

"Bloody hell mate, I can't ever remember feeling sorry for another team's fans before". Prudence, cowardice and the need to get a pint have led me not to want to divulge my allegiance before but never shame. This is a new low.

In our defence, it's not our fault. Trouble is gallows wit, a carefree attitude, belief in ourselves, respect for our club and the honour of the tribe have been kicked out of us by liars and bastards.

We have been betrayed by everybody and our blood is black with hatred.

And there is more to this than the present shambles which is merely the most recent and cruel kick in the head. We have all over-reacted to Mike Ashley's mistakes because we were already sick to death. It's not long since Liverpool were in our wake, now we are drowning while they hit the ski jumps on the horizon and this situation is entirely down to bad management from Newcastle United – on and off the pitch.

Most recently the sale of Milner helped nobody except Aston Villa and Leeds *(there was a sell-on clause when we bought him*. Whoever sanctioned the sale was being short-sighted and stupid. Something we have seen far too much of.

Slumped in my seat in the Leazes End, silent, arms folded and scowling at players, some of whom I wouldn't take the time to drown in their own piss, isn't helping anybody. And I'm not alone, can you remember the last time we got behind an individual player who needed, or would have appreciated, a lift? Meanwhile the press bite chunks off us and jeer sarcastically. The fascinating thing about Joe Kinnear's outburst against the media that nobody picked up on was that he came into this situation and was shocked by the sneering, undermining tone of reporting. Whereas we fans barely noticed because that's the way we are treated by the press in Newcastle. All the time. Little wonder we have become demoralised.

Away from home it is difficult to imagine any fans beating our numbers + miles travelled + noise made to tangible reward ratio, despite the fact that you can't go away without agreeing to let some greedy chairman molest your wallet with his sweaty fingers and the Portsmouth game being shifted to an early kick-off tells you how much everybody else cares about our welfare; but at home we have got mean, lazy and flabby.

OK gobshite, you may say, so who is better? Well nobody in this country for a start so you have to look abroad. Argentina, Brazil, China? I haven't been.

Be?ikta? of Istanbul caught my eye. I saw them at home to Liverpool last season on TV in the Champions League and was gobsmacked. The ground was full three hours before kick off and the noise was unrelenting. Their team gave

Liverpool a hell of a game but in the away leg without the support they lost 8 – 0. It would be patronising and wrong to say that game was a one off, "their big day" – I went last month to check it out for myself, a UEFA Cup game against Metalist from the Ukraine and despite the ground not being full the support was thrilling and the hair on the back of my neck prickled for 90 minutes.

With a ground on the banks of the Bosphorus, Be?ikta? (The Black Eagles), apart from having cool little tails on their S's (? = sh – Beshiktash), play in black and white stripes and are traditionally the left wing/anarcho team of Istanbul's five top flight teams. The hardcore fans, the Çar?ı, have a motto "Çar?ı is against everything" and they have displayed banners protesting against racism, nuclear power, child pornography and while officially defunct from May this year their "rebellious spirit" remains as does the logo on a lot of the fans clothes.

In the stadium the P.A. hammers out banging techno before the match and at half-time which provides a sense of urgency (unlike *Local* fucking *Hero*) and the mascots (two people dressed as tins of Turkish cola with big goggly eyes stuck on) dance and jump into one another. A fire engine emerges from behind one of the goals and squads of riot police circle the pitch. A sprinkle of Ukrainians start to sing and the Be?ikta? support machine growls into life.

Quality of support is relative and difficult to judge but Be?ikta? are the loudest recorded football crowd ever at 132 decibels. The organisation is stunning with a call and response thing from the centre of one stand to the corner of another, then up and down the centre stand then side to side, then they all hush themselves before starting again only louder. Then louder. Then louder. Then so loud you feel dizzy. They do that thing where the crowd link arms and pogo from side to side within their row of seats with the next row down going the other way and so on, then all their arms are pumping in unison and it is relentless and thrilling. And me...? The cynical old 'seen it all before' veteran of Toon trench warfare? I can barely look at the pitch despite Besiktas having that most piratey of footballers Rustu in goal and a tidy team captained by Argentinean Delgado and Brazilian striker Bobo on as a sub.

The Black Eagles won 1-0 (they lost the away leg 4-1 and are out) but that hardly mattered. My sister, an Istanbul resident who got the tickets and took us, asked why Newcastle fans didn't support their team like that and I could barely begin to list the reasons. Apart from anything, joy and honour are now alien concepts to us. Perhaps when the present nightmare is over and we are all on the same side again....

...... hang on someone is coming.

Well the Bunnymen finished with the song Ocean Rain and we all cried with happiness.

Chapter 74

October 2008

Bragging Rights

So we woke up on the 26th of October the day after Newcastle lost at sunderland and the world hadn't actually ended after all.
We hadn't all had to commit an honourable suicide, throwing ourselves, sobbing, into the Tyne.
No one came for us to order a barefoot walk through the streets, filthy and shamed.

We just woke up a bit pissed off.

I was surprised; we hadn't had our airport confiscated, our cathedral knocked down and all our best pubs closed. Last Shadow Puppets, Rancid, Kings of Leon, Flogging Molly, Slipknot, Aggrolites and the Killers hadn't all moved their gigs to sunderland. Yes, Oasis are doing charity work down there but how many times have they played Newcastle? Seven if you include that time they had to cut the show short after that daft mackem punched Noel at the Riverside.
No complaints about the match either; they probably shaded it. Fine. But seriously, beating Newcastle this season then showing off about it is like jumping Joe Calzaghe when he's in hospital having his appendix out and then claiming to be Light Heavyweight Champion of the World – you're fucking well not. Bragging rights the local press claim they get, and what does that involve? Making sure the whole country knows that after something like 47 years they finally beat us at home in a top flight game? They want to draw that to people's attention, do they? While claiming that all that time they were at least our equals? Excellent, I'm right up for that.
The problem is people watching that game outside the region will mostly have been thinking, "Look at all that litter blowing across the pitch. Scruffy bastards

– do they live in a rubbish dump?" Yes they do and don't mock the carrier bags, that's designer luggage down there.

A shift in the balance of power possibly? Well, when we've been in Division Three, when we've been officially the worst team in the world in the same season they qualify for The Champions League and when they've played over a hundred games in Europe and gone eight years unbeaten against us, maybe. Until then go back to your filthy houses and see if you can stop interfering with the dog long enough to work out how to spell class or dignity.

All season we have been told by the country's foremost chinscratchers that sunderland, unlike Newcastle, have been doing things right. Yet if we gave Tottenham the fat end of £40 million for a load of players they didn't want, bought Diouf, spent £8 million on Anton Ferdinand and allowed our fans to invade the pitch in their hundreds, that would presumably be reported as being very bad. Fortunately they haven't scored many goals against us at home but every time they have done so (including that time they celebrated a late Kevin Kyle goal for ages not knowing, as we did, that the goal had been disallowed) there has been a pitch invasion and have they ever been punished at all?

In the darkest of moments before this game I feared how I would cope with losing at sunderland. I had a back-up article half planned about a recent trip (from our airport) to see Roma play at home to Inter (they lost 0-4 and the 15 year old kids in front of us never stopped smoking spliffs – Wifey and I were soooo mellow after, that we sat outside a bar drinking and smiling at the beautiful Roman night until way past our normal bed time) but this is really easy. I'm alright with it. I long since stopped buying local papers so the deluded crowing of cross-eyed ding-bats hasn't entered my life and the stupid bastards think that the season is over and that all their dreams have come true – meanwhile they have just lost their third game in a row

Of more interest to us is all the players we had injured are coming back, the club might be on the brink of new ownership and in recent weeks Joe Kinnear has galvanised team and fans in difficult circumstances. None of that has got anything to do with the points we didn't get at sunderland.

The noticeable thing is how everything they do has to be measured by what we do and they seem oblivious to how pathetic that makes them look. Unless something mad happens I doubt we'll need to mention them until the game at our place. Stupid fuckers.

Chapter 75

October 2008

Russell Brand, Jonathan Ross and Joey Barton

Newcastle played West Brom while the world was awash with outrage. Russell Brand and Jonathan Ross were being vilified for a hoax call from a Radio 2 show to actor Andrew Sachs. Barton, while warming up as a sub at sunderland, got in a debate with some of the home fans.

In the immediate aftermath of the recent game at sunderland a charming young lady from *The Sunday Sun* asked me for a quote regarding Joey Barton kissing his badge. I was, understandably, in something of a bad mood so didn't think to pass the request on to the new Toon Politburo who are actually responsible for telling the world what we all think. "Joey is our boy. As long as he stands by us, we will stand by him," said I and they printed it. What they didn't print, presumably down to space, was the next bit I gave them; "and everyone else can go to hell." I mention it now not just because I hate being edited but because it is the important side of the Barton debate nobody seems to want to talk about. Joey is our player, for us to deal with.

The priorities of the anti-Barton lynch mob and those of Newcastle fans are not the same: for a start, not upsetting the delicate sensibilities of squealing gibbons in red and white shirts isn't very high on the list of things we want him to care about.

Joe Kinnear was asked if it was wise to play Barton at sunderland when the only mistake he made was not to start with him as captain. Joe, bless his heart, seems to like telling the press to "fuck off!" – making Barton captain would be sticking his fingers up and farting in their faces at the same time. The timing of Barton's return could not have been better because any Newcastle fan feeling the misguided urge to boo him would put themselves on the side of sunderland

supporters and sometimes in life it really is "whose side are you on?"
The press have been falling over themselves to demonise Barton and I'm sick
and bored of it and I won't be told what to think by bastards, people who
manufacture outrage, liars and hypocrites. How many of the papers witch
hunting Joey printed disgusting lies about the parents of Madeleine McCann –
and then they have the fucking nerve to moralise at us – fuck them. But they
don't stop; scapegoats are not allowed to defend themselves from a press-led
hate mob – witness Barton laughing off a pathetic dive by Nasri of Arsenal after
a fair challenge being reported as him smiling smugly after a foul. It seems all
you can do is keep your head down and wait for some other poor mug to incur
the wrath of people looking to scream "disgrace!"

How Joey Barton must have loved Russell Brand and Jonathan Ross taking on
the role of baby-peeling, granny murdering, goat molesters or whatever it is that
the *Daily Mail* think is going to end the fucking world this week.

This is from BBC Radio Ulster:

Noel Gallagher said he was "outraged" that columnists in the press had "dictated
the tone and are telling people how to behave. It's so typical of the English in
general - 10,000 people get outraged, but only five days after it has happened.
You know what? There's now a massive divide. Them and us," he added.

As the complaints about Ross and Brand hit 30,000 and phone-ins went into
their third day of asking people how outraged they were you couldn't help but
think: five million dead in the Congo, the world on the edge of financial
Armageddon and this is what people are up in arms about? People are idiots.

For a start anyone who ever says, "If I did that at work, I'd get the sack" when
being outraged by anything are hoisting a little flag with a downward pointing
arrow and the word "tosser" written on it.

It is Joey Barton's job to be aggressive. It is Russell Brand's job to be silly and
he is very good at it. In this case he was admittedly too silly but that was still his
job. It's probably not your job to be silly, much like if you said, "If I went to work
and started punching people in the face, I'd get the sack" – that's because you are
not Ricky Hatton. "If I turned up for work in leather chaps with my arse exposed
and started dancing to techno music in a cage, I'd get the sack" – that's because
you are probably not a dancer in a San Francisco nightclub. "If I turned up for
work and blew the building up, I'd get the sack" – that's because you are

probably not a demolition expert. "If I turned up for work and started telling people to 'Fuck Off', I'd get the sack" – that's because you are not me – now be a good chap and fuck off!

"But I'm a licence payer…." yeah and so am I and I could just about stomach the BBC paying Eamonn Holmes because *The Russell Brand Show* was the funniest thing that has ever been on the radio and now thanks to the bellyaching of sheep a programme that they never listened to isn't on anymore. Trust me, there has been something *Daily Mail* readers would have hated on that show every week for two years. And what do they come after next, *Mock The Week*? *Never Mind The Buzzcocks*? Russell Brand is so articulate and bedazzlingly funny that his Guardian articles are essential reading on a Saturday despite the fact that said paper is still employing mackem witch Louise Taylor to spit poison at all things Newcastle on a daily basis.

Anyway, the West Brom game happened amidst all this rhubarb and Joey Barton was man of the match. Captain in all but armband, Barton dominated the first half, encouraging his team mates and at the hub of some of the best passing we have seen from our lot in weeks. Twinkle-toed Shola Ameobi was brought down in the area, Barton took the ball and with big brass balls coated in molten steel, told regular penalty taker Oba Martins that all was in hand, and confidently put us 1-0 up after 9 minutes.

After 42 minutes of confident passing and moving Newcastle went 2-0 up, Beye crossed and Martins, despite being off balance, jumped to head in off a defender's leg.

Lots of reasons have been put forward for our awful form going up to this game – mostly along the lines of we are all self-deluded idiots finally getting our come-uppance, the manager's a foul mouthed fool and all the players are rubbish, especially compared to lovely sunderland. Not much mention of a small squad having nine first choice players missing.

Beye, Enrique, Guthrie, Barton, Gutiérrez, Martins and Shola for various reasons haven't seen a lot of action this season and it is fantastic to have them back but between half-time and about 55 minutes they all seemed to run out of gas, which made for a very long and nervous second half. Fortunately West Brom were content to weave patterns with the ball rather than try to put it in our net and we had to hand them a goal on a plate with Ishmael Miller going round Given to give us all the heebie-jeebies.

We would never have held out against a half decent side – Barton made a final burst from deep to support Duff and was ignored and was out on his feet. Martins seemed to resent even token gestures of tracking back and Geremi coming on as a sub didn't give us much more than another player to lump the ball clear.

When four minutes came up on the board for injury time, there was a 40,000 person groan, all the clocks and watches in the place were broken and another cruel late goal seemed inevitable.

Credit to those still standing that it didn't happen and the cheer at the end was the only sound louder in the second half than the cheer for Barton being given man of the match.

I also told the lass from the paper, "Joey is going to be chased by shit stirrers all his life – fuck 'em." I didn't expect her to use that despite it being the fundamental point – he and us will continue to be treated unfairly as will Brand and Ross (and now Jeremy Clarkson) but as long as we all remember whose side we are on…..

This was our first win in six games. It was followed by a 2-0 win over Aston Villa with two goals from Obafemi Martins.

Chapter 76

December 2008

Who Are You Calling Racist?

One would think *The Guardian* newspaper a publication the least likely to single out a minority group for insult. Perpetuating unfair and inaccurate stereotypes and using hurtful and offensive language against a group of people offered no chance to defend themselves? Surely not – yet Louise Taylor within her match report from The Riverside once again chose to abuse her position by stating that some Newcastle fans were "morons" with "the fleeting whiff of Islamophobia" when singing "he's got a bomb, Mido" at the Egyptian Middlesbrough striker.

Many of you will have been bored and irritated by this piffle last season when Ms Taylor succeeded in whipping up quite the little witch hunt. When the truth is that the only people insulted during this pathetic non-story were the fans of Newcastle United.

It had been pointed out in various places before the Newcastle game at Middlesbrough last season that Mido bears a striking resemblance to shoe-bomber Richard Reid and this was considered funny or satirical. Some Newcastle fans point this out and we are racist. It is apparently laughable that Newcastle fans might read or watch topical quiz shows – presumably we are all too busy beating our whippet-wives with a coal allotment or something.

Regrettably some of the older members of the tribe have seen real racism from Newcastle supporters, so we know what it looks like, and this aint it. They used to sell National Front papers outside St James's Park in the '80s and the club did nothing about it, so some fans took it upon themselves to spit in these people's faces and threaten them until they went away.

We fought this war and we won it on our own so don't you dare call us racist. Can I vouch for the character of every Newcastle fan at The Riverside, can I speak for over three thousand individuals? No, of course not – but here is the vital point – neither can anybody else.

You come to my house and call me racist or Islamophobic and I'll bash you to death with half a dozen Asian Dub Foundation CDs, you call me a racist in print and I'll sue you for defamation of character. How many mosques have you been to this year Taylor? I've (respectfully) been to half a dozen, you can't beat me on this argument because I'm violently anti-racist, so where does that leave you? In the fucking wrong, that's where because the counter case is that ALL look-a-like comparisons, ever, are racist.

Louise Taylor throws accusations about with unacceptable abandon – happy to have the word racist in a sentence also home to the words Newcastle and United for what can only be viewed as malicious intent. Witness the reporting of Joey Barton's spat with Aston Villa's Gabby Agbonlahor: Barton was accused of saying something racist, nothing came of it, people asked why and Agbonlahor was praised for letting it go. A lip reader was employed by one of those crap lad's magazines and Barton seemed to say, after an Agbonlahor foul, "What the fuck was that, you fucking wanker?" I've tried really hard to find something pertinent to the Villa player's colour in there and there's nothing – the story ran in *The Guardian* for three days and any likelihood of Barton's innocence was never mentioned.

One of the many problems we have got with our club being half-run on a day to day basis by people who don't want to be here is that nobody gives a crap about our players or fans being treated in such as shabby way. Would former chairman (and lawyer) Chris Mort have stood for Barton being given a six match ban for a crime that, not only didn't happen during an actual match, but was a crime he'd already been punished for, twice. For the most part lawyers should stay out of football but the threat of them should make people act fairly – in the present climate we are being openly accused of things that are offensive to us.

And where is our new supporters group during this latest round of media lies: surely if it has a point, if it's going to be worthwhile having an organised voice, they should be issuing very strongly worded statements and be getting lawyers onto *The Guardian*. A letter with the word "defamation" in near "millions of pounds" brings this vendetta to an end.

Mido looks like Richard Reid and the idea that he has a bomb about his person like that character on *The Muppet Show* who used to blow himself up every week is funny. What the hell has that got to do with his colour or his faith? We used to sing "fat Eddie Murphy", at Jimmy Floyd Hasselbaink – no one thought that was racist.

What's the difference, except for the absence of evil and deliberate misinterpretation?

I won't be bullied and brought to heel by a hysterical media's kangaroo court.

The FA and Middlesbrough said they were disappointed that the two lads lifted by the cops didn't get banning orders. I don't know the gentlemen in question and wouldn't presume to guess their intentions or what happened in their case (just as I would be unwise and wrong to suggest regular accusations of Islamaphobia would put off wealthy Arab investors) but I was disappointed the case wasn't thrown out for being trumped-up bullshit.

The two people lifted were found guilty. Make of that what you will. The match finished 0-0.

Chapter 77

January 2009

Stupid Useless Fucking Bastards

On the 28th of December Mike Ashley took NUFC off the market. Newcastle's march towards relegation was interrupted by getting knocked out of the FA Cup by Hull.

Over the years you get to recognise patterns in your own behaviour and how the day progresses the morning after getting dumped out of a cup here in Newcastle becomes as traditional as The Changing of the Guard; alarm clock goes off like a malicious little twat. Wake up in a foul mood before you can remember why. Remember why. Pull the duvet over your head in the stoic and determined belief that the world and everyone in it can fuck off. Already late for work you have to come to terms with the fact that no one is going to believe that you suddenly and convincingly fell ill straight after a match that everyone at work knows you were going to. Not going will be a sign of weakness and laying about feeling sorry for yourself never got Newcastle United reinstated into any competition. You hope a mouthful of strong mints and flippancy will mask the stink of stale beer and crushed hope and the only way to get through the day is powerful coffee, fatty foods and to mentally torture anyone who so much as looks at you funny. The phrase "stupid useless fucking bastards" rolls around behind your grinding teeth and it applies to your team, the match officials, work mates…. people.
Mostly, however, it applies to yourself and the fools like you who dared to think a cup run might be on.
"Stupid useless fucking bastards!"
Yes we know how this day goes, we've been living days just like it for years.
Odd then that I'm halfway to work, clear of head when the man on Radio Newcastle says something along the lines of, "Another year without a trophy for

Newcastle after a 1-0 defeat to Hull City at St James' Park last night."
I laughed out loud, firstly (and worryingly) I had forgotten that I had even been
to a game last night but more because…. well, who in their right mind thought
we were going to win the FA Cup this season? You might as well say, "Defeat
last night means that Newcastle will now be unable to occupy the Gaza Strip."
Oh aye – we expect success here in Newcastle alright.
Yes, we had more than enough chances to win, yes, we would have been at home
to Millwall in the next round with every chance of getting to the fifth round and
yes, teams as crappy as Cardiff and Portsmouth got to the final last year. But we
all know that this present Newcastle team would have come up against a good
side with even more of our players injured and been spanked stupid. Better off
out of it before we got a repeat of that Birmingham FA Cup game where we
conceded five.
Check out our famous "unreasonable expectations."
Instead of a pointless and depressing trudge towards humiliation and
disappointment we can have at least two weekends blissfully free of Newcastle
United and all the stupid useless fucking bastards who come with it.
A friend e-mailed to complain that the Furious website hadn't been updated
since early December – the same lad asked if I had had a good Christmas/ New
Year – yes I had a brilliant time thank you and don't think those two things aren't
related. The absence of Newcastle United from my thinking was a considerable
plus when it came to my mental well being and I resent the re-imposition.
How can anyone expect to make sense of the present situation, in fact when
anybody starts to explain what they think is going on at St James' Park this
season I mentally switch off because it can only be speculation and I'm bored to
death with speculation.
If Mike Ashley wants us all to "move forward together" then he needs about £20
million worth of peace offerings on the table, which doesn't look like happening.
And Joe Kinnear is clearly a fucking ding-bat.
Don't get me wrong, I'm developing quite an affection for Joe and his getting in
Phil Brown's smug face at this game only enhanced that feeling but does he ever
say anything that he doesn't entirely contradict later? "My agent informed
me…" – "I've never had an agent". In a recent press conference he named a
couple of players he wanted, then wouldn't name another because the deal wasn't
done yet; when at the time of writing no deals had been bloody done. He said no

one would be leaving before nipping off to pack Geremi's suitcase. I'm sure Joe is a warm and loving husband but if he carries on like this at home he must be a fucking nightmare; "Mrs Kinnear, I should very much like peas with my fish and chips tonight. Peas! Peas! What the fuck are you doing giving me peas, I've never eaten peas in my life because I am violently allergic to them. I would go into anaphylactic shock if I so much as looked at a fucking pea.... oh are these the peas? Lovely."

Giving Shola Ameobi a new contract? Apart from the fact that the lad is no less erratic and annoying than he was eight years ago he's now injured all the time as well. Who was it who said, "Never in the field of human conflict have so many football fans been irritated by one man for so bloody long. Except for Alan Green, obviously." Yes, it was me.

This game came shortly after the best run of form of the season as mad Joe Kinnear seemed to be making progress. The draw at Boro was after a creditable draw at Chelsea. Only an injury time equaliser from former Newcastle player Abdoulaye Faye stopped us beating Stoke. We won 3-0 at Portsmouth and a 90th minute goal from Damien Duff saw off Spurs and put us 12th in the League. But the wind was taken out our sails with another loss at Wigan where Emile Heskey struggled from the halfway line with Sebastian Bassong pulling his shirt only to run out of strength an inch into the penalty area (by which time Bassong had stopped pulling his shirt) thus guaranteeing not only a penalty but Bassong's sending off. A humbling 1-5 defeat at home to Liverpool followed two days later.

Chapter 78

January to April 2009

You Don't Have To Read This Bit

Misfortune and incompetence continued to pile up, flickering embers of hope were stamped out. The curse of the ex-player took a new twist as Craig Bellamy scored for two different teams against us in January as he moved from West Ham to Manchester City in a month that saw a single point added to our total.

During the time he was a Newcastle player, Charles N'Zogbia, constantly expressed his ambition to play for Arsenal. He was sold to Wigan in a deal that brought Ryan Taylor the other way. Manchester City had tried and failed to get goalkeeper Gianluigi Buffon from Juventus despite offering a huge transfer fee. Mark Hughes claims Sir Bobby Robson advised him that Shay Given would be better and cheaper. Despite Man City having bundles of cash to waste and Newcastle having little to gain from Given's sale the negotiations, as I understand them, went something like this:

Man City: We'll give you £6 million for Given.

NUFC: No.

MC: We'll give you £6 million for Given.

NUFC: That's not enough.

MC: We'll give you £6 million for Given.

NUFC: £10 million.

MC: We'll give you £6 million for Given.

NUFC: £8 million.

MC: We'll give you £6 million for Given.

NUFC: Throw in Michael Johnson: he's injured and he's never going to get in your team of international superstars anyway?

MC: We'll give you £6 million for Given.

Shay Given joined Man City for £6 million.

We brought in Peter Lovenkrands and Kevin Nolan.
Shola Ameobi scored a penalty in a 1-1 draw with sunderland. Joe Kinnear was taken into hospital with chest pains on the 7th of February and his team responded with a 3-2 win at West Brom. Chris Hughton was put in charge of minding the shop until Kinnear recovered from his heart surgery. Newcastle failed to win any of the next ten games.
On the first of April Alan Shearer came in as manager, bringing Ian Dowie as his assistant. Dennis Wise resigned from his job as director of football.

I could go into more detail but I doubt you, dear reader, want to read it and it would be disingenuous for me to attempt to catch the mood on Tyneside because I wasn't even in the country. In fact when I got a text saying Shearer was in charge I assumed it was a sick and unfunny April Fools joke.
Wifey and I were in Wellington in New Zealand when we finally bothered to check our emails and nufc.com. New Zealand is spectacular – ideally Kaikoura is on the lookout for someone to set up a South Island NUFC supporters' club but I doubt it because the whole country seems to be afflicted with a rugby fixation. We did however see Andy Carroll's first Newcastle goal in a bar in Palmerston after a long Sunday evening drive back up through the North Island.
So rather than a painstaking autopsy of Newcastle's descent to 18th place I could tell you at length about the quality of the beer, wine, food and people of one of the world's most beautiful countries. But I'm not going to do that either. As they say in New Zealand (to everything) "Awesome".

We were back for the final five games – three of which, crucially, were at home: the first of them was Portsmouth on a Monday night. Does anybody at The Premier League even pretend not to be taking the piss out of fans any more?

Experts have predicted that this swine-flu thing will kill nine million people and the first cases have already broken out in the UK. All across the world impotent politicians, who have been busy throwing around billions of pounds of non-existent money failing to prop up our dis-proven notion of capitalism, have a plague to deal with. At the same time the bees that pollinate a third of our crops are dying out because the planet's eco-systems are collapsing; five sub-species

of tiger are already extinct along with all manner of frogs, birds and minor celebrities.
Is this what the end of the world feels like?

As we stamped, in the dark and through the rain, up to The Church Of Saint James, fevered with nerves and a grim determination not to think the unthinkable (yet), you could feel the foreboding. For Newcastle United this season The Footballing Gods have been maniacal skull-faced jesters throwing loaded dice and cackling at us. How could we expect that to change with a team that looked like it was picked on salary and reputation ahead of form?
The following night after (what seemed like) only two hundred lads but every Geordie lass capable of holding a drink, had watched Pink at The Arena skipping around an insane carnival set with clowns and harlequins singing, "This used to be a fun house. But now it's full of evil clowns" – I walked through the worsening rain past our be-shadowed football ground and thought, "We have our metaphor".
Opera singer Graeme Danby employed for his muscular voice and ability to put some solid oak in our hearts, bestrode the field crazed and roaring. Flags were waved, individual cards were held up in unison to make walls of black and white as we shouted and sang in an effort to crush Portsmouth before a ball was kicked.
Pompey brought 300 – yes the FA and Setanta have shown a vicious, almost criminal, disregard for them by moving the game to a Monday night - but here is a message to all those Premiership fans thinking they will laugh at the back of us. Except for the top four teams, who else is going to buy all your overpriced tickets when it's wet and midweek?
It was an awesome display of raw passion. Tinged with a desperate, urgent and awful need.
But this season isn't about passion. This season passion and beauty bounce off walls of enemy castles like rubber arrows because from fifth place down it's all about organized systems, smothering, closing down and shape. Portsmouth's shape may have been ugly with Peter Crouch at its point but it was maintained and disciplined while we looked like a mess. When Enrique's hamstring twanged him out of the game and Duff went to left back that mess got messier.

"Shearer's got nothing to lose," has been the mantra of the clueless in recent weeks. Oh but he has and he's losing it by the second because at this stage of proceedings a manager has only made a right decision if his team wins, so the gamble of playing three up top failed. Oba Martins and Viduka are clearly not fit but our manager knows all about that from his last two seasons as a player so can expect a shift out of both but our problem is Owen, Shearer's mate. What does Owen give us if he's not scoring goals? In this game, not much. And how likely is he to score a goal standing out on the wing? Not very. And what does Alan Smith actually do anymore? Kick people and complain, is that Everton on the phone or are those bells ringing just in our heads?

The ongoing frustration that is Nicky Butt was underlined when three times in the opening ten minutes he passed a ball quickly off with his first touch – to nobody. But then spent an hour turning up with a brilliant tackle here, a smart pass there, a calm presence, grim professionalism and then there was our complete inability to even get the ball after he went off.

Butt was replaced by Gutiérrez who looked like he had the nerve, will and ability to make something happen but we seemed reluctant to let him have the ball. Our midfield that has all too often undermined our decent defenders also lacks the speed of foot and brain to get the ball to players who can do damage. We had chances; a low Duff shot and Martins launching for the roof from eight yards out in the first half and Viduka and Owen failing to seriously trouble David James when well placed in the second. Carroll on for Viduka looped a header just over but, on the plus side, the expected sucker punch from them, a header, hit the post.

A point – a single point from a must-win game.

It's been a while and many fans won't or couldn't be expected remember this situation but down the bottom of the table must-win games come round every couple of weeks. That point takes us above Boro and within reach of Hull so we ain't dead yet.

And the swine flu? Forgive my flippancy but two people in Falkirk having a bit of a cough is hardly an epidemic now, is it? In three weeks time Newcastle could be relegated and/or half the world could be dead. Sleep well.

The next game was a 3-0 loss at Liverpool where Joey Barton was sent off and then we beat Middlesbrough 3-1 to make sure that if we went down they were *coming with us. But in 17th place our destiny was now back in our own hands. At the time of going to press, 8,999,998 potential swine flu victims have gone on to worry about something else.*

Chapter 79

May 2009

The Goal That Relegated Newcastle United

On top of all the other mental torments suffered this season *The Mag* end of campaign poll made me feel like I was 16 and sitting CSE Physics again. In front of me a page of questions that I hadn't a clue how to answer; "Player of the Season", "Most Improved Player", "Goal of the Season" ?? Goal, Goal Goal – if you keep saying the word it makes no sense, Goal, it's just a noise - Goal. gOal. *Gooowwl* Ahhhh!

Did we score any goals? I can't remember any. Calm down, I can do this. We scored over 40 but I can't remember ….Oh hang on, Duff against Spurs in the last minute, Martins against Boro, Martins against Man U. Put one of them down as the answer and wait for the end of season DVD to remind myself of the others. What do you mean there is no end of season DVD, why ever not?

Except that these goals and all others are not the right answer, the Newcastle United goal of the season came in the game at home to Fulham. A single goal, a defining second, a goal that summed up Newcastle United in 2009; trailing 1-0 after the latest misunderstanding between Taylor and Bassong and desperate for an equaliser, attacking the Gallowgate in the second half. A corner swings in and Viduka meets it at the near post to head smartly into the Fulham net. An explosion of relief and joy snapped off before it could draw a second breath. Disallowed (as it turns out) for nothing at all. There are moments in football that are less memories and more brain scars, you can recall them with a horrible raw clarity; An offside Kevin Phillips running clear to score at sunderland, Collymore celebrating Liverpool's fourth in the first 4-3 at Anfield, Cantona, Fenton, Poyet at Wembley and Gascoigne sliding in and just missing the ball for England against the Germans in the semi-final of Euro 96 – (see it again and you still think he's going to get it) – this goal joined them. A horrible ghost goal that will remind us of wasted hope and cruel misfortune in a crappy season where we fell for the want of a single point.

The tired calls for technology and video replay appeals do nothing but mock our self-inflicted plight. Technology promises much but the hidden complications are more trouble than the problems themselves. Dishwashers? Turns out they ruin your glassware. Games consoles? Yes I can finally be Wolverine, Vin Diesel or a pirate but I'm supposed to be working on a book. I haven't showered, been outside or spoken to anybody since the last day of the season because I've been playing *The Punisher* and can't stop shooting people in the face and throwing their bodies out of windows.

iPods? 30,000 songs in your pocket but iTunes marches into your computer like the Wehrmacht up the Champs Elysees and starts bossing you about, "click here", "download this", "register these" "wait for five hours while I bum rape all your other music files", "if you like that song, why not click here to be told what other songs you will like?" Don't tell me what music to listen to you jumped up little fucking tape recorder and I won't "register now" you bossy shithouse bastard.

On the way up to the Fulham game we were discussing the vital need for the invention of the hover-trouser. High specification pantaloons that whisk you along six-inches above the ground to save a chap or chapess the tiresome business of walking. You could program your hover-trousers in the morning before you go out and never be late for anything again and they could fly you home even if you have passed out. Brilliant. Brilliant except that Apple will invent the iTrouser and the bloody things would be impossible to get off and they would constantly be flying you off to places you don't want to go to and ordering fucking Coldplay downloads. In five years time they would still be flying us all up to the match because we can't work out how to cancel our season tickets. People will be clinging to the bar, trying to order a pint but the iTrousers won't be denied and they will literally drag you by the legs up Gallowgate, past folk crying and grasping desperately at lampposts. It gets worse when you get to the ground because the club has installed The Windows Turnstile 2014 which is incompatible with iTrousers which means thousands of us will be screaming "Reboot Reboot!" as our iTrousers relentlessly pound us against unopening gates. And that's how it ends for us if we trust technology to solve our problems; our lifeless corpses hanging out of soiled electro-pants being dragged round places we used to enjoy going to before the world ended – a bit like now really. What else can I moan about to avoid thinking about this game? Ah the new kit. It's rubbish. Why would you buy one, when it's not even finished – are adidas taking the fucking piss or what? Did the designer just give up when he got to doing the back and leave it: "It's got stripes on it, daft Geordies will buy anything with black and white stripes on it, anyone fancy a pint?" You'd think it would look better with a name and number on the back but it doesn't, it looks worse, the same crappy font as this season only inverted – look at some of the snazzy writing and numbers on the backs of the shirts in Spain, then look at ours. It's the worst home kit we have ever had, recall them all and start again, you idle useless fuckers.

Speaking of useless fuckers: the Fulham match; the most notable thing apart from our non-goal was the last five minutes when the sky went black and the wind turned and threw freezing rain from Gallowgate to Leazes in the face of our final attacks. It was hard enough what with being down to ten men after Bassong was sent off after what looked like a tangle of legs. At one point a ball going out for a Newcastle corner appeared to be blown back for a throw in. It was like the footballing gods were making damn sure we didn't score and that we all suffered while failing to do so. Yet still there was a chance with Butt (who had been terrible all game) nearly scoring only for Schwarzer to dive full length to turn it away. This season has obviously not been one you would choose to remember but moments like these are horribly unforgettable.

Chapter 80

June 2009

Right, Can Everybody Just Fuck Right Off!

That went well then.

The post-Villa Sunday evening "aw fuck it, no more than we deserved, let's get drunker" was replaced by a Bank Holiday Monday morning of cold realisation that this relegation shit is a humiliation we are going to have to live with for some time. Sky Sports News showing Phil Brown's elephant's knacker-bag face didn't help but their disappointment that we weren't all up the ground wailing and complaining definitely did. For once even our dumbest fans weren't prepared to jump through hoops to make us all look like knuckleheads and long may it continue. About as much chance as a quick sale of the club and us turning up for next season with our shorts on the right way round in reality, but such is life.

The plan, at least on my behalf, had been for us to get enough points to stay up and then tell the Premier League and everybody in it to fuck off anyway. To go away and play in The Championship, or Scotland, or the Italian League just because we wanted to, not because we have to.

Now saying The Premiership is an over-hyped sack of shit just sounds like sour grapes, but bollocks to what it sounds like because it's true. The Premiership is an over-hyped sack of shit; riddled with cheats and liars, bastards and cowards, it's boring and it's been missing a strong Newcastle United breaking up the top four for five years. Now it's missing any kind of Newcastle United which many seem to think is hilarious, which is fine, we can take it. You all get on with your Super Sunday Best League in the World without us, who's on, Burnley v Wigan, Bolton v Fulham, Stoke v Blackburn, Aston Fucking Villa against sodding Everton? Sounds a treat, especially that last one. If the subject of Newcastle

United comes up on a national radio station nobody from the North East can get on for Everton and Villa fans ringing up to tell everybody what a big club we're not. Villa fans had banners taking the piss out of us on the last day of the season and Everton fans reportedly sang "Cheer up Alan Shearer" at the Cup Final. Can you imagine ringing up a radio station with an opinion about either of these clubs? Can you imagine making a banner slagging off Villa or even sparing a thought for fucking Everton at any game, never mind a Cup Final? If we're not all we're cracked up to be how come you thimble-dicked dum-dums even give a shit, huh?

What have these clubs got in common, a lack of identity that's what; Villa are from Birmingham but don't like Birmingham, Everton are from Liverpool but don't like Liverpool. We have an affinity with Newcastle, the place, the word, the people. If a contestant turns up on a game show from Newcastle we naturally side with them, they showed an otter swimming at night under the bridges on the Tyne on *Springwatch* and we look at the beauty of the scene with unflinching pride. We know who we are and if that is a bunch of drunken gobshites from time to time, fair enough but here's another thing – fuck you!

Our friends from sunderland are a different matter – we know how they operate; crawling out from under their rocks in their filthy underpants and tatty shirts to gloat. Fine, we have been giving it out non-stop for 15 years, now we have to take it like grown ups. I did take issue with a mackem who said us going down was revenge for '97 when they and Boro were relegated and we qualified for The Champions League, pointing out that they hadn't just won 5-0 and finished second in the League and were only really gloating about being slightly less shit than us and Hull. Not quite the same – the fact that he didn't seem to get it tells you all you need to know. We also know that the rat faced, inbred pigfuckers eat their own shit and a good proportion of them will get overexcited and spend their benefit on a dog that bites their children's faces off.

Truth is the piss-taking is mild compared to the shit we give ourselves, what really burns is the conceited way some people say, "If they had stuck with Sam Allardyce they wouldn't have got relegated this season." No, we would have got relegated the season before and even if we didn't, what was the likelihood of that hippo-headed snake-oil salesman bullshitting his way through another year and a half up here?

I would love to have watched the Champions League final with Allardyce, Tony Pulis, and Gary Megson as Barcelona passed Manchester United to death. That, you fuckers, is how to play football, now take your "Best League in the World" and stick it up your arses.

Chapter 81

2008/09 postscript – A Distorted View

The traditional reason for a team getting relegated is them being more rubbish at football than a significant number of other teams they share the same division with. Ignoring financial irregularities and points docked for not turning up at Blackburn, because a couple of your team have got a tummy upset, relegated teams lack sufficient quality players.

Newcastle got relegated in 2009 with a squad chocked to overflowing with proven international footballers, so how the hell did they end up in the Championship?

Because we only went down by a point we could blame either A): Selling Abdoulaye Faye to Stoke who scored home and away for Tony Pulis' red and white monsters. Bringing in Dennis Wise to help Keegan with player recruitment might have seemed like a good idea (Wise brought in Nile Ranger for example) but we have always hated Wise and he wasn't welcome here; not because he is a Londoner but because he is a twat (in my humble opinion), his presence was poisonous. Selling James Milner was idiotic for the money we got for him. Not replacing Keegan with an adequate coach in the mistaken belief that a new owner would be along in a minute who could then hire his own choice of manager. Blackburn at home: Chris Samba was so far offside for the first Blackburn goal he was nearly in the fucking crowd. Making Joe Kinnear manager; not because he was a particularly bad coach but because he physically wasn't up to it, not many people remember that by the turn of the year Joe had turned things round to the point that we were up to 11th in the League. Home to Man City Habib Beye was incorrectly sent off in the 12th minute (the red card was later rescinded – which was of little use on the night), we conceded a late equaliser in a 2-2 draw. Home to Wigan and Habib Beye headed out a ball that was going straight to Shay Given and Titus bloody Bramble scored another late equaliser from the resulting corner. In the same game a Lee Cattermole "tackle" put Joey Barton out for five months. When Joe Kinnear fell ill we waited for him to spring from his hospital bed rather than getting in another manager. We waited five games to appoint a new manager in which time we got two points. Alan Shearer came in as coach and made all the same mistakes his predecessors had, most notably thinking that Michael Owen would score the goals that would save us. Owen didn't score a single goal in seven games under Shearer. The goal we had incorrectly disallowed at home to Fulham. At various points we had up to nine first teamers injured and rarely had anything close to a fully fit squad all season. Despite this we let Shay Given and Charles N'Zogbia leave in the January. A lack of communication, leadership or competence from the boardroom meant a state of panic and confusion was allowed to fester from August until May.

Or B): Newcastle fans are all deluded fools, it's their own fault they got relegated.

And the nation voted for B.

Player of the Season: Sebastien Bassong.

Goal of the Season: Mark Viduka's ghost goal against Fulham.

Chapter 82

August 2009

What Are We Fighting For?

Facing up to life in The Championship.

People ask us and we ask each other, "So what do you reckon then?" About what? There is nothing to reckon on or with. Newcastle United has been a ghost ship drifting in a midnight fog all summer long. The new season has been an immovable iceberg looming up at us, now we have crashed into it and Admiral Mike Ashley still seems to be sitting under a table with his head in a bucket. Reports of David O'Leary trying on captain's hats isn't going to enliven anybody. The news that Obafemi Martins was seen leaping overboard and swimming towards Germany, although predictable and disappointing, was at least a sign of life. So many of us have grown so numb that bad news is like self-harming; welcome, in that at least we can feel something. Splash! There goes Bassong on the cheap and Beye going to Villa feels like good news because at least he didn't go to fucking Hull.

Wednesday 29th of July, an impressive gathering of Leeds fans sang "Your support is fucking shit" at those of us in St James's Park for a pre-season friendly and we didn't respond. This may be because looking at Leeds feels unnervingly as though a mirror from our future may have opened before our eyes and cold dead arms are reaching out to pull us in by the face or, it may be that confused, bewildered and betrayed we don't know who we should be fighting or what we would be fighting for. If it wasn't for the continued sniping and spiteful bile being spat at us every time I make the mistake of tuning into Talksport Radio I'd think Newcastle United had ceased to exist.

"I distinctly remember being at St James' Park on Boxing Day 1986 in a crowd of 7,000 Everton fans with only 18,000 in the ground," said one caller who had rung up, supposedly, to talk about The Toffees selling Joleon Lescott to Manchester City. I know I shouldn't have let such a deluded, cretinous tosspot get to me but I looked it up; 35,079, and can anyone remember Everton ever bringing 7,000?

It seems that we are at the whim of sentimental revisionists – "the decline of Newcastle United began with the sacking of Sir Bobby Robson" – is a very neat and tidy way of paying tribute to a grand old fellow as well as sticking the knife into us again as being the masters of our own destruction. Shame it's not true but then pissing in the wind seems to be my allotted vocation.

The media get blasted by other teams' fans for covering us at all but everything to do with us is wrong so we are a journalist's dream: where there should be dramatic action there is nothing, yet the mundane can be alarming even on a personal level; last year when I went to the ground simply to renew my season ticket Sir Bobby blew up the brewery. No honestly he did, it was a Sunday morning and he said it wasn't as loud as he expected – it was deafening and terrifying, car alarms went off for miles and people were running away from the cloud of 9/11 style dust. This year I was in the box office (breaking my vow not to put any more money into the club until it was sold) when the news came in that Our First Knight had finally dropped his sword. The lass behind the counter had tears in her eyes, my lip trembled.

As fans, our nature is to be defiant in the face of adversity and to want to fight for our club so we pace like caged tigers or we sleep the restless sleep of the wrongly imprisoned.

But what are we supposed to be fighting for? A club run by daft people who hate us, players who would hate us if they had the capacity to feel anything, players who have let us down but lack the decency to fuck off? The shirt? The shirts are the worst shirts we have ever seen. The home kit is half arsed and presumably botched together by designers whacked out on pints of chimp piss. The replica shirt buyer has the revolting predicament of the shirt looking stupid without a name and number on the back but not daring to add a current player's name in fear that they will be gone in the morning.

People were actually queuing up for the putrid abomination that is our new away kit. Blind loyalty is one thing, colour blind loyalty has to be openly mocked, surely, although I thought my mate Loud Mark saying the shirts are high visibility vests for idiots, and a warning of people not to enter into conversation with, was going a bit far.

Perhaps when this is all over we might be able to make some sense of it all – at the moment anybody from the club saying anything is probably lying so we can ignore them along with anyone who says or writes "just when you thought things couldn't get any worse…" because things can still get A LOT worse.

In the end we will (metaphorically) climb the rigging, stripped to the waist with a cutlass in our teeth because that's what we do.

Now brace yourselves – we're going in.

Chapter 83

September 2009

And Justice For All

It's been a good year for those of us who enjoy seeing the privileged and the seemingly untouchable having their pants pulled down in public: MPs being hog-roasted for their expense claims by the media, with the *Daily Telegraph* of all papers reading like a copy of *Class War* – "Filthy thieving parasites are robbing us blind while the nation goes to the dogs, stuffing their fat faces while good people are thrown out of work, dissolve parliament! Smash the state!" – they didn't write at any point – but I'm sure it's what they meant.

Next we had rugby being exposed as a sport peopled by rogues and cheats during the "bloodgate scandal," wherein an uninjured player chomped on a stage-blood capsule and staggered about a bit to allow a tactical substitution. What actual advantage was being gained is as irrelevant and uninteresting as rugby itself, the great joy was adding 'premeditated cheating' to a charge sheet that also includes; rugby players hoovering 'class A' narcotics up their big posh hooters, punching, biting, stamping, raking and sexual-deviant-bum-fondling (they call it a scrum – the perverts). In the process the moral high horse rugby fans have been trotting about on for years has been turned into dog food – hilarious, and now every time some pompous nit starts slagging off football by saying "well of course in rugby...." we are allowed to laugh, spit and fart in their stupid faces.

Most recently, Chelsea have been effectively banned from registering players for a year and a half by FIFA for stealing children from other football clubs. They were found guilty of "inducing" a boy, Gaël Kakuta, who was already signed to Lens: for legal reasons the media has to be careful because the case is going to appeal. So presumably nobody is allowed to write, "Chelsea have pissed off a whole host of clubs, in this country and abroad, by stealing their best young players and yet none of these boys are ever seen again, what is Abramovich doing, sacrificing them and bathing in their blood?" so nobody, I repeat nobody, is allowed to even think that OK?

(It is of course possible to add to this list of misfortune befalling the high and mighty a Premiership club with one of the biggest grounds and wage bills in the world being so badly run that they got themselves relegated but to do this you would have to admit that the club in question is massive and we're not, apparently. We are also not, by any stretch of the imagination, posh.)

When the posh are accused of anything untoward they move through four distinct stages: 1. Outrage and indignant denial; "how dare you", "I've never been so insulted" etc. 2. Bargaining; "I'm sure this is all just an unfortunate misunderstanding, my wife went to school with the Arch Bishop of Canterbury den-cha-know." 3. Dismissal; "Oh everybody's doing it, it's only stealing from taxpayers / undermining the reputation of an entire sport / keeping myself young by bathing in the blood of talented children. It's not a proper crime, like poor people should go to prison for." 4. Pretending to be sorry when we can all tell that the only thing they are sorry about is getting caught.

In the end if these outrages are going to be more than just an opportunity for us peasants to point and hoot, if we are actually going to make the world a better place it's what happens next that matters most. I suppose it was only an idle dream that the politicians could have been dragged screaming into the street along with the bankers and beaten within an inch of their fucking lives on *Ant and Dec's Saturday Night Takeaway*. Unfortunately the system is made by the posh for the posh so they know that a proportion of the country will, instead of chopping off heads and rising in open rebellion, get distracted by celebrity magazines and…. "hey look at Jordon's tits!" The correct way to protest we are told, is at the ballot box, a mass vote for the Greens or some spunky independents would cause a storm but depressingly the reaction of the country seems to be; "We've had enough of career politicians who have never actually worked running the country and lining their own pockets so let's show them how sick we are… by … voting Conservative." Which is monumentally bloody depressing. So the country is still going to be run by the same people or their friends.

Rugby is irrelevant but keeps a sizeable amount of insufferable toffs away from football so let them get on with it, we never cared in the first place.

The football is saveable but we have to realise whose side we need to be on. The rich English clubs are trying to get us on their side by accusing FIFA and UEFA of being anti-English which is bullshit. Platini wants clubs to only spend what they earn when recruiting players and to not steal children from smaller clubs. This would stop teams becoming rich men's toys like Chelsea and Man City, stop Man Utd spending £30 million on a player when they are already £600 million in debt, stop the top teams hoarding and not playing players who could be superstars at smaller clubs and stop the creepy child-catchers luring children into their nets. Most importantly, Platini could make The Premiership interesting enough for Newcastle United to consider re-joining as an option.

On appeal, Chelsea had their transfer ban lifted, which is a shame – they shouldn't have been allowed to bring anyone in or let anyone leave. Like a grotesque version of a haunted house they could have been forced to play with the same players for twenty years.

Chapter 84

October 2009

Nee Fukkaz

"The Lies That Damned United" - *The Journal* silently screamed at us from newsagents' shelves. Finally, after a year of guessing and assuming, the truth was out on Keegan's departure from Mike Ashley's substantial bosom and that truth was "constructive dismissal." Keegan's claim that he was entirely vindicated by the tribunal initially looks a bit of an overstatement when he wanted over £25 million in compensation and they only awarded him £2 million, like they were saying, "yes we can see your point, well kind of…." but it's the wording and the tone of the tribunal's findings that must really sting Newcastle's hierarchy. The tribunal clearly didn't believe a word that came out of Ashley, Wise or Llambias's faces. They all said Keegan knew he didn't have final say on transfers from the start, Keegan said he knew no such thing. The tribunal found "he knew no such thing."

The judgement in full is truly a savage and extraordinary insight into the way our club has been run recently – reading it you constantly think that if you gave an ape a big bag of crack and a black and white shirt it would have made a better and more dignified fist of things.

Disappointingly, the report jumps from the initial meetings Ashley's mob had with Keegan to the signing (against Keegan's express wishes) of Ignacio Maria Gonzalez Gatti which the report describes as "the final, final straw". We want to know about the previous final straws dammit - but no official light is shone on the idiot sales of James Milner and Abdoulaye Faye and no mention is made of Keegan's supposed bonkers transfer wish-list that (as I understand) included David Beckham, a Bratz Doll, the world's biggest hat, Frank Lampard and Darth Vader.

Dennis Wise, poisonous little turd that he is, turned up on Sky the next day to say taking Gonzalez on loan was doing two agents a favour in return for which Newcastle would have first refusal on "all the best young players in South America." It's been a year now Dennis, where are they all, why aren't there hordes of Brazilians, Argentineans and Venezuelans swarming up Northumberland Street? And what planet do you have to be living on to believe that Real Madrid ring up Boca Juniors to ask about a player and Boca say, "It doesn't matter how much you offer, he's going to Newcastle United"?

Send me ten thousand pounds Dennis, you won the Nigerian lottery. You fucking idiot.

In the end no one has come out of this well, the previously well thought of Chris Mort turns out to have been lying right in *The Mag's* face when he told us how the transfers would work and Keegan unashamedly wanting £25 million out of us means the morally acceptable side to be on now that the dust has settled is "nee fukkaz."

Chapter 85

November 2009

Piers Morgan Has Been Horribly Murdered

Newcastle United announced they were prepared to change the name of St James' Park, for a price, and Jonas Gutiérrez scored a goal.

One of the lasting side effects of our club being for sale over the summer has been my habit of turning Radio Newcastle on in the car of a morning with an increasingly pathetic air of optimism. Instead of good news like: "Last night Newcastle United was sold to some fabulously wealthy space monkeys" or "It turns out, if we concentrate, humans can fly" or "Piers Morgan has been brutally murdered by a gang of midgets with extremely powerful fireworks" - what one usually hears is a studio full of people who don't know anything about anything talking rubbish. Unless it's one of those, all too rare, mornings where darling Mick Lowes turns up or Gemma (who used to sing like an angel for Newcastle's own Hug) is guesting on travel (because it's like having a swear-bomb in the studio that could go off at any moment – thrilling radio) it's pointless. For example; "I don't get punk." "No." "Me neither". Good, well done, that kept the world turning, thank you.

So the re-naming of Le parc du Sainte James story breaks and naturally the region is up in arms. Hilariously the Radio Newcastle breakfast gaggle and their enraged listeners can't decide if it's St James or St James's or St James's'zz' – like, "this is an outrage you can't change the name of... er... whatever it is we call it, it's always been.. er .. you know... it's a disgrace!"

Naturally any idea the present regime comes up with is going to be viewed as if Mike Ashley has wandered stark naked to his seat just before kick-off and spent the next 90 minutes waving his genitals at us, shouting "Waaaaay" in a manner that only cockneys can, drawing a Hitler moustache on a photo of Jackie

Milburn and sticking it up his arse on the final whistle.

Playing devil's advocate here for a second, is changing the stadium name that bad an idea? If some mugs want to give us twenty million pounds a year to pretend to call our ground something else and that money all goes straight into strengthening the team where's the real harm? We're not going to call it anything other than St James' and ever it shall be so, ask anybody sitting in The Sir John Hall or Exhibition Stands. Also what if it ends up being "The San Miguel and Playstation 3 @ St James' Park Stadium in conjunction with Pringles and Jaffa Cakes" – I would be actively supporting the team for up to 30 hours a week.

Also, we overlook the fun of changing the ground's name on a weekly basis just so that's what they have to print in the paper above the match report and what they would have to say on Radio 5 Live and on TV. So you would hear Alan Green saying, "I'm here at the What The Fuck Are You Looking At Stadium in Newcastle" or behold the joy of John Motson introducing the game from the "We Were Here When We Were Shit Park". Yes, I know I'm being frivolous but frankly I'm sick of being told to sit up and bark whenever the media expects me to be outraged.

You want to know what I really think? Black kit, thin white stripes, skull and crossbones where the club badge used to be playing at the Amnesty International Stadium with the candle/barbed wire logo on the shirts that we give Amnesty £10 million a year for. Instantly coolest club in the world selling so many replica kits that we can't make them fast enough even at £100 a throw (75% off for season ticket holders.)

(Jarringly violent change of subject.)

Am I correct in understanding that Jonas Gutiérrez has been keeping a Spiderman mask in his knickers for every game since he got here but left it in the dressing room for the recent game against Peterborough? Unencumbered by unlicensed Marvel paraphernalia in his keks he has the ability to run from the halfway line, through the entire opposition team before scoring with a previously unwitnessed confidence?

He then refused to celebrate his goal at all because he was upset about speculation that he was about to leave us to play for Roma? I bow to few people in my own love for Spiderman, have long hoped the Jonas mask when revealed would be the black and white version first seen in the mid 1980s and was myself firing imaginary webs at the Leazes End roof seconds after the goal BUT are you telling me that he could have scored a goal or goals like that before now if he had been a bit pissed off and didn't have a Spidey mask in his pants. Given that we got relegated for the lack of one goal.... no I must have got that wrong.

Chapter 86

December 2009

Blissful Ignorance

Christmas. How did it get to be fucking Christmas, didn't we just have one of them? Ho-hum, better buy some Baileys as well this week.

It's at this time of year that we start to think of our families. Specifically what we think is what a fucking nuisance they are. My friend Keith is the fifth of six children and Christmas to him is an endless chore of guilt, tears and driver conscious sobriety. Fortunately most of my immediate family are all nice and dead, or at least pretending to be to avoid me trying to borrow money off them, so I love Christmas.

I do have an uncle I adore; hilarious, charismatic and with sarcasm deadly enough to conquer Russia in a ground war - who crucially lives far enough away for neither of us to be bothered by any obligation to each other. I mention him here because he knows nothing about football. When I say he knows nothing about football I don't mean he doesn't understand the offside rule or know the second verse of The Blaydon Races (which secretly nobody does except my friend Guy), I mean my aunt had to tell him who Cristiano Ronaldo is. I accused him of this being an affectation, surely the world is soaked in football, it sloshes all over the papers and spills out of the radio 24 hours a day but no, he just filters it out. He has no interest in it, no love or hate for it and as a result his life is utterly free of it.

How wonderful to be able to wilfully ignore the bits of life you can't be bothered with, I thought, and have been enthusiastically taking on the role of the Blissfully Ignorant for over a year now. If you try it with work they stop paying you unfortunately, unless you're a politician or a judge, but otherwise it's been great. Occasionally I catch a bit of Eastenders and merely think, why are these awful people shouting in that silly accent before flicking to a channel that might have snow leopards on it.

At the Tyne Tunnel on the board that's supposed to warn you of things, it instead flashes "Vote Joe!" in urgent orange. Like if we don't "Vote Joe" the Tunnel will fill with smoke or the river will start seeping into it. It's hard enough trying not to think that every time you drive through the bloody thing as it is without what looks like a threat flashing at you.

Joe is/was apparently on *X-Factor* which I would know if I didn't flick straight to a Frank Turner CD every time they even mention it on Radio 5 Live. Do I need to know who Joe is or is he just another interchangeable bag of skin and teeth twitching across the television beneath the invisible strings of rich and evil people? People who have broken music as an art form down into a formula to be repackaged as high-definition disposable brain-drugs for the feeble minded, where folk are treated like sheep to the point where they actually care what people like Simon Cowell and Piers fucking Morgan think. There are parasitic fish in the Amazon that enter the host's body by swimming up its urine. Once inside they have got painful barbs to stop them being dislodged. That's what Britain's Got X Dancing is. Well Piers Morgan can try and swim up my piss if he wants to, I'd like to see him try but I won't have it, do you hear me?

I tell you what I want to watch on a Saturday shall I? All the judges from every talent show sitting behind little desks with their smug fucking faces on, waiting to sneer at the peasantry, being told to "FUCK OFF!" It would be called "Why Don't You Fuck Off?" and every time one of them opened their stupid fucking faces to speak someone with a baseball bat wrapped in razor wire would shout, "Why don't you FUCK OFF!?" at them. I'd watch that for hours.

Which brings me to the picture in this chapter; have I taken this Blissful Ignorance thing too far, only I don't know who any of these people are? Yet this poster is everywhere in Newcastle at the minute, outside the actual Theatre the pictures are 20 feet tall. And quite frankly I find them terrifying since my splendid friend Davey Todd suggested the show should be called "Cinderella – Up The Wrong 'un" as all the cast appear to have been subjected to a sudden and uninvited back door invasion (as I believe the Viz Profanosaurus would have it) just as their picture was about to be taken. And look at Clive Webb, he doesn't look like he's acting, I fear he walks the streets dressed like that shouting at strangers and whispering into the bins. David Ducasse, the poster informs me, belongs to Scooch. What the bloody hell is a Scooch? It sounds like an inflammation of the scrotum.

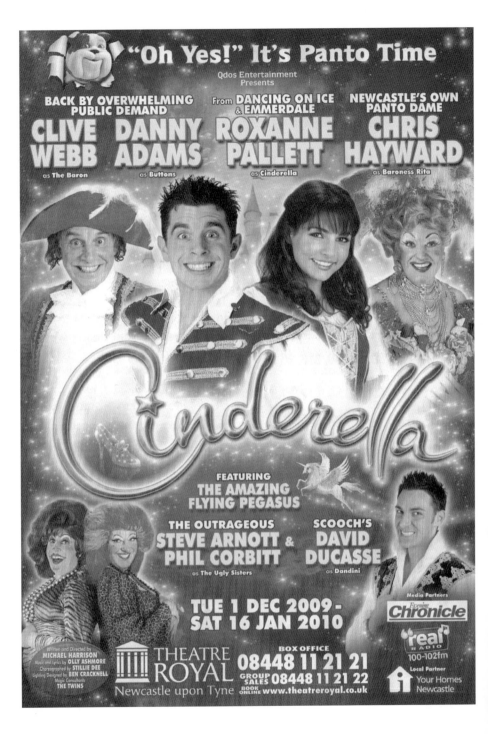

The problem is my Blissful Ignorance is raging out of control which means we all might have a problem because it's spreading to football. Maybe it's just a symptom of being in this division but I don't know or care who anybody is who doesn't play for Newcastle United. For your entertainment dear reader (assuming anybody is still reading after the phrase "inflammation of the scrotum") I am supposed to write match reports and pass on informed opinion but I can't do that if I don't recognise the enemy and what we're up against. I can only write, "Hey everybody, let's kick Piers Morgan down some stairs" so many times before you'd get sick of it. Or maybe you wouldn't – don't ask me, I don't know anything.

Happy Christmas.

I didn't "vote Joe" - like many other freedom fighters (as guitarist Tom Morello called us) I supported Rage Against The Machine's Killing in the Name successful attempt for the Christmas number one slot. And now understand that it legally has to be added to every compilation Christmas album ever made – but I might be wrong about that as well.

Chapter 87

February 2010

I Love A Referee & I Don't Care Who Knows It

We all know watching a football match where your own team of choice is not playing only becomes interesting when you have taken sides. The process starts even if you walk past a parks game, be it on kit, hair or because one side has a left back who looks like the bloke who played drums for Joy Division. Ambivalence will make any game boring, which is one of the reasons The African Cup of Nations was virtually unwatchable. You just couldn't build up sufficient hatred or admiration to really get into it.

With embittered and damaged fans such as us most games, not involving Newcastle United, boil down to, "who do I hate least?" Watching *Match of the Day* for specific, obscure or complicated reasons you can pick who you want to win for each match of the entire Premiership season. Even though it has nothing to do with us.

However, I was watching Birmingham v Manchester United a few weeks back and was really enjoying myself. I was right into it despite not really caring what happened. It's funny when Man U lose but does that mean you want Chelsea to win the League? And I refuse to support Birmingham because Lee Bowyer plays for them, a man must have principles. I eventually realised I was supporting the referee, which came as a bit of a shock. The ref was Mark Clattenburg who has never pissed us off because he's not allowed to ref Newcastle matches as he's a fan. He did Shearer's testimonial if you remember and gave us a penalty in the last minute. So we can actively enjoy Clatters when he turns up on screen and not just because he's so damned handsome. He is often wildly erratic, he's unafraid to give inconsistent and crazed decisions but best of all, his job is to annoy the horrible, selfish cry baby liars who populate the Premiership. Alex Ferguson slaughtered him after the game for sending off Darren Fletcher and the incidents in isolation did make the red card seem a bit harsh – but watching the whole game you could see the situation as it developed and the build towards the inevitable climax was thrilling. Fletcher never stopped moaning from the start. In his own words Clatters "bollocked him for dissent" then booked him for a foul. You could see him gradually lose patience with Fletcher who kept complaining, then he finally snapped after a cynical trip and produced a second yellow, then flourished a red, with a "go on, fuck off" look on his face. By which time I was bouncing up and down clapping my hands with giddy glee. When reffing Man City recently, Clatters clearly sent Craig Bellamy off for getting on his tits, which was brilliant.

So I have taken to supporting the ref in Premiership matches with some enthusiasm and am considering a replica kit and replica cards to brandish. Refs have got a chance to revolutionise the game for the better and they can do it because most people hate footballers at the minute. In the recent Milan derby a player was sent off for being sarcastic – we need more of that. I want to see a ref say to Wayne Rooney, "If you come spitting and swearing in my face one more fucking time boy, I'm gonna fuck you up."

Who knows, we could even play the game by the rules, not the rules as interpreted by Sky TV's Andy Gray. Like offside; the rule is that the benefit of the doubt should go to the forward but it never does because refs and linesmen are terrified of what a manager will say if they get one wrong. Bollocks to managers, tell them to go away and learn the rules. Managers who say, "we should go back to the old rule where offside meant offside" should be openly derided as the fools they are, shouldn't they Mr. S. Bruce of Corbridge? The offside rule is fine, it's just interpreted by cowards. Handball is only an offence if done deliberately, not when some poor sod has the ball blasted at them from an inch away. Refs really should get after Stoke City in particular with their constant rule bending as well. In the first half of their FA Cup game with Arsenal they spent nine minutes taking throw ins. Drying the ball with towels, moving everybody into position. Honestly, nine minutes on taking throw ins. The soft ref told them to hurry up once or twice then added two minutes. Tough on Stoke, tough on the causes of Stoke; no towels, and bookings for time wasting, Pulis would have a blue fit, which would be great because he's a horrible bastard who is trying to ruin football. Get 'im Clatters, get 'im.

More power to refs in the Premier League, get the fourth official to stop fussing pointlessly around the technical areas and into the stand with a monitor and wire him up to the man in the middle. "I got the ball ref," squeals John Terry; "That's ours," squeaks Steven Gerrard; "(insert white noise here)", screeches Jamie Carragher. "Oh really?" says the official with his finger on his ear piece and a twinkle in his eye, "would you care to bet a card on that? Thought not, now shut up and bugger off!"

Obviously my support of refs does not extend to the Championship where be-whistled ding-bats have been ganging up on us for weeks.

But in the Premiership we should demand brutal justice and support referees unreservedly. If that means Mark Clattenburg carries on wreaking vengeance on those who have wronged Newcastle United and starts sending players off for looking at him funny and then kicking them up the arse as they walk off, all the better.

Chapter 88

March 2010

Run To The Hills

Somebody suggested the Premier League should introduce a playoff for the fourth Champions League spot and some tool is always suggesting the fourth Champions League spot should go to the FA Cup winners. Here's why not.

Probably the most underrated thing about living in Newcastle is how easy it is to get the hell out. Main line station, international airport – whoosh – "see ya" – gone. But one of our great secrets is that you can be in the heart of our magnificent, multi-cultural urban conurbation and half an hour later be in a forest, up a hill or by a lake with barely another living soul for miles. Stretch that to an hour and you can be in Kielder near the massive man-made reservoir that is going to make us all rich and powerful come the great water wars that are due to break out around 2025. (By 2025 I mean the year not the time, we are not going to be at the centre of a world war before half past eight tonight however frenzied the media get over the Tweedy girl and Wayne Bridge.)
I fucking love Kielder; the people at the Bird Of Prey Centre will take you out walking with a hawk on your arm for some quids and the mountain bike trails are brilliant even for wobbly old guttersnipes whose knees are shot from too many slide tackles across the wooden floors of the Lightfoot Centre's 5-a-side courts. A 26 mile track around the reservoir was recently completed that twists and undulates through breathtaking scenery – "get the bike out and bollocks to the football" I increasingly think. But no, because here comes Steve bloody Cram on the local news barking up a thousand person marathon run around it on October the 17th (2010). "Following on from the success of the Great North Run…" – what success would that be then? The number of people who have successfully died or the number of perverts who have successfully videoed ladies going to the toilet before the race starts?

Before Steve bloody Cram flew off to the Winter Olympics to be publicly baffled and confused on national television he made a short video encouraging people to join him in Kielder in October. You can see it on youtube: "It's so quiet," he says. Aye, it is at the fuckin' minute but it won't be when you turn up with your thousand runners and your volunteers and your St John's sodding Ambulance crackpots and your high visibility vest wearing Nazis and your police and friends and idiot families and their bored horrible children and your ice cream vans fighting each other over the right to sell overpriced 99s and your perverts. This is just "year one" as well – they plan to expand it year on year. You've seen long distance runners – not the harmless ding-bats dressed up making thousands of pounds for good causes - I mean the bug eyed obsessives who run and run and run and run in an apparent attempt to stop any thoughts wandering into their pointy heads. "Every corner you turn there is a fantastic view," says Steve bloody Cram – yes there is but you won't dare look at it because here comes yet another sweaty, emaciated freak in ill-fitting day-glo shorts looking like it's about to have a fucking heart attack.

If Steve bloody Cram wants to have a run with a thousand of his friends wouldn't it be better for everybody if they all ran south down the A19 against the traffic the next time the ambulances go on strike? I think we all know the answer to that is yes.

When fools try to change something that is already fine they usually end up spoiling whatever it was that made that something good in the first place. So it's good that England has four places in the Champions League because our top four teams will generally do OK (except when we were last in it, or Everton) and that will keep the co-efficient up so every half decent team in the Premiership can fancy their chances of having an exceptional season and getting a go. So who the hell came up with the idea of play-offs with fourth to seventh battling it out for the last spot? Seventh place is invariably some well-organised chancers who would plop out of the qualifying rounds like an undercooked King Prawn Balti. Too many high profile games with millions of pounds riding on them is what has bolloxed up the FA Cup; the idea that we need to squeeze some more in is absurd. There was a time when winning the FA Cup was a goal in itself, it remains important, we would kill for it and Portsmouth effectively swapped their very existence for it but most teams can't afford to put it above their League campaign. Quite obviously many fans can't afford a Cup run either with cup games across Europe played out before blocks of empty seats this season. But the FA Cup itself is fine, ask any Leeds fan who saw their team win at Old Trafford, ask any fan whose team gets to the semi-final and witness the outrage as proper fans can't get tickets for the final. All very good, all very traditional. But have you seen the "ideas" to "improve" the FA Cup? Extra officials – Oh I can't wait. Scrap replays? – The game we beat Spurs 6-1 here in '99 was a replay. Or that traditional red flag warning of idiots approaching: give the fourth Champions League spot to the FA Cup winners.

Anyone who says "give the fourth Champions League spot to the FA Cup winners," or thinks we should have a fourth to seventh place play off should have their trousers set on fire before being chased up a tree – football works because, despite all its flaws, greedy men, cheats and knacker-bags, it's a meritocracy which means that teams are rewarded on what they achieve. If they over-achieve by spending money they haven't got they will crash and burn. Which is why no one should have any sympathy for Portsmouth now and will hopefully have no sympathy for Manchester United and Liverpool in two years' time. The idea that a team can get its undeserving snout into the Champions League from seventh position is as stupid as finding somewhere tranquil and then importing two thousand freaks and lunatics to run around shouting.

Chapter 89

March 2010

Bring The Noise

Newcastle played at Middlesbrough and the Boro fans had a banner with "trophy virgins" written on it and an arrow pointing to the Newcastle fans.

I don't get dignified silences: somebody says/does something nasty or unfair about you or yours and you are supposed to remain quiet? And dignified? Surely the best way to deal with being accused of something is undignified noise. In the work place, even when stone cold guilty, surely the best options are 1; to deny it, abuse your accuser, publicly humiliate and destroy them so they think twice about ever crossing you again or 2; claim that what ever you did wrong was actually a brilliant idea that, through no fault of yours, went a bit wonky. Let nothing lie, always attack, with charm or with the threat of a pick axe handle, nothing goes unchallenged - attack!

So when Boro fans make and wave a banner with "Trophy Virgins" on it and wave it at us do I say nothing and let them assume I am stumped for a response in the face of their sparkling Teesside wit? Or do I say; "How can we be virgins when we have fucked you lot so often? And we have won a lot of trophies, just because the major ones were some time ago doesn't reinstate our purity. You can't become a virgin again given time, whatever your special uncle told you as he wiped himself off on your mother's curtains."

When manager of Newcastle, before he went mental, Ruud Gullit was accused of spending more time in Holland than in Newcastle and didn't defend himself. *The Mag* got first hand evidence that Gullit was at the training ground first nearly every day and stayed behind on afternoons to coach the kids. But the damage was done and the lie was repeated until it became the accepted truth. Over the years Rob Lee, Kenny Dalglish, Laurent Robert, Graeme Souness, Nicky Butt and Michael Owen among others all quickly came to the conclusion that the best way to deal with the prattling idiocy of one local hack was to ignore him. And not one of the above is universally well thought of, while other unnamed quote-happy players, never received a match rating of less than 7 in the paper of the journalist in question and remained adored however badly they may have played.

In modern football you are damned by silence and silence has been one of the Ashley regime's greatest mistakes. Derek Llambias shuffles into public and politely points out a few things in Mike's defence from time to time but he lacks credibility because so much misinformation has been allowed to fester. He also lacks the confident charm or dangerous menace needed to pull it off. So since January, we are told, Ashley has put £25 million into the club, brought in the six players we needed to stop the wobble we might have been about to have and he still daren't go out for a pint in the town for fear of being burnt at the stake. But this situation has been dragged out more through an infuriating lack of communication than by anything else. Everybody has got an uninformed opinion about Newcastle United and that has given license for unrelenting attacks on our football club to the point where we fans find it difficult to stick up for ourselves.

It's an unfortunate fact that football clubs can survive on hot air and bullshit and that PR is vital. Look at Saint Niall down the A19; for the last two years we have been told, "Newcastle is not the way to run a football club. Look at sunderland, aren't they clever and professional and forward thinking?" – well, not according to *The Journal* (Wednesday 17th of March.) Our neighbour's wage bill is 80% of their turnover (50% is good, over 60% in considered to be unsustainable), they lost £26 million last year, their shirt sponsor, Boylesports, is pulling out with no one any the wiser as to what the hell it is that they do and chief executive Steve Walton has admitted the club would consider selling sponsorship rights for their pink seated stadium. Excuse me? Where are the headlines, where is the national outcry, the abuse, the two year scoffathon? Oh and get this on their poor attendances: "And we are the furthest away of anyone. It takes three hours for us to get to the nearest match for us. Plus we don't have the advantage of having any home derbies. So our average gate took a hit because Middlesbrough and Newcastle are not in our division." So they thought it was so damn funny us getting relegated and it turns out they can't even begin to manage without us. Yet everybody I have shouted this information at over the last week was unaware of it – how the fuck does that happen?

Silence, that's how – fuck silence – as Public Enemy said "Bring The Noise!"

Chapter 90

April 2010

You Can't Bring Me Down

After a 0-3 defeat at Derby in February, Newcastle went on a 12 match unbeaten run to secure promotion which for some reason attracted the media's vultures of impending doom.

"You. Can't. Bring me down, bring me down you can't bring me down!" ("You Can't Bring Me Down"- Suicidal Tendencies)

When it was announced towards the end of the Sheffield United match that the Newcastle United players would be staying on the pitch to say thank you to the fans after securing promotion I must admit my heart sank. Promotion was surely nothing to celebrate, being mathematically superior to Nottingham Forest and Swansea was, and is, of little interest to me. Suffice to say my sunken heart rocketed from its watery grave and blazed towards the stars as the players gave a polite clap but emphasised the job wasn't finished, Chris Hughton said we still had work to do and the club refused the indignity of an open top bus parade through the streets. Good.
Promotion.
Balls!
I want to be 100 point Champions standing on the bloodied corpses of this entire division before I will consider the first celebratory sip from glory's fickle cup. I feared the season celebrated prematurely would fizzle out and it is a credit to the grit and determination at our club now that it has not been allowed to do so. Instead we have been instantly swamped with the unwelcome and dismal opinions of journalists and fans, who have had no interest in us all year, turning up to piss on our chips and tell us how hopeless we all are. It seems on arrival in the

Premiership we stand less chance of avoiding a good buggering than an unattended choirboy in a Catholic vestibule. Our old chum at the stupid stupid *Daily Express* Mick Dennis at least had the decency to admit he was wrong about us spiralling ever downward like a burning Messerschmitt (my simile not his – make of that what you will) before sticking the boot in. "Deluded fans" (yawn), demanding Keegan or Shearer as manager on phone-ins, crowds not that good etc.

Our much publicised and derided "delusions" were, on reflection, reasonable expectations based on back to back top four finishes, crowd size, wages, transfer budget, facilities and having one of the largest turnovers in Europe. It was the players and managers within that structure that let us down not the unreasonable burden we placed upon them. Suffice to say those expectations have long since been readjusted by the majority of us who can't be held responsible for every crackpot allowed on national radio. (I actually agree with Dennis on the attendance and find the clamour for tickets for our coronation against Ipswich from the previously absent physically sickening. There was a lad within my earshot at the Sheffield United match who said, "I haven't missed this shit through not having a season ticket this year." And you think we've missed you and your bleating? Do you? Fuck off back to the golf course! - but that's a different argument). Mick Dennis thinks we would be mad to replace Hughton, whereas Rob Shepherd at *The News of the World* thinks we should part company at once, with his sources claiming that is exactly what will happen when the club is sold in the summer. Shepherd's entire career is based on his contacts (it can't be on his ability as a writer) which he will bark about rudely regardless of how wrong and misinformed he is. Shepherd also managed to include a sideswipe at our own darling Joey Barton within the same piffle. Rob Shepherd is a name you need to know when the Joey Barton argument comes around again (as it will) because Rob Shepherd did four months of a 14 month sentence for biting a man on the face in a wine bar in 2004. (*Guardian / Independent* online.) That's Rob Shepherd, who gets paid to moralise at us by the News of the World. Got that – OK?

At *The Sun* we have the Newcastle supporting Custis brothers; Neil long since denied himself any credibility by passionately supporting that hippo-headed gasbag and snake-oil salesman Sam Allardyce so we can ignore him but Shaun (the prettier one) when asked of our promotion on Sky rolled his eyes and insisted it was the same players that got relegated and that Hughton had already been found wanting in The Premiership.

The media are falling over themselves to kick all the joy and optimism we've found this season out of us before it has even ended. Like the world can't be doing with happy Newcastle fans. 5 Live's commentary of our game at Reading was 45 minutes of Clive Walker explaining why we "wouldn't get away with that in The Premiership" before I thankfully went to see The King Blues and the next day Talksport reporting on a game we had won simply listed the players who would have to be replaced including the line "The Angel of the North has more chance of scoring in The Premiership than Andy Carroll." That's Andy Carroll, who as you know, already has scored goals for Newcastle when we were last in The Premiership and has now blossomed into The White Drogba. I hope every team we play thinks he is not worth marking.

People forget Newcastle didn't get relegated due to a lack of ability; they got relegated because of a poor attitude and a catastrophic tactical policy that saw the team picked on salary and reputation ahead of astuteness and necessity. No one as yet has challenged my firm belief that this season's Newcastle United would have beaten last season's Newcastle United easily and last season's Newcastle United only went down by a point.

No one here thinks we are going to outspend Man City or pay better wages than Chelsea (and I suspect most of us don't want us to try to) or outplay Arsenal in our first year but we won't have to. We need to be better than both the teams we come up with (which we clearly are) and one of the teams that don't get relegated to survive – then look up from there – see how high you get before someone screams "deluded" at you. Wigan, Wolves, Birmingham? Then we hang in there until the rules on debt and foreigners come in and watch the teams above crumble into oblivion.

I know nothing beyond the twinkle in Mike Ashley's eye but I don't expect the club to be sold and I do expect Chris Hughton to be our manager next season. Hughton has evolved from reluctant stand-in to thoughtful tactician and has kept his dignity whilst doing so. Wherever you want to draw your own imaginary line between the influence of our coach and the enforcers of determination within our squad you can't argue that it hasn't worked. And it's also hard to argue that Alan Shearer would have done better, we will never know. What we do know is that the players who grasped and preserved the very soul of this club when everybody else, including a lot of its fans, was prepared to let it rot deserve our gratitude and demand respect from all others. History tells us it is a respect they are not going to get from anybody but those of us who have stood with them. Newcastle United Football Club has changed in the last year, changed in what it has lost and in what it has gained, it is still changing and it could be into something good and something happy to be underestimated. Just don't expect us fans to be quiet about it.

Cheers.

The unbeaten run was extended to 17 matches of which 13 were victories

Chapter 91

2009/10 postscript – A Distorted View

Villa Park, Sunday the 24th of May 2009, Newcastle United have lost the game 1-0 and are relegated as a consequence. The TV cameras are scanning across the Newcastle support. The sun is shining brightly and it provides a horrible clarity for those watching at home, the camera zooms in hopefully onto individual fans, then it swoops away to others, then on again. In this slick modern era of live television this had a noticeably jarring effect on the viewer. That is until you realised what they are looking for, then you could imagine the director's instructions becoming increasingly frantic in the cameraman's earpiece. "Find me one that's crying, come on they are bloody Newcastle fans, it's what they do, no not him, over there, her, no, bloody hell, what's wrong with them? I want tears, shoulder lurching sobs, individual pain, give me my shot for the ages, for posterity, where's a fucking cliché when you need one? Cry damn you. Cry!" And they never found it; when people write or talk of "the tears and recriminations" of that day they lie because try as they might no evidence was found. Maybe I'm wrong, maybe you blubbed and boo-hooed all the way home but I don't think so and all the pictures I have seen of tearful people in black and white shirts were not from the people at the actual game.

Instead, betrayed and blood black with hatred, the Newcastle support stood or sat, rarely even blinking in the sunshine. Fear can make you cry, joy can make you cry, loss, disappointment, pain or the perfect song at the right moment – but cold hard fucking loathing and stomach churning primeval disgust never made anybody cry. Hate for the players, hate for the dysfunctional club management, hate for dismal and tedious Villa fans and their thick classless gloating.

And that was how we were left to feel for the entire summer. Blood blackened by hatred. Sick and confused. To make matters worse, football itself looked rotten and disgusting. Newcastle United hadn't even been relegated out of a good division, well organised was enough to survive, vulgar functional teams directed by tedious and joyless men were looking down on us from the putrefied stinking carcass that was all that was left of top-flight English football.

What joy then to see the Premier League Champions scalped, eviscerated and torn to shreds by beautiful Barcelona in the Champions League Final. That single game reminded us that we didn't entirely despise football and everything about it.

The next part of the Newcastle United story you all know by heart, owner Mike Ashley clearly thought the Shearer blueprint for promotion too expensive so he tried and failed to sell the club while players were shipped out and we all waited helplessly to see what would become of the club we consider our own. Unknown to us at the time the remaining players had come together with a collective determination to put the situation right. Alan Smith later said that the players who wanted to leave were helped on their way, those who remained would have to fight. Bizarrely we got help from arch villain Diego Maradona who said it would do Jonas Gutiérrez's World Cup hopes no harm to be playing in The Championship. Eventual Championship Player of the Year to anybody who bothered looking, Jose Enrique Sanchez Diaz turned down any idea of leaving, earning a special place in our hearts by saying, "Why would I want to go there?" when asked of a move to sunderland. The club was taken off the market and we would run with what we had. What we had was a core of players who were simply too good, too mentally tough, too galvanized for anything The Championship could throw at them.

The season started with a draw, followed by five wins. Then we lost a game, won two, drew two then lost two to spend a brief period in second place while people told us West Brom were better than we were. We then went unbeaten for 15 games of which we won 10. Against who? Does it matter?

Thought not.

Most surprising of all when the campaign looked to be faltering under a heap of injuries in January it was Mike Ashley who stumped up for six new players and as a consequence Newcastle went up two gears and pulverized the League. After a 0-3 defeat at Derby in February, Newcastle went on a 17 match unbeaten run of which 13 were victories

But what next? The celebrations in the crowd at our coronation after the Ipswich game seemed muted. Again, this was not what the media expected of us. Yes, we were pleased but the champagne popping, the fireworks and the unreserved glee on the faces of our players didn't seem to be reflected in the faces of anyone clapping them near my seat – this was underlined by the irritating bloke from Real Radio with the microphone as he tried and failed to whip us into some kind of celebratory frenzy. Yes, some of us stayed out late that night but the only people wanting an open top bus parade were the few with no understanding of what we have become. Solid, realistic and actually bloody dignified.

I was glad to be out of the Premiership so I don't see much to be gained in going back apart from the money. But we clearly need the money. It feels less like we were relegated and more like we have been on holiday and now we reluctantly have to get back to work. My sensible suggestion of a paid sabbatical in the Italian or Turkish league seems to have fallen on deaf ears so we just have to get on with it.

The cartoon cliché view the world has of Newcastle fans was never entirely fair or accurate but now it seems a million miles away. Yes we've got our daft lads who treat every game like a stag party but as far as I can tell we've never been so realistic. We know we're not going to win the League but relegation holds little fear for us any more.

The people saying our players aren't good enough for The Premiership are the same people who said we were going to drop straight out the bottom of The Championship and we've got 102 points saying those people don't know shit. As usual, the people with the most to say are the people who know the least. The rest of us seem to have learnt that all the worrying and all the pontificating and all the hating got us nowhere a year ago so why bother now when our situation is clearly so much healthier? For example, we actually like a lot of our players again and the club has lost dead wood on and off the pitch – what's left is leaner and harder but only we seem to know that.

Everybody outside Newcastle thinks our team is shit and that our fans are going to cry about it. Let them. Fuck them. But we'll see about that eh?

Player of the Season: Jose Enrique Sanchez Diaz.

Goal of the Season: Jose Enrique Sanchez Diaz v Nottingham Forest.

Chapter 92

October 2010

So How Is This My Fault?

Newcastle United have made an erratic and bewildering start to this season and, presumably like everybody else in Newcastle who has successfully intertwined massive ego with thundering self-loathing, I'm trying to work how it's my fault. The league table on *Match of the Day* last Saturday showed that if Newcastle had won their previous two home games this season (hardly wishing for the moon to be painted purple given that we were playing Blackpool and Stoke) they would have been second. Conversely without the three points provided by a surprising and delightful win at Everton we would have been stone cold bottom. How many of our fans will spend the week leading up to our next game desperately trying to remember what it was they did or didn't do before we shredded Aston stinking Villa 6-0, in our first home game, that was omitted from or added to their pre-match ritual before we played The Seasiders and Tony Pulis's red and white abomination? The answer is probably - a lot.

For my own part I am gripped in the teeth of a fearsome dilemma: it seems the less enthusiasm and interest I show in the fortunes of Newcastle United the better they do – and as soon as I allow myself to get excited the sooner those fledgling hopes turn to ashes and crumble through my grasping tired old fingers. Best to stay off the subject altogether: fucking cruise liners; have you been somewhere where one turns up? If one barged up the Tyne and smashed through the Millennium Bridge, you could stand on the roof of the Castle Keep and not be able to see either The Baltic or The Sage. They are massive and are a hideous cross between a prison ship and a retirement home for people whose family really hates them. They park up, blocking out everybody else's view of Istanbul, Venice or wherever and spit out thousands of fucking morons who have been given the collective and mistaken belief that the world and everyone in it has been provided for their comfort and convenience. People who despite having twice as much luggage as any other traveller are always appallingly dressed; socks and sandals obviously but generally beige shorts belted up to man boobs with polo shirt tucked in, dragging around some moaning she-ape in a floral smock. Somebody give me a fleet of U-boats – Now!

"Nobody wants to read about your bloody holidays," Wifey helpfully informs me as we walked through the streets of Maltese capital Valletta. We were in search of a bar called Chiaroscuro in the hope that it would provide mystery, beer and the football scores, when we passed an old man listening to the BBC World Service on an ancient transistor radio. "They are not holidays, they are adventures," I complain, "and when I finally rid myself of the embarrassing affliction that means I keep buying a season ticket and bugger off for good what the hell else am I going to write about? Anyway this stuff is virtually writing itself." Which Wifey did have to concede was a good point because the only thing we heard out of the old man's radio as we passed was "Everton 0, Newcastle 1" and what we thought was "Ben Arfa."

The old fella confirmed the score when we marched back and demanded details but when we asked "Ben Arfa?" he obviously assumed we said half-time and would do no more than smile, nod and say, "No, it's the end. 1-0." Bar Chiaroscuro provided mystery in so far as it had vanished without a trace so consequently there was no beer or further match details. The Pub, a straightforward no-nonsense name for a pub I'm sure you will agree, had beer but the TV showed nothing but The Nazi-pope waving to his cult's UK contingent. The Pub is where Oliver Reed took his last several drinks before collapsing and dying on his way to hospital. "He died doing what he enjoyed most," somebody said, "which I guess is the best any of us can hope for" - unless what you enjoy doing most is - not dying. A massive heart attack while shitting on the mutilated corpse of Piers Morgan would at least be memorable for your family.

Then a cruise ship the size of Romania came in and we couldn't move for bastards. We rushed to Rome to see if we could declare Wifey Pope before the real one got back but we were too late and missed the Carling Cup game at Chelsea as well. Checking in with nufc.com to see how many goals we got buggered by we looked at the 3 they scored and thought "OK" then we sat blinking at the 4 next to Newcastle United like we couldn't work out what it meant.

"You guys cost me 10 euros last night," said my new friend Gerry in the Scholars Lounge – "You mean you bet on Newcastle to win at Chelsea?" – Gerry just shrugged.

"So what 'append there then?" Gerry asked after we had witnessed Newcastle's insipid surrender against Stoke. I didn't know then but after seeing the terrible injustice and sickening injury of Ben Arfa at Manchester City I feared I was beginning to see a pattern.

If I remain oblivious to what's going on, Newcastle seem to enjoy better fortune. However, trying to steer clear of the present drama is difficult because I have grown fonder of this group of players than virtually any season's Newcastle United squad in about eight years. But darling Joey Barton hasn't scored since I wrote about him in such glowing terms last month, Ben Arfa clearly went down under the weight of my intoxicated enthusiasm for him ahead of anything De Jong did, Andy Carroll looks to have had his wings clipped since I assured Gerry he could actually fly and I daren't begin to tell anyone how impressed I am with Cheik Tiote lest he spontaneously explodes.

So like being at home or at work when there is a mess or a fault; I understand that it is always my fault – just once in a while it would be nice if someone explained why.

Chapter 93

Sunday Oct 31st 2010

Newcastle United 5 v sunderland 1

The week before

All season we in Newcastle have had the impression that sunderland consider themselves to be superior to us on and off the field now. Having spent years accusing us of being smug they have taken to the role themselves without so much as a flicker of self-awareness.

Fucking brilliant.

Consequently we were always going to win this game. I said so beforehand and I've got witnesses. I told everybody who would listen and several who wouldn't that we would win simply because "Newcastle are nowhere near as shit as sunderland think we are." I don't write this to try and appear clever or insightful because most of you have been reading my rubbish opinions long enough to know that I am neither but simply to point out that our greatest weapon in this derby was sunderland's extraordinary stupidity.

Listening to the local radio, sunderland's fans seemed to only disagree about how many they were going to win by. If they were so far and away our betters how come they had only a point more than us? The league table didn't appear to cross their minds. I was working in South Shields – two men were talking in the street – "They have only got Carroll, and he's shit."

"Aye that's true."

I turned to them and said, "What?"

"Oh, must be a Maggy."

"Shit?" I asked.

"Aye."

"We'll see about that, eh?" Idiots.

In Steve Bruce's defence he had done his homework, he came to see us play Wigan the other week and Wigan was a bloody abomination of a performance, Perch imploded and Joey Barton was wretched (although he never tried to hide – this is important). Many of our number would have been reluctant to admit it at the time but there was also a massive Kevin Nolan sized hole in the team that day. Nobody played well and Newcastle were relatively fortunate to get out of the game with a point *(in a 2-2 draw – late Coloccini equaliser)* but crucially Steve Bruce was there to see it. Much of what he thought he had learned at that game was wrong.

So I convinced myself that I was confident and deliberately tried to put the game out of my mind. Jim Jones Revue, Playstation and drink. The tiny nagging doubt will never go away so you have to remain constantly distracted. The Black Keys live at the O2, *Match of the Day* and bed.

Sunday October the 31st

The Metro into Newcastle is packed and the windows are steamed up, people have to shuffle up closer to each other than they would like. Strangers are pressed together, I try to exhale through my nose because there is doubtless Jack Daniels on my breath. Groups of lads without football shirts are eyed suspiciously, it takes too long to get to town.

The air is damp and heavy with rain and expectation. The pub is busy but good natured, Guy is bracing himself to lose, Bront has money riding on us winning. The rest of us bicker and laugh like thousands of others across the city eager to get on with the game. Pub time usually flies over, today it crawls too slowly, the walk to the ground takes too long, the queues are too big. But all this masks the real irritation; having them in my ground.

Circumstance has conspired to allow the enemy to be above and behind me – this is contrary to all strategy of battle and I don't like it. I pull my hat down and vow not to turn and look up.

The teams come out, the ground is a mass of black and white as carefully placed cards create vast stripes – the din is astonishing. I can't hear them at all. They have impertinently worn black shorts and make us kick towards the Gallowgate in the first half. Steve Bruce, who earned credit in the week for his genuine backing of Chrissy Hughton against an unwelcome round of fabricated bullshit, shakes our manager warmly by the hand and compliments his suit.

We kick off and the game starts at a cracking pace with Newcastle pressing, forcing sunderland to turn and retreat; a throw in from near the corner flag, a free kick that Barton whips in and Bardsley heads behind for a corner, from which Carroll gets up highest. But sunderland break quickly with Wellbeck, and Bent is in the middle. Danny Simpson manages to cut off both the run and the pass at the expense of a corner from which Bramble heads well wide. Our defensive high line combined with the threat of Bent has been our major concern, until Tiote gets booked in the fifth minute. By the 14th Carroll has been booked as well and Coloccini has got away with a crunching challenge on El Mohamady. Both sides are aggressive and urgent but twice Bardsley has to make excellent challenges to stop Carroll who is spreading panic amongst the sunderland rearguard. They can't deal with him and, as yet another ball is headed across the area by our number 9, only a desperate bat away from Mignolet in the sunderland goal stops Coloccini heading in.

Joey Barton might not like playing wide but out on the right he has the time and space to get the ball down and slash into the heart of the enemy, fizzing purposeful balls terrify sunderland and when he does drift inside there is danger and Mignolet has to dive to turn a low shot round the post. The respite is brief. Six players jump for Barton's corner before the ball drops and Kevin Nolan hooks the ball over his own head into the roof of the mackem net. St James' erupts as the players bundle on top of each other in the Gallowgate goal.

You fear we will retreat and they will attack but instead they start reeling and we smell blood. Malbranque is booked for a desperate hack at Barton as we attack quickly down the right. Two minutes later Shola brings a ball down with surprising grace and powers through the middle. Jonas and Nolan link up and a shot is blocked from Jonas which leads to a scissor kick from Carroll which is only partially blocked - before Nolan is suddenly clear in front of goal, with no flag in sight. The ball is slotted calmly into the bottom corner and Nolan is away, elbows flapping. St James' Park goes utterly berserk with celebration.

On Friday, Gary "Benno" Bennett on Radio Newcastle said that Newcastle would have to change tactics to live with sunderland's midfield. On 40 minutes

Bruce hooks off Ahmed El Mohamady and brings on Asamoah Gyan who despite paying a colossal fee for he rarely trusts to start a game.

Onuoha dives in on Jonas and doesn't get the ball and gets booked, Simpson dives in on Wellbeck and does get the ball but receives the same punishment by which point players on both sides should have worked out that ref Phil Dowd isn't going to look kindly on reckless tackles.

Then on half-time Onuoha dives in on Jonas again, only this time in the penalty area and to our surprise and delight we get the penalty. Things are going far too well, a penalty miss could be pivotal. Shola hits the inside of the side netting with a clean strike, with his captain standing on a hat-trick – damn but that boy has got some balls. 3-0.

Checking out the highlights at half-time, Nolan was onside and it was a penalty. Why am I nervous now? I've carried the serenity of a stone cold killer for a week and now it gets to me?

Carroll clears from within his own penalty area twice from open play in the first five minutes of the second half and the lad behind me complains about us being too deep. I think he might have a point. Nolan walks the ball out of one of those hideous goalmouth scrambles that we insist on involving ourselves with and calmly passes to Barton, who is on the touchline near the East Stand where Cattermole knacked him when he was playing for Wigan – and who is that flying in from the side? Barton kicks the ball out and that was possibly the first time today he didn't find a black and white shirt.

We've heard a lot about how good Bramble has been for sunderland this season. We know how good he can be but we also know how bad he can be. Booed throughout, and clearly intimidated by our forwards, Bramble has already been having a poor game, slicing clearances into the air and passing into the stands - then Carroll bursts forward. It is a challenge so late, violent and reckless that it could have been a straight red on the halfway line but with Carroll clean through the ref has no option. Bramble trudges off, the home crowd somewhat less than sympathetic.

"Pogo if you love The Toon" and the whole ground is jumping, the concrete beneath my feet is actually bouncing – I've never noticed that before, have we ever been this happy? The last of sunderland's brittle discipline splinters into shards. Cattermole comes in late and sneaky on Nolan and gets his ear bent ("Hey wanker what was that?" if my lip reading skills are up to scratch); he comes in late on Enrique and gets a shove and hopefully an invitation to the car park afterwards. Turner cynically takes out Shola and finally another sunderland player is booked as Bardsley upends Coloccini. Krul makes a smart low save from Bardsley before the already booked Malbranque drags back Jonas Gutiérrez. Cattermole eventually gets booked for a foul on the exceptional Tiote and you know the unrepentant shithouse is incapable of calming himself down by this point.

We break down the right with Simpson, Barton, back to Simpson and a cross right onto the head of the flying Carroll who rattles the cross-bar – Shola, rushing in, jumps to smash a rocket through Mignolet for our fourth. Again we erupt - Wifey turns round and looks at the away support, I refuse the temptation but ask what they look like. "Ugly and mostly gone," she reports.

The extended roar of "one Chrissy Hughton" will have made something of a point.

Turner is booked for bringing down Carroll. You kind of don't want them to get another player sent off because that would become the story but you sort of do and look at the reception Joey Barton is getting as he goes to take that corner. It's turned behind, Barton runs to the other corner for yet another ovation before hanging a ball into the air that Shola flies onto, slamming a header across goal straight onto the forehead of Nolan who thunders in his third and our fifth. There are 15 minutes left and anything could still happen.

Steve Bruce removes the desperately thick Cattermole and the first act of his replacement, Mensah, is to wipe out Carroll. A man dressed only in his socks runs around on the pitch. Mensah is booked for persistently fouling Nolan at a corner, then carries on fouling Nolan despite being warned, twice. We are cruising through this now, keeping the ball, careful despite the urging of a raucous and blood-thirsty crowd.

Nile Ranger replaces Shola with five minutes left by which time our players have settled for five goals. Nolan has spent most of the second half walking around utterly dominant over our humiliated foes. Tiote has been immaculate, Gutiérrez a constant threat and Barton would be man of the match with a performance like this normally. The defence has snuffed out the threat of Bent and our forwards have brought shock and awe to our neighbours – it would be greedy to want more and petty to be shouting, "Nothing, I want them to have nothing!" while on TV

Martin Tyler is saying, "Absolutely no crumb of comfort for sunderland today at all" – then we let them score. Turner clearly fouls Ranger on the edge of their area before they break to get a corner and Bent hooks in from in front of Krul's fingers.

If the remaining mackems celebrated – I couldn't tell you.

We in the stands are annoyed – it could have been 8 or 9 nil and we have to settle for this. But we clap our hands sore on the final whistle and wide smiles mask our disappointment.

The week after.

The euphoria and the goals would rush into my brain again whenever I half woke up making extended periods of sleep impossible. Newcastle fans spent the week meeting each other with massive smiles of astonishment. At times it was almost too much to comprehend and because nothing controversial happened it was all beyond argument – it was just a battering, pure and simple. Our old foes couldn't have been more humiliated if we fed their hearts to our pets and used their empty skulls for toilet roll holders. You would think they would shut up for a while but by Thursday I was bored of all the waffle and more concerned about having to play Arsenal. It took Steve Bruce that long to find his angle, complaining about our etiquette (what is the correct etiquette in these situations? I've looked on the Debrett's website and there is nothing about how one should act after defeating a tedious gas-bag) and moaning on about how they were going to exact revenge in January. Obsessing about us – doesn't look like a lot has changed.

Except for the small matter of Five fucking One!

The win 1-0 at Arsenal the week later is actually more impressive and I think banging on about it to our sunderland friends could bug them even more.

Chapter 94

December 2010

Ьоё судно на воздушной подушке полно угрей
(My Hovercraft Is Full Of Eels)

I can't begin to express how frustrated, angry and disappointed I'm **not** about England not getting the 2018 World Cup.
Eight years of "football's coming home", eight years of tin pot clubs with ideas above their station demanding to right to host games, eight years of fuss and piffle while we wait for the chance to pay seventy quid a ticket to see Belgium play Ecuador in Milton Keynes. We'll not get to experience any of that now.

Instead now all we'll get is a couple of weeks of daft journalists pointing their fingers at the BBC before they get back to slagging off Fabio Capello and wondering where Wayne Rooney's first touch went. The leader of the English bid, Andy Anson, accused the BBC of being "unpatriotic" for uncovering bribery and corruption within FIFA at such a sensitive time. Like the correct way to go on would have been to turn a blind eye, treat Sepp bloody Blatter like he's the Lord Jesus Christ, and pretend a bunch of sticky-fingered layabouts are actually angel-hearted philanthropists. If Mr Anson wants to grease up to FIFA Vice President Jack Warner, stroke his hair and tell him he's pretty, fine but don't do it my account - the man is a self-serving bandit as far as I can see. Surely doing what's right above what's profitable is one of the more noble English traditions.

Of course, not all our journalists are wailing and gnashing their teeth at not getting the World Cup, check this out from Martin Samuel at *The Mail:* "All you need to know about the men who made this decision is that FIFA requested, as a condition if England had mounted a successful bid, exclusion from a range of UK laws including one governing Banks and Foreign Exchange Operations. FIFA had asked for 'the unrestricted import and export of all foreign currencies to and from the UK' and, worse, they got it. So, had England hosted the World Cup, FIFA executives were free to move around with sacks of unexplained cash, exempt from the inquisition of customs officers. Is it only me that is beginning to feel the need for a shower?"

Meanwhile at *The Times* Matt Dickinson pointed out that the 2006 World Cup cost German taxpayers 3.7 billion Euros and that FIFA walked away from that tournament with 1.4 billion, tax free.

You wonder why we bothered bidding at all. Until you take into account that the FA is still paying for building the catastrophically expensive National Stadium in the wrong place and that they might be able to justify their ego-maniacal stupidity and actually pay for the bloody thing by hosting the World Cup.

So they sent a delegation in the hope that actually meeting David Beckham and Prince William would make FIFA's executive committee get all wobbly at the knees and girly and star struck. Surely nobody thought David Cameron was going to help did they? Being glad handed by Cameron must be like looking at a startled hen's face reflected in the back of a spoon, very disconcerting. I'm still amazed we are not at war with China after his recent visit. Of course Mr Cameron was keen to help, working on the ancient Roman tradition of bread and circuses he would think that he can spend the next eight years putting people out of work then getting Ian Duncan Smith to accuse them of being benefit scroungers; because hey - we'll all be thrilled to bits by the chance of seeing Poland play South Korea in sunderland.

Not having to lower ourselves to the bickerfest that was about to start with St Niall and his Legion of pig-fuckers about who should get to host games is a massive relief as well. Eight bloody years that would have gone on for with nobody allowed to tell the truth about sunderland in the media because they get awful touchy if you point out that most people flying or getting a train into the region would have to come through Newcastle. If somebody actually asked Niall Quinn why the hell anybody would want to come all the way to Newcastle only to have to then travel on to an inferior stadium with faded pink seats set within an ugly, sprawling slum, he would most likely burst with indignation.

England has got some great stadiums, and enthusiastic fans but that was never important because FIFA is all about revenue streams and the English football market in saturated. Russia on the other hand is largely untapped. In fairness Russia looks like a fascinating and beautiful country that we can learn a lot from. How to deal with snow beyond panic buying eight loaves of bread and complaining all day would be a good start.

You fear that FIFA will actually be proved right the second the first bomb goes off during the London Olympics. Not that security was an issue. Neither was transport infrastructure, stadiums or anything else despite the fact that FIFA have had inspectors enjoying a five star pampering across the globe who were supposedly checking such things out. How the hell then do you explain the 2022 World Cup being in Qatar? Easy, the average age of the executive committee is 64. 2022 is 12 years away.

Chapter 95

December 2010

A Bath Full of Drugs and Vodka

A quiet week. Newcastle sacked Chris Hughton and employed Alan Pardew as manager. Newcastle then played Liverpool, during which Joey Barton pulled at the contents of his underpants in a fine Shakespearean tradition while saying something to Fernando Torres which got some elements within the media a bit cross. In retrospect Andy Carroll might have played a little too well.

Here's a mildly interesting thing: I spent the week of Chrissy Hughton's cruel sacking dodging press interviews. Despite the obvious danger of them finding some dribbling baboon to speak on behalf of the Geordie nation in my stead, I don't take naturally to the job of media whore (there is rarely any money in it and the role of celebrity football pundit is not, unfortunately, going to lead directly to me sharing a bath full of drugs and vodka with Yulia Volkova in Moscow after the opening ceremony of the 2018 World Cup).

However, on the Friday before this game I was invited onto Colin Murray's Radio Five Live Sunday show to comment on events surrounding our match with his own Liverpool. I kind of owe Colin because his excellent Radio 1 show used to keep me awake and consequently alive on a nightly drive back to Newcastle from Birmingham. Also my friend Guy bet me a pint that I wouldn't dare say "we have to respect Alan Partridge" instead of "Alan Pardew" before the nation and I like Guy buying me pints.

Anyway they didn't use me. I was bumped by Ian Dowie and the latest non-revolution on Gallowgate was bumped right down the news by Carlos Tevez demanding a transfer off his Manchester City slave-ship. It seems if we Newcastle fans are not ripping our own faces off for the amusement of everybody else then everybody else isn't interested.

Quite simply we weren't supposed to win this game – Liverpool were supposed to thrash us as some sort of punishment for Mike Ashley's shocking treatment of Chrissy and we were supposed to spiral straight down the divisions and it would serve us right!

Instead Liverpool became the latest team to underestimate how mentally tough this Newcastle team is and I can't believe I'm still having to argue with some people about what a brilliant signing Kevin Nolan was.

Referee Lee Mason was a gift from the gods for Uncle Mike and Mr Pardew, with his standard approach to any game being his belief that his job is to award privilege to the big name team. After 15 minutes of giving Liverpool everything they asked for, Mike Ashley and Alan Pardew could have been kissing each other in the technical area and most of the crowd wouldn't have noticed because they were so annoyed with the official's blatant favouritism.

Then Newcastle were awarded a free kick at what should have been a safe enough distance from goal. Safe if you ignore Joey Barton's uncanny knack of picking out Andy Carroll's head, Andy Carroll's unnatural ability to fly and Kevin Nolan's determination. Carroll had headed the ball down and Nolan had popped it into the bottom right hand corner before anyone in red noticed the danger.

Sol Campbell just failed to get his head to another free kick minutes later then Liverpool took control of the ball for three quarters of an hour. However, except for a Jose Enrique clearance off the line, most of the talking points were about Liverpool's behaviour. Torres kicked Sol Campbell then went down holding his own face and while Lee Mason waved away a Maxi Rodriguez dive he should have gone back and booked the bastard.

The second half started with more of the same, but the goal when it came was scabby as hell. The ball hitting Campbell on the back before Dirk Kuyt's shot took a horrible deflection off Steven Taylor before dribbling into the Leazes End net.

It could have got worse three minutes later when yet another non-foul led to a quick free kick and Torres was clean through. Krul blocked brilliantly.

Most of our forward work was being done by Andy Carroll who started and finished a move that ended with a flying header. Kyrgiakos tried to bully him out of the game from the start and like all before him utterly failed.

On the other hand, Shola Ameobi's inability to control a football has been driving us insane for 10 years and Alan Pardew won't be risking the wrath of anybody if he gave him to Norwich City (I like Norwich and I could carry on wishing him well if he went there.) Shola's departure from this match and the introduction of Nile Ranger won us the game. Innit. (Nile says "innit" a lot – it's a young man's thing, I shall be using it post-ironically and not in a pathetic attempt to seem twenty years younger than I am. Innit.)

Ranger matched Carroll for effort and determination and it rattled the hell out of Liverpool. Almost at once he nearly scored, Carroll headed him through and his shot on the stretch just missed the far post.

I didn't notice until I watched the game back that Joe Cole was on the bench and I can't remember when I last thought , "who the hell is that?" about so many Liverpool players. Jovanovic? Meireles? Hoothafuk? The other thing I noticed from the second look is how soon Joey spots that the Liverpool defence are about to fall over themselves. He is running onto the loose ball while they are still wondering where it is. 2-1.

On the third goal Carroll seems to be moving his leg too slowly to shoot – then it arrows into the net for his 10th of the season.

A really important point about this game was the home crowd who demonstrated noisily before and after about the way our club treated Chris Hughton but during the game supported their team whole-heartedly.

I haven't mentioned the Barton incident because nothing really happened and Colin Murray would have been better off talking to me about Alan Partridge than whittering on about it. Innit.

(Yulia Volkova is the dark haired girl out of t.A.T.u. who shamefully was the only Russian girl I could think of apart from Barry's wife in *Auf Wiedersehen Pet* and the ginger one out of t.A.T.u)

Chapter 96

January 2011

Mike Ashley; Waving His Willy at God

I sit bleary-eyed before the screen even more confused and befuddled than usual. It's that strange hinterland betwixt Christmas and New Year where a reality bends, where you can drink yourself sober, where you might not have to get out of bed as early as usual but if you do you can be rewarded by the sight of Australian cricket captain Ricky Ponting having a little hissy fit as England win another test match. Like an enraged Penfold from *Dangermouse* but with hairier arms and a dafter hat. Also there is an air of sick disappointment hovering over me and I can't work out if its cause is yet another double deflected ball spinning into the Leazes End net in our loss to Manchester City or our team's collective inability to put their elbows through Nigel De Jong's fucking teeth. Like what we would all have liked them to – in the spirit of peace on earth and goodwill to all men.

Hunkered down at Castle Furious, Wifey and I are oblivious to much that is happening beyond our own kitchen and events in 15th century Rome (*Assassin's Creed Brotherhood* – Playstation) take precedence over North and South Korea warming up for a nuclear Armageddon. So I have missed much and details from my match crew yesterday appear unreliable. Apparently some people died in Coronation Street and one of our Princes (not the one who looks like James Hewitt) has got engaged to Jayne Middlemiss. Congratulations, your esteemed Geordie Highness.

Also in the wake of the sacking of Chrissy Hughton and Sam Allardyce being dismissed from Blackburn I missed the apology to us Newcastle fans. You know, the one from everybody in the bastard world. Surely out of common courtesy everybody got together and issued some sort of statement along the lines of:

"Dear Newcastle United supporters,

we, everybody in the bastard world, have long been of the opinion that you were responsible for the state of constant chaos at your football club, with your impatience, unreasonable expectations and ignorant disregard for the obvious tactical genius of Mr Sam Allardyce. Recent events have proved that you have in fact been innocent victims all along, playthings in the hands of powerful despots even. Also it has now become all too clear that Mr Allardyce is a buffoonish bell-end of a manager and even Blackburn fans, with their limited understanding of decent football, couldn't stand watching his team's brand of non-football. In short we are all sorry and would like to buy you all a pint sometime but could you all please put more clothes on.

Thank you, yours sincerely, everybody in the bastard world. XX"

That sort of thing.

Amidst the initial outrage of Chris Hughton being sacked somebody said, "It was like when Bobby Robson was sacked," which seemed daft at the time but in retrospect was right but not for the reasons they meant. In both cases decent men were treated in a shabby fashion but the other similarity is that while other teams' supporters were quick to condemn us if you replied, "If you think he's such a good manager put him in charge at your club," few of them would take you up on the offer.

Like most of you (I think) I had no desire to see Hughton sacked and was very proud of him and what he achieved. I'm happy to admit that he proved me wrong on several occasions; for example given that he was a reluctant manager in the first place I assumed his scouting network would be virtually non-existent but it turns out he had been watching Cheik Tiote for three years. Also who thought playing two strikers at Arsenal would work? On the downside you have to mention the impact Leon Best hasn't had, making a half-fit Shola captain, playing Guthrie on the wing for half of last season and why have we seen so little of Vuckic, Ranger and Shane Ferguson? Not playing Campbell at Bolton, West Brom away and Stoke, Wigan, Fulham and Blackburn at home and never saying anything interesting.

But the biggest plus hasn't been mentioned as far as I can see (at least not in *Assassin's Creed* which is about as far as I've looked) – which is for the first time since the pre-Lee Bowyer era Bobby Robson reign, Newcastle United players have been noticeably improving. Since 2003 players have been coming into the team here and getting steadily worse. Hughton changed that and his tactics at Arsenal were impeccable. But doesn't that make the battering we took at West Brom less forgivable. Like I said at the start, I'm confused but at this stage in proceedings I'm distrustful of anybody who isn't. The timing does actually make sense if you think Alan Pardew has got a month to look at the squad before the transfer window opens but the timing also makes sense if you consider that at the time of his removal Hughton was 12 to1 to be the next manager sacked and those odds were only ever going to get worse with this hard run of games we are in. Martin Samuel at *The Mail* has been publicly suspicious of the speed with which Hughton's sack-race odds plummeted. Suggesting that somebody or somebodies made a lot of money on it.

I'd rather not think about it and obviously hope that Alan Pardew has the time, money and ability to make Ashley's decision to recruit him be declared brave. Because Hughton had us all happy enough just to avoid relegation, now the stakes have been raised.

It seems that for no good reason Mike Ashley has put his head on the block, or hung his arse out the window, or waved his willy at God. Choose your own metaphor because I haven't got a fucking clue.

P.S. It's that time of year again where people offer you their hand and say "All the best". This is starting to annoy me; all the best what? Venereal diseases, car accidents, house fires, redundancies? Don't bark half-finished sentences at me you fuckers. It's like saying "Have a lovely…." or "I hope you die in a…." – think about it and stop it.

Happy New Year. X

Chapter 97

February 2011

Everything is Better When There's Girls

On Sky Sports, Richard Keys and Andy Gray made disparaging remarks about lines-lady-person Sian Massey's understanding of the offside law based on her gender. Within a week, leaked footage of the gentlemen in question being less than polite, about or to, other women saw them dismissed.

The beautiful thing about football is how inclusive it is. All you need is a ball and a working foot and some kind of game can start. All you need to be a football writer is an opinion. What level you take that to should only be decided by your ambition and ability, not on the possession of dangly stuff in your underpants. Obviously.

Andy Gray and Richard Keys' departure from Sky Sports after making ludicrous remarks about assistant referee Sian Massey and further revelations that they are a pair of thundering boorish pillocks might seem like a massive over-reaction to some people but in the long run it could be in football's best interests. For a start Gray's constant sniping, moaning and undermining of all officials had become tedious beyond endurance and Keys' apparent certainty that Sky owns football and that as the top man at Sky that makes him Emperor of Football was a bubble that needed bursting.

The wider argument as to women's involvement in the game has been the subject of much debate ever since – I even broke my own boycott of *The Guardian* to get the view from the Mujahideen of political correctness. Wherein I found the reason for that boycott, Ms Louise Taylor, rehashing her story about Bobby Robson calling her a "stupid tart" to show how even football's finest gentleman could make life difficult for ladies looking to make their way in the game. I fear

Ms Taylor would regard many people objecting to her pursuing her chosen career as sexism and not because they object to her deliberately abusing her position to perpetuate falsehoods about Newcastle United's players and supporters. Your homework this month children is to put the words "louise taylor private eye Qatar" into your search engine then write me a short piece on journalistic integrity.

This distrust is nothing to do with sexism. In fact we need more women in football; for a start Jo Brand should get the Richard Keys job and all referees and linespersons should be ladies.

I can't believe more people haven't come forward before now to point out this glaringly obvious improvement to the modern game. Ladies know where things are, sensible men know this and will ask the nearest lady where something is before even beginning to look for themselves. This is apparently annoying for the lady in question but it is in fact a massive compliment, we are tacitly saying, "you know where everything is, where things should be and where things shouldn't be, I couldn't begin to comprehend such knowledge." So ladies should be encouraged to bring the same fearsome certainty to football they bring to supervising the drying up – "That doesn't go there!" – as a fork is placed in the spoon slot becomes – "he shouldn't be standing there when that player kicked the ball to him – offside!"

It was especially rich of Andy Gray to scoff at Ms Massey's knowledge of the offside laws when his own understanding of the rule is reprehensible. He barked out this ignorance whenever he reviewed a goal and did that "mmmm he was justabowt onside" thing that has got really irritating to those of us who noticed how often he did it. "Just about onside" is like being "a little bit pregnant"; the rule is that if there is any doubt the benefit of it should go to the forward, so you can't be "just about onside". When not clearly offside a player is on-fucking-side. But thanks to Gray and the other professional gas-bags the game is riddled with, linesmen all too often flag at the merest hint of offside because it is less bother to stop a move before a shot than allow a goal where the HD cameras will pick up that the tip of a forward's boot has stretched beyond the last fibre of a defender's sock in the build up.

There are few more frustrating sights in football than a through ball into the path of a perfectly timed run being flagged offside. And Gray is partly responsible for this with his sneering attitude and refusal to admit he is wrong. Gray should have apologised to Sian Massey as soon as the replay proved her right and him wrong but not just because he's a sexist div who should be made to go back to living up a tree and eating his own shit – but because he questioned a decision, was wrong and that is the grown up thing to do. The gender of the official shouldn't enter into it. Sian Massey is going to make mistakes because linespersons are in a terrible place to see the pass and the last defender at the same time and until officials are suspended on moveable wires above the touchline human fallibility is unavoidable. Regardless of which public toilet one is expected to use.

Male refs can't begin to assert any kind of authority over the modern game's spoilt little shit-pots, we could be onto something giving the gals a go. I have thought this for years after being involved in a particularly bad-tempered encounter down at Newburn. My own informal Sunday morning gatherings of rag-tag drunks, pill-merchants, students and hung-over maniacs agreed to play a pre-season friendly to help another mate's 11-a-side team prepare for a new season. The game was on a proper marked pitch with nets and a ref. We beat them 11-3 and some of them thought we were taking the piss and one of their players said something racist to the Nigerian doctor who played on our right wing and the qualified male ref couldn't stop it turning into a blood-bath.

They asked for a re-match but the ref didn't show up so Wifey very reluctantly took on the job. All she said as the teams lined up was, "Alright, don't take the fucking piss!" and everybody behaved beautifully; "sorry that was a foul", "I handled that" etc. Only when she gave a penalty against us was a lone voice of dissent heard and she told me to "shut the fuck up" so I did.

What the hell she would do to an enraged and screaming Premiership player could range from a chilling icy stare to kicking Wayne Rooney in the face both of which would make the game better. But it wouldn't happen because the men would be forced to behave better. Male pride would stop them pretending to be injured or to be seen publicly abusing a woman. And football would be all the better for it.

We would of course be at the whims of different types of refereeing inconsistencies; for example an unshaven Niko Kranjcar would be virtually unbookable but if he tidied himself up and signed for sunderland he would get a red card in the tunnel for "betrayal."

But we would learn to live with it because everything is better when there's girls there.

All the above opinion has been authorised by An Woman.

Chapter 98

February 2011

Andy Carroll

Everyone is going to have their own opinion on Carroll going to Liverpool which is fine. But we shouldn't get wrapped up in this he said/she said bullshit because if either the club or the player had said "No" it couldn't happen. So he wasn't forced out and the club didn't have to sell him – truth is both parties are very happy with the outcome and saying otherwise is just fear of a fan reaction. Carroll was always going to leave, he was never going to stay here for ten years unless we started spending silly money and looking like we might win something. Good players go to the richer clubs; Man U lost Ronaldo to Real Madrid. Promising local youngsters are snapped up by other clubs; Barca had Fabregas stolen by Arsenal. Football stinks – this isn't news.

Keeping Carroll long term would cost us a reported £80,000 in wages to him, not to mention what the likes of Barton and Enrique would then expect because of it. The club would be hundreds of thousands of pounds worse off, every week, with no new players added to the squad. This is where football is for mid-table teams. You overspend to stay mid-table or you drop into a relegation battle. Any thought of moving up a level comes with a ludicrous price tag.

The idea that the Premier League can become more competitive through teams progressing on a purely footballing front is ruined by the unmatchable spending power of Manchester City and Chelsea. Newcastle were not the victim of Liverpool's wealth when losing Carroll but of the wealth passed onto them by Chelsea. Chelsea, who keep saying they are going to be run as a business, then Abramovich bungs another £70 million on the table. Like the aliens in *Mars Attacks* who keep shouting "We come in peace" as they continue grinning whilst shooting unarmed earthlings.

The people running our club are clearly happy with the thirty five million pounds. Dabbing metaphorical handkerchiefs to their faces whilst pointing Andy Carroll in the direction of the already whirling blades of Mike Ashley's own helicopter was fooling nobody. One of the things that really sticks in the throat though is how Newcastle apparently held all the power but ended up looking like mugs. Liverpool reportedly wouldn't let Torres go to Chelsea unless they could get Carroll which meant nothing happened unless we released our best striker. And we let that happen without having a plan to replace him. So Newcastle held the strings of the puppet master for once and we dropped them to pick up the money. Did anyone ever say, "Square the circle, Chelsea how bad do you really want Torres? Enough to give us Anelka? No, then forget it" – for a gambler Mike Ashley doesn't half blink early.

Andy Carroll's role as victim would be more convincing if he wasn't shovelling a quadrupled wage packet down the front of his trousers. Letting him go saves us a fortune in wages and he might spend half his time at Liverpool injured or in trouble.

Having said that I saw a Liverpool shirt with Carroll on the back this evening and I wanted to puke poisonous black hatred all over the telly.

I calmed myself by watching *Rastamouse* on C Beebies. I recommend it.

Chapter 99

February 2011

Newcastle United 4 v Arsenal 4

Marvel Superheroes as Premiership football teams: The Mighty Thor = Manchester United; the most powerful, even when he wins, it's expected, he's Thor, boring. Iron Man = Chelsea; essentially a rich man's plaything, lacking in soul. The Hulk = Liverpool; can bully anybody but as soon as they're not pissed off with the world they turn into a feeble weakling. Spiderman = Newcastle United; not one of the most powerful and knows it but has a part to play and does so while taking the piss out of everybody else. His life is one disaster after another, even when he thinks he has won there is loss, tragedy befalls him at every turn and he blames himself, misunderstood and the victim of a malicious press, he regularly gets battered to within an inch of his life but won't compromise. Hilarious but loaded with pathos.

In old school Spiderman standard storylines came around that even if you are unfamiliar with comics (philistine) you will recognise from Newcastle United. Old enemies return stronger than ever, catastrophe strikes and everyone blames him, a costume change, just when he thinks everything is going to be OK, everything gets worse. The storyline I hated most was when he would lose his powers, when his secret confidence was taken away and he had to face his chaotic and perilous life as a regular person.

That's what losing Andy Carroll is, losing our secret confidence. For example we wouldn't have won at Arsenal without Carroll because no one else could have scored the goal he did. You could see it all over our team in the recent loss to Fulham. Yes we tried, put a shift in, all that old gubbins but the underplayed assurance that saw us win at Everton, Arsenal, West Ham and should have been enough at sunderland was absent. Even though we all knew that the injured Carroll wouldn't be playing for us anytime soon we somehow lost more than the player. Everybody in Newcastle seemed to look down and contemplate the fall with only the promise of £35 Million to land on giving us any hope, except we are not sure it will be there come splat time.

The air stinks of defeat, we look and sound like a team and a crowd grinding our teeth in the face of the inevitable. 44 seconds and Walcott runs clear and puts Arsenal 1-0 up. 48,000 pairs of eyes roll heavenward. Never mind Arsenal are weak in the air, if we could get the ball up and at them.... Arsenal free kick, Djourou rises above all our lot with an apparent ease and bang 0-2. Less than 10 minutes gone and Walcott goes wide and pulls the ball back for Van Persie 0-3. We are stunned, our players have lined up to kick off again out of habit surely, some kind of muscle memory, they are clearly in shock. Everybody in black and white has been appalling, even Tiote and Enrique and Coloccini, Barton had been giving the ball away, Nolan had not been in the game and our forwards Best and Lovenkrands may as well have not been on the field. Williamson was having a total bloody nightmare. Two things: Danny Simpson is keeping his side of the defence tight and Gutiérrez will not stop running at Arsenal players whenever he gets the ball. Granted he generally loses it but at least he's trying to make something happen, can we salvage something from this game? A goal maybe, or a corner? No, because Arsenal sweep forward and Van Persie has nodded in the fourth, utterly unmarked.

Useless fucking shithouse bastards.

"Where's your famous atmosphere," sing the Arsenal fans. The lad three rows down from me stands up and sticks his fingers up at them. Ignore them you daft bastard, you're only making it worse. I'm sending texts, but mentally I'm on a beach away from this Hellmouth, too sick to be angry – this is going to be double figures. This is going to be the worst defeat in the history of football, our lovely goal difference has been torn to pieces by these bastards. "Are we brilliant or are you rubbish?" texts Bully, an Arsenal fan. "Both," I reply. I hate people who stare at their stupid phones when the game is on but this doesn't count because my team is dying and I can barely stand to look.

Tiote rattles into a tackle and the crowd are stirred – encouraged by the sign of life, we string some passes together, more people cheer. Like we can stop this ignoble defeat, this humiliation. Diaby takes out Barton with a late and cynical challenge and the crowd are angry, on their feet. Newcastle get a corner and they roar. What the hell is wrong with us – surely this is hopeless.

We make it to half-time and it is only 0-4 which feels like a tiny victory but the team are booed off. How many people who claim to never boo cracked, how many people who never leave early left? I didn't but only because I lacked the strength of will.

I trudged back up the steps towards my seat for the second half and was surprised by the amount of people who had stayed.

Djourou limps off and Arsenal's best header of a ball is out of the game. The crowd sensed a will to fight and liked it.

There is a throaty roar as Barton rattles cleanly but hard into Diaby and people leap enraged to their feet as Diaby jumps up, grabs Joey by the neck then throws him to the ground, then he shoves Nolan. "He's only going to book him. Bloody typical."

But no; the card flashes up red and 10-0 isn't going to happen anymore.

Our blood is up, Arsenal scramble clear a couple of crosses, Nolan has a shot blocked and Barton is fouled again. Indignation becomes energy, Simpson bursts through a couple of challenges and shoots low and hard, Szczesny saves. Szczesny gave the score in the League Cup a lopsided *(0-4)* look by being brilliant, he gets down smartly again to save a curling Nolan shot.

Whatever force is driving us is no flash in the pan, the crowd applaud every tackle and as Arsenal get a corner Nolan is too busy chasing Lovenkrands and Gutiérrez up the pitch to notice it is being taken. Walcott cuts in to shoot and Danny Simpson arrives out of nowhere to block it, we break and get a corner. The ball drops in the area, bouncing awkwardly. Leon Best is attempting to shield it, Koscielny pulls him, pushes him and trips him, Best crashes to the ground. Penalty.

Joey Barton thumps the penalty hard to the left, 1-4, then turns to get on with the game, remembers the ball and goes to get it. Szczesny clutches onto it, Nolan grabs him, Szczesny goes down and gets booked for time wasting. Nolan gets booked for being rough, Jack Wilshere is having a little fit about it. Arsenal are not comfortable, Newcastle's players and supporters are full of hell and sparks are flying, twice Fabregas tries to weave into our area and twice Simpson slams the door in his face with immaculate challenges.

Williamson heads wide from a corner before Ranger comes on for Lovenkrands. Again the crowd turn it up, Simpson in to Barton, a cute ball into Best who scores. But there's a flag up. The player blocking the linesman's view of Best was

Rosicky which should have told him something which, one assumes, is what Joey is forcefully explaining.

Nile Ranger, full of muscle and purpose, holds the ball up amidst a mass of red, he feeds Enrique who twists and curls in a cross. Best heads it onto the defender's back but reacts first to stab home and make it 2-4.

Arsenal cannot get us off them, Gutiérrez feeds Ranger whose powerful shot is saved. Gutierrez crosses, Barton crosses from the other side, Simpson crosses, Enrique crosses as we swarm. Nolan puts in Ranger and Szczesny has to be out and down fast to thwart him. From another fiendish Barton corner Ranger heads back and Best leaping in, heads over. Why is Coloccini, our centre half, on the left wing?

Barton swings in a free kick to the far post; two Arsenal players are around Williamson as he jumps, one jumps with him, the other, Rosicky, shoves him, two handed, in the back while he is in the air. The linesman is looking straight at it, penalty. Surely.

Penalty! Yes!!

Barton clips it arrogantly down the middle, Szczesny nearly gets enough foot on it but doesn't, 3-4. St James' goes thermo-fucking nuclear. The whole world seems to be bouncing black and white, the air visibly shakes.

There's our famous atmosphere – do you like it Arsenal? We do because it means we're alive. Even if we lose now, we're alive and while we live we fight.

Tackles, tackles, tackles. Energy, belief, passion, more tackles. Thrilling stuff.

Barton jumps for a ball, Rosicky nudges him in the back, another free kick, this time out on our right. Barton, swings ball in, defender heads ball out, Tiote is running onto ball. Ball has flashed violently into Arsenal net before anyone has time to think "Tiote is brilliant but his shooting is shocking." A multiple sonic boom explodes around us, wide-eyed screaming people are in a frenzy of disbelief and ecstasy. Tiote is running half the length of the pitch, mouth wide open, team mates in pursuit. He collapses to his knees, falls forward and they pile on top. For some reason Harper elbow-slams into Leon Best's arse. Best grabs said arse and has to be removed from the game but we are too busy being shocked and ecstatic to take it in properly. Guthrie comes on.

Enrique up to Ranger, Ranger chests it down brilliantly to the forward rushing Nolan, who hammers a low shot narrowly wide and we all clutch our heads for the loudest ever recorded "oooyafukka."

Van Persie scores for Arsenal but the flag was up so long he had to be miles offside. He wasn't.

In the pubs afterwards our hands and heads were shaking, with the conversation limited to variations of, "I have never seen anything like that before in my fucking life." The flood of relief and belief is tangible, empowering. What character, what balls, what a team, what a crowd, what a day.

Oh and Arsenal as Marvel Superheroes – The Fantastic Four because while their fans might think they are as tough as The Thing and their manager is Mr Fantastic clever they are in fact Human Torch style arrogant gobshites, but when the going gets tough they are Invisible Girls.

Chapter 100

2010/11 – A Distorted View

Before the start of the 2010/11 season Newcastle-supporting Shaun Custis from *The Sun* was asked of Newcastle's prospects for the coming season and he rolled his eyes heavenward and said, "They have got the same players as when they were relegated."

And he was right: of the team that beat Birmingham 2-1 to mathematically assure our survival on May 7th only one player, Cheik Tiote, wasn't in the squad that suffered the humiliation of the lonely plop into the Championship. Tiote was undoubtedly player of the season, with his tackling, immaculate positional sense and tidy passing but was he good enough to keep Newcastle United afloat alone? Hardly, and what this proves is firstly: Newcastle didn't get relegated in 2009 because their players weren't good enough; and secondly, the quality of teams in The Premiership isn't as good as some people like to tell us it is. Manchester United won the League with a team so far off their own high standards that they deserved their loss when playing at Wolves. But who did they beat to win the title? Chelsea went through a period where they were so poor they lost 0-3 at home to sunderland, Arsenal were so flaky they lost at home to West Brom and Newcastle, and Liverpool flirted with relegation until Dalglish took over (I told you he was a good manager). Manchester City threw millions of pounds around with the same careless abandon an in-bred ape flings its own shit, but mired in their own boring bitterness they only finished third. They celebrated scraping into a Champions League place when they could have won the League simply by showing more imagination and courage. They did win the FA Cup but that was only good because it pissed off Man U fans and stopped Stoke winning it. Stoke are despicable.

All the teams at the bottom were capable of beating anybody else on any given day and The Premiership was the better for it, so what of Newcastle United? Exacting bloody revenge on Aston Villa for taking pleasure in our relegation with a 6-0 battering was pretty sweet. Thrashing sunderland 5-1 was a very special afternoon but the 1-0 win at Arsenal was probably our best team performance in years.

Unfortunately the season was defined by one point in time, BC to AD; Before Carroll fucked off to After Dalglish swiped our best striker. It hurt us mentally (and he looks daft in red) but in moaning about it we overlooked how hideously inconsistent we were before he left; bad beatings at Bolton and West Brom away and awful home showings against Blackpool, Wigan, Stoke and Blackburn came before we had the no-Carroll excuse. The magnificent recovery against Arsenal, commendable draws at home against Manchester United and away to Chelsea, not to mention the sound thrashings administered to West Ham and Wolves, were without Carroll and under Alan Pardew.

The Chris Hughton sacking in December made Newcastle look shabby and didn't seem to gain us anything, especially as his replacement, Alan Pardew, did nothing positive when the transfer window was open. Mike Ashley clearly didn't fancy Hughton as a long term option and saw a five game winless steak where we dropped from a heady 5th to 11th as opportunity to heave a popular and dignified gentleman into the street.

Mike Ashley was either being brave or brazenly antagonistic in firing the popular Houghton with few people lining up to shower our owner with praise. The club's hierarchy believes that silence or late and clumsy statements is the way to communicate with fans which means nothing gets a positive spin. So Ashley, despite having kept Newcastle United afloat with tens of millions of pounds of his own money, remains reviled while John Hall and his family took millions out of the club and they named a fucking stand after him.

For example, Kevin Keegan claimed while doing some punditing on ESPN that Ashley would spend none of the Carroll money on new players when that was already untrue; the club having made Hatem Ben Arfa's loan a permanent deal for a cost of £8.5 million. Ben Arfa, the victim of a shockingly brutal challenge from Manchester City's midfielder/ fucking shit-house Nigel De Jong, looked a real class act in the 180 or so minutes we were allowed to enjoy him this season.

In the first season after promotion 17th was what most of us were aiming for what with our unrealistic expectations and all. It went better than that but the nagging feeling that with Carroll and Ben Arfa in the team all season it could have really been something exceptional contributed towards the disappointment that we only managed 12th.

Player of the Season: Cheik Tiote.

Goal of the Season: Cheik Tiote v Arsenal.

The End

So what happens in the end? It's a book, it has to have an end?

But it's a book about football and football doesn't end, that's its great power and its greatest frustration. Everything in football is transitory: for example, Chelsea won the League and Cup double in 2009/10, does that mean they get to live happily ever after? No, a year later Chelsea won nowt and the manager who led them to that double, Carlo Ancelotti, got the sack. Some time ago, our dear friends in Middlesbrough won the League Cup and got to a European final before vanishing in a puff of indifference but apparently they do still exist down the League somewhere. Wimbledon Football Club was essentially murdered and disappeared yet in 2011 the reformed club made it back into the Football League.

If the story of Cinderella was a football story she would marry her Prince Charming and the next day the papers would be linking her with a move to Robin Hood. Meanwhile in Newcastle Puss in Boots has been neutered but it hasn't stopped him climbing up the curtains.

What?

Never mind.

Football doesn't end; in the future as the diseased and dying planet spins into the sun when nearly every living thing is dust, the last giant cockroach is arguing with the last mutant rat over the offside law.

What?

Fuck off, I'm metaphoring.

Football is a multi-layered soap opera that runs and runs powered by itself. There is a cliché that says "players and owners come and go but fans stay the same" –

no they don't. Are the people who watched Newcastle in 1892 still going? I know football crowds are statistically getting older but we are definitely missing a few 130 years olds. Everything dies except the football but football can make life worth living.

This is a book about Newcastle United; mostly about and for the fans of this magnificently mental football club in this vibrant and thrilling city so I was hoping for a final chapter that didn't have "and then we were relegated again" in it.
So the story (so far) ends with Newcastle getting back into The Premiership and not only surviving but thriving; smacking sunderland 5-1 silly, taking a brutal 6-0 revenge on Aston Villa for relegating us, coming from 4-0 down to draw 4-4 with Arsenal (a game we only failed to win by the width of a post) as well as gaining creditable draws with Champions Man Utd and second place Chelsea. (There were also a lot of terrible games but we will forget about them.) We scored more goals at home than every team in the division who wasn't Manchester United (we will also be ignoring that all the relegated teams scored more away goals than we managed) and apparently have tens of millions of pounds to spend on new players (which we will believe when we see the receipts) – a happy ending.

Then in the Old George public house (before what turned out to be a monumentally irritating last game of the season against West Brom where we led 3-0 and were on course for a top half finish but pissed it away to draw and finish 12th) a lad told me the club was definitely getting sold. Within the week, he says, the information provided from a copper-bottomed source.

Newcastle is constantly awash with bullshit rumours; an old boy up at the training ground insisted to me that the only reason Alan Pardew was manager was because he owed Mike Ashley money, which seems a cruel and unusual punishment. If every rumour was true Bobby Robson would barely have got a wink of sleep when in charge here what with the amount of bed time he lost dragging errant footballers out of nightclubs. But sometimes the most outrageous and fantastical things turn out to be true in football; suddenly players and managers are gone, a club is bought by wealthy Arabs or Indian chicken farmers, players are impregnating women they oughtn't. Constant drama awaits, every day could bring fortune or disaster to a football fan with no any actual footballs required.

I pride myself on being the World's Worst Glory-hunter and in Newcastle that is up against some very stiff opposition; the first time I saw Newcastle play for 90 minutes on TV was the 1974 Cup Final that we lost 3-0. My first ever live game was a 1-4 loss to sunderland and I have been to Wembley four times with Newcastle and the score stands 10-1 against my lot. Despite having helped to pay for some of the planet's finest footballers I have never seen a trophy more significant than the elaborate urn you get for winning the second division. But it's not about trophies, it can't be; why would nearly 52,000 people turn up to see an end of season, mid-table game between Newcastle United and West Bromwich Albion if silverware was of any relevance? You couldn't be further from a trophy if you were in a rocket heading towards the sun. Newcastle United fans have been mistreated, lied to, exploited, sold out and let down for years and then blamed for being part of whatever crisis is afflicting us this week. And yet here we all are like our fucking lives depended on it, with tens of thousands in our extended family spread right across the globe; watching on dodgy TV channels or on the internet or listening to a radio. Then there are those who choose not to engage with a live match at all but fret intensely until it has finished. All infected with an incurable black and white virus that makes the game seem more important than it probably is, all on the same side even when we are shouting in each other's faces, all defiant and gobby and magnificent in our collective lunacy.

We really don't care if people outside the tribe don't 'get it' – 'it' is not theirs to get – 'it' belongs to us and 'it' will still be here when we are dead. 'It' doesn't end.